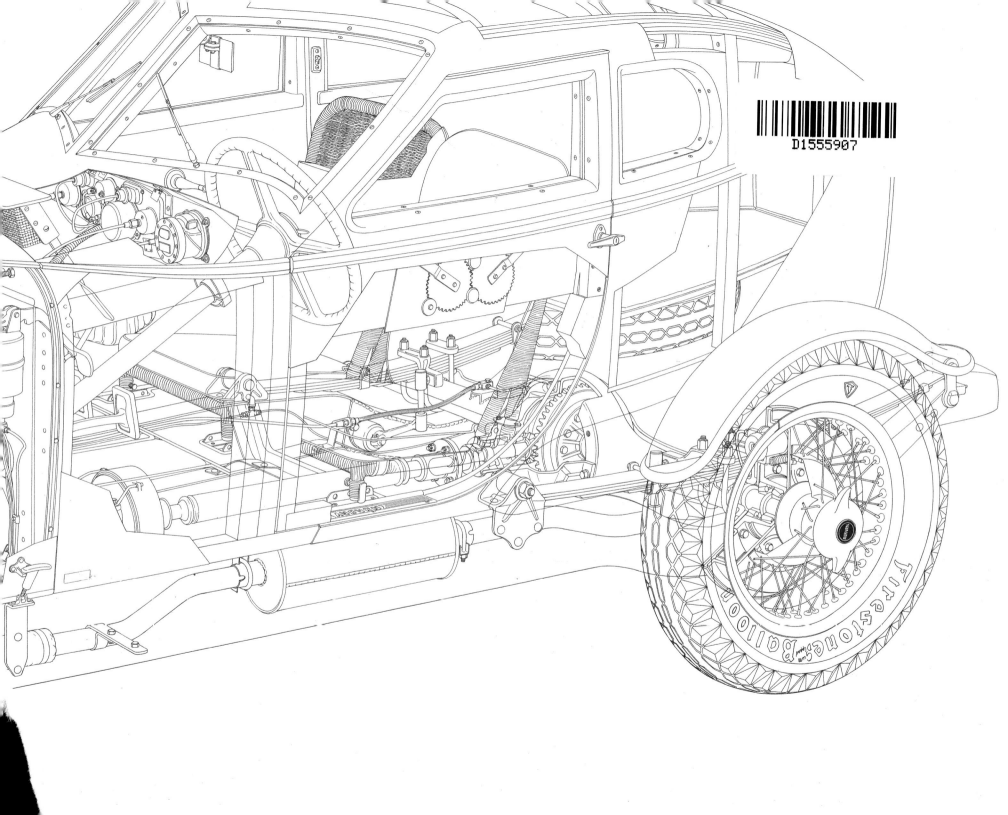

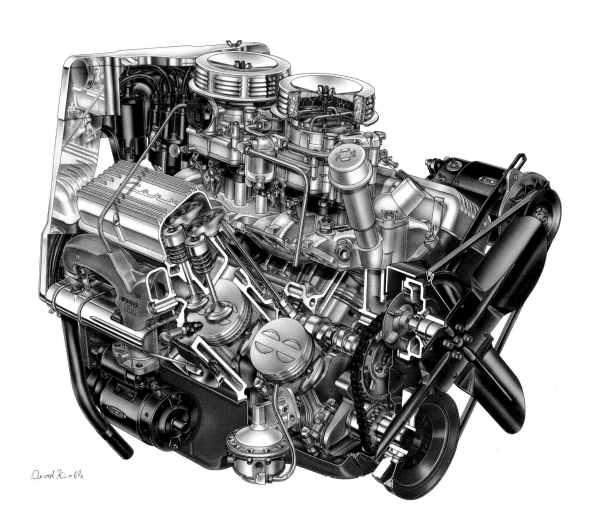

DAVID KIMBLE'S Cutaways

TECHNIQUES & STORIES BEHIND THE ART

CarTech®, Inc.
39966 Grand Avenue
North Branch, MN 55056
Phone: 651-277-1200 or 800-551-4754
Fax: 651-277-1203
www.cartechbooks.com

Edit by Bob Wilson
Layout by Connie DeFlorin

ISBN 978-1-61325-173-7
Item No. CT535

Signed Limited Edition: ISBN 978-1-61325-291-8   Item No. CT571

Library of Congress Cataloging-in-Publication Data Available

Written, edited, and designed in the U.S.A.
Printed in China
10 9 8 7 6 5 4 3 2 1

Front Cover: McLaren M8A

Front Flap: I have been using two of these 12-compartment watercolor trays since I started airbrushing. I use them to mix colors and thin the Winsor & Newton gouache with distilled water for spraying. These tubes of gouache are the three principal colors used for rendering metal, I use a separate nylon bristle brush used for each color.

Back Flap: Author David Kimble. Photo Courtesy Chris Endres.

Front Endpapers: This 1929 Auburn Cabin Speedster is the only illustration project that has ever shown up like a lightning bolt out of the blue in the mail, and it was well worth doing. The photos I received were of a re-creation of the car in progressive stages of assembly and showed a lot of insight into what it took to draw a cutaway illustration.

Back Endpapers: It was only supercharged when the driver put the pedal to the metal to engage its compressor, which added 40 to 140 hp. The 540K was a legend, and it was my privilege to illustrate this one. It was the first 540K built by Mercedes-Benz in 1936, and to do justice to its long, low Sindelfingen Special Coupe bodywork, this drawing was my longest yet at 44 inches.

Frontispiece: This is a 1956 265 equipped with the Order Code 469 dual Carter 4-barrels.

Title Page: Sterling Marlin's win at the 2001 Pepsi 400 in Michigan driving the No. 40 Coors Light Dodge for Ganassi Racing was the team's first win in NASCAR and Dodge's first win since 1977. Sterling scored another win later in the season, while his team car, the No. 01 Singular Wireless Dodge driven by Jason Leffler, won a pole, scored one top-ten finish, and led 15 laps.

Back Cover: Four rolls of frisket, dozens of sheets of velum, and many tubes of paint later, here is the final result of cutting frisket and spraying paint for 18 days. This cutaway is of the first 1949 Hydra-Glide to roll off the Harley-Davidson assembly line, equipped like the bike they used for studio photography.

Author Note: Over the years General Motors did and did not use hyphens in option codes. For consistency I have used hyphens in all option codes.

OVERSEAS DISTRIBUTION BY:

PGUK
63 Hatton Garden
London EC1N 8LE, England
Phone: 020 7061 1980 • Fax: 020 7242 3725
www.pguk.co.uk

Renniks Publications Ltd.
3/37-39 Green Street
Banksmeadow, NSW 2109, Australia
Phone: 2 9695 7055 • Fax: 2 9695 7355
www.renniks.com

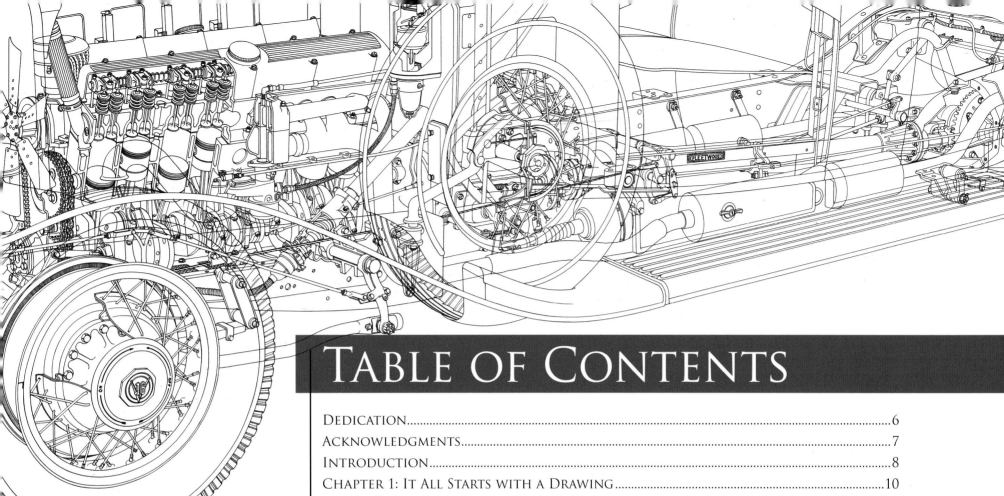

TABLE OF CONTENTS

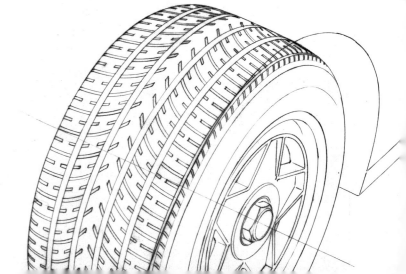

DEDICATION

This book is dedicated to my longtime friend and rep, Melanie Kirsch. For many years she stood by me, through thick and thin; she was there to support and encourage me even when no one else did. I miss her.

Acknowledgments

Over the years a lot of people have contributed to my success: Austin Kimble Jr., my father, whose connections gave me the opportunities that started my career; Mildred Bowen Kimble, my mother, an elementary school teacher who enrolled me in the right schools and never gave up; Bob Falcon and Ted Halibrand, who gave me a shot early on; Bill Young and Jerry Titus, who got me into magazines; Don Edmunds, who, more than anyone, was my mentor; Jerry Isert, who first let me in on designing a racing car; Al Bartz, who had me help design an engine; Gary Knudson, who brought me to Chaparral; and Neil Nissing, who introduced me to the film positive, and with whom I shared a studio for 14 years. Neil, with the film positives, and Dick Bruton, who taught me to use an airbrush, were the main contributors to the development of my signature style, which makes my work totally different from anyone else's. Thank you, everyone.

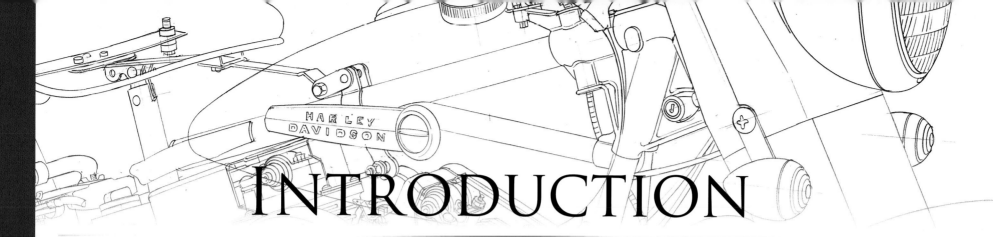

INTRODUCTION

Fifty years is a long time, and it is amazing to me now that I did my first automotive cutaway illustration in August 1964 of Ted Halibrand's *Shrike* Indy car. I grew up in Southern California during the 1950s when it was the center of racing car building, and Frank Kurtis built most of the Indy cars early in the decade. Frank, a friend of my father, had raced midgets in the 1930s and was generally well connected in the motor sports community. He visited Kurtis Kraft every spring with me in tow when the new Indy cars were under construction, which left a lasting impression on me. Encouraged by my mother, I covered rolls of shelf paper with drawings of these cars using crayons, showing not only their exteriors but also their frames, suspensions, and engines.

Watching racing cars being built was the inspiration for what would become my life's work, but it didn't start out that way. After attending two art schools and graduating from a third, it was not enough. The course I completed at the Pasadena Academy of Technical Arts gave me an understanding of engineering graphics and the realization that I needed to understand cars as well as their designers did. I soon became more interested in designing racing cars myself than illustrating them, and in 1964 Dad showed my work to Bob Falcon, the art director at the Bendix Aerospace Division in the San Fernando Valley where they both worked. Bob moonlighted as advertising manager

for Ted Halibrand, who produced most of the wheels, drivelines, and chassis components for midgets, sprint cars, and Indy cars.

Ted had built a Lotus-style, mid-engine Indy car that was tragically destroyed in that year's 500, but he was going ahead with plans to build them for customers. Bob Falcon asked me to do a cutaway illustration of the Halibrand *Shrike* for a sales brochure he was producing (for which I will always be grateful), even though I had never tackled anything that complicated. My dad showed the *Shrike* brochure to Lotus dealer Bill Young, an SCCA national champion who was a friend of Jerry Titus, the technical editor of *Sports Car Graphic* magazine. Jerry liked the *Shrike* illustration, and in another leap of faith asked me to write a 1965 Indy 500 technical preview and to do another Indy car cutaway for the magazine.

While putting together the article for *Sports Car Graphic*, I visited the shops around the Los Angeles area where Indy cars and engines were being built, and made some very important contacts. Interviewing Don Edmunds at his autoresearch shop in Anaheim soon led to me moving my drawing board to autoresearch. Don, perhaps unknowingly, became my mentor. Farther south in Costa Mesa I spent a lot of time with the Harrison racing team illustrating their cars for *Sports Car Graphic*, but good looks didn't translate into speed. Jerry Isert, the car's builder, took a chance and asked me to participate in the design of his 1966 Indy car, and even though I knew less than he hoped or I thought, the *Harrison Special* made the starting field.

History repeated itself in 1968 when I interviewed Al Bartz, a popular builder of Chevrolet-based racing engines for the Can-Am, Trans-Am, and Formula 5000, for a magazine article. Al had a contract to develop a 303-ci Trans-Am racing engine for Pontiac and asked me to work with him designing the cylinder heads and intake manifold. Through Al I met the McLaren Can-Am team and, most important, their engine builder, Gary Knudson, while I was working at Bartz Engine Development. Gary and I shared an office when he was in town, and in 1969 he was returning to Chaparral Cars where I met their resident engineer, Mike Pocobello, who was struggling with the 2H Can-Am car. Mike needed an assistant, and Gary recommended me. When I received the call I jumped at the opportunity, even though it meant giving up club racing in California, and moved to Midland, Texas.

The 2H was fast. However, it was also the first less-than-successful Chaparral, which put a cloud over everyone working on it. My stay in Midland was brief. I left California in late April and was back in early August, but having worked at the legendary Chaparral Cars I came away from Texas with a great credential.

I met my future wife in 1969 while working at Chaparral Cars in Midland, and we were married a few months later after I returned to California. Now back home, I made my first attempt at full-time freelance illustration, but I couldn't make enough money to support us. I soon returned to engineering because I wanted to spend time with my wife. I stayed away from racing, which is as all consuming on the drawing board as it is on the track. I started designing motor homes and ended up as a chief engineer for a lawn sprinkler timer company where I was so bored I began freelancing again, illustrating oil field valves. This was in addition to an occasional cutaway for the car magazines, but the Willis Oil Tool Company became a steady client, allowing me to leave my day job when the time was right.

My work seldom appeared in *Road & Track*, the holy grail of car magazines. But, in January 1976 I had to choose between doing an illustration for them or keeping my job at Tymevalve. That was the end of my career in engineering, but it gave me the insight I was looking for to do in-depth cutaway illustrations of mechanical subjects with the eye of an engineer. John Steinberg, the top artist representative in Los Angeles, recruited me in the spring, and almost overnight I was on my way, working for the largest advertising agencies in the country. Every project John brought in was a new challenge, illustrating everything from snowmobiles to the starship *Enterprise*. My skills developed so quickly that in a year my paintings looked like the work of a different artist.

The next big break came in 1982 when *Motor Trend* magazine asked me to illustrate the all-new 1984 Corvette, which led indirectly to a long-term relationship with General Motors. This was my first in-depth cutaway illustration of a production car. It was also the first in a eight-year series of *Motor Trend* foldout covers that, more than anything else, put me on the map. By the end of the decade I was working for Ford and Chrysler as well, along with most of the European and Japanese manufacturers, with "Kimble" becoming a synonym for cutaway illustration in Detroit. For years, my illustrations were seemingly everywhere in the automotive media. With most of them available as prints, people started collecting them and following my work.

This book is intended to answer the question I am most often asked: "How do you do it?" To which I usually respond, "A little at a time," which gets a chuckle, but it doesn't really answer the question. In this book, for the first time, I disclose fully not only how I developed my approach and technique but also how this artwork is done, along with the stories behind some of the illustrations. I followed an unconventional and circuitous path to at least come close to realizing my vision of how to illustrate the anatomy and physiology of machinery. I'm coming close to what I want to see.

1

IT ALL STARTS WITH A DRAWING

Whether it's sketched by eye, plotted geometrically, or traced from a photograph, every automotive illustration done by hand starts with a line drawing. When it comes to cutaways where internal components have to fit correctly within the car's body, eyeballing is not the way to go, and although plotting is effective,

When my work is shown as contemporary art, the drawings are sometimes compared to Leonardo da Vinci's. But he didn't have the benefit of ellipse guides and I am dependent on them. Triangles, curves, and dividers are also essential tools for technical drawing, which I do with a mechanical drafting pencil. (Photo Courtesy Chris Endres)

it's also very time consuming. This leaves photos as the best starting point, but if a vehicle isn't available in time to meet the client's deadline, math data will do to get the project under way. Cars have been designed electronically for some time, and the 3-D digital files of their parts can be assembled, reformatted, and printed out in perspective as an alternative to a photo.

MCLAREN M8A

Cutaway has become a generic term for any illustration showing a car's anatomy through its exterior, whether internal details are revealed by cutting holes or seen through a transparent body. To show the steps involved in laying out a "cutaway" car drawing, I have resurrected an image from a simpler time that is both easier to follow and more fun than a current production car. The McLaren M8A Can-Am car was drawn as though it were transparent, done for the team in 1968 and never published; this book is the first time it's been seen in print. Both my work and the art form have come a long way through the years, and ever since I started airbrushing in the late 1970s, I have wanted to see this illustration in color.

Car magazines of the 1960s had little inside color, and cutaways were typically black and white, making it necessary to redraw the McLaren to make it suitable for a full-color airbrush painting. This also

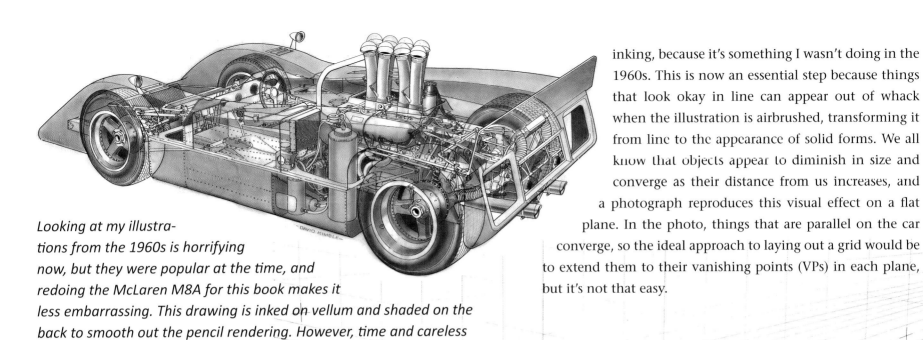

Looking at my illustrations from the 1960s is horrifying now, but they were popular at the time, and redoing the McLaren M8A for this book makes it less embarrassing. This drawing is inked on vellum and shaded on the back to smooth out the pencil rendering. However, time and careless storage have made it look mottled anyway.

inking, because it's something I wasn't doing in the 1960s. This is now an essential step because things that look okay in line can appear out of whack when the illustration is airbrushed, transforming it from line to the appearance of solid forms. We all know that objects appear to diminish in size and converge as their distance from us increases, and a photograph reproduces this visual effect on a flat plane. In the photo, things that are parallel on the car converge, so the ideal approach to laying out a grid would be to extend them to their vanishing points (VPs) in each plane, but it's not that easy.

gave me the opportunity to bring it up to my current skill level, which involves most of the same steps as starting from scratch. The photos are long gone, but I still have the preliminary layouts and finished inking shaded with pencil on vellum, which was unfortunately not stored carefully. It was quite a chore tracing this wrinkled and yellowed inking onto the plastic drafting film, which I now use instead of vellum as a starting point.

Perspective Grid

Before going any further with the drawing, I develop a perspective grid from the tracing of the photo, or in this case the

Tracing the wrinkled and yellowed McLaren inking onto drafting film was made even more difficult by leveling out some details while adding others from old preliminary layouts. A perspective grid was added to the tracing, which is something I wasn't doing in the 1960s, but airbrushing makes perspective more critical.

Even though the McLaren drawing is only 26½ inches long, about a foot shorter than I work with today, its horizontal VPs are spread 97½ inches across the horizon. Even worse, the virtual VP is more than 10 feet below its rear tire, but there is a stupid simple way to get around this dilemma. The photo's perspective can be kept on the drawing board by extending two converging parallel surfaces in each plane to the opposing edges of the drawing with the distance between them stepped off with dividers. These points are marked along the length of the edges, and lines drawn between them over the car simulate their perspective vanishing point. The hard part is that these parallels have to be on the vertical, longitudinal, and transverse axis of the car to be of any value, which is sometimes difficult to determine.

Layout Layers

Even though the M8A's body was easily removed and I photographed the car both with and without it, I made the layout a single layer, which is how I worked back in the day. For this go-round the addition of exterior graphics and complete tire tread made it necessary to separate the layout into two layers, which is how I now work anyway. For the new final layout, the chassis is logically on the bottom layer and gets the perspective grid with the near-side wheels

By applying the basic principles of geometric linear perspective to a photograph, its horizontal and vertical vanishing points (VPs) can be found, but this method isn't practical for laying out a grid. The problem is size. Even with the McLaren being a foot shorter than my current work, its horizontal VPs are spread 97½ inches across the horizon.

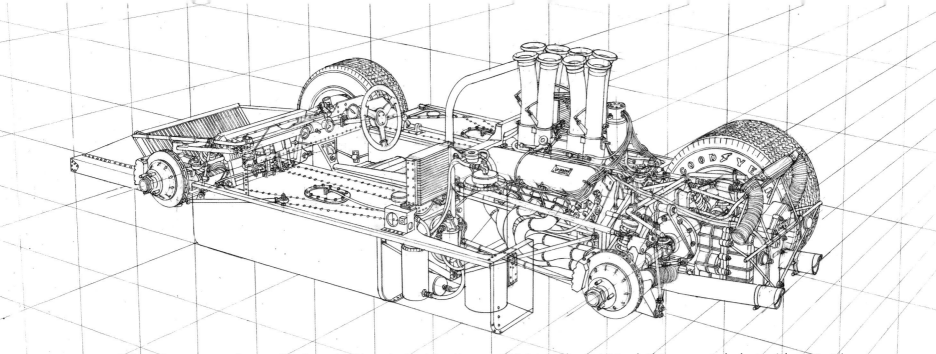

Today I routinely separate a car's exterior from its chassis, and for the new McLaren layout I took this approach, but without cutting away the engine and transaxle because of the low angle. Logically the chassis is on the base layer along with the perspective grid, which has registration marks added in red near the corners.

removed. A simplified tracing of the monocoque chassis tub's side is included to complete the picture, and a small supplemental layout of the engine and transaxle was traced in.

To demonstrate how unseen surfaces and components are plotted in, I have made a simplified tracing of the McLaren chassis structure with construction lines drawn using a red pencil. This is a monocoque structure made up of stressed aluminum boxes riveted to bulkheads at

both ends fabricated from square steel tubing. The bulkheads provide hard points to mount the suspension and pedals in front, along with the engine and roll bar at the back, among other things. Showing them through the sheet metal gives the drawing continuity. It's just as

To demonstrate how unseen surfaces and components are plotted into a transparent car, I have isolated the McLaren's monocoque tub by projecting from areas that could be seen in my photo. A red "X" is drawn between the corners of the tub's top surface to find the longitudinal centerline. From there, anything can be plotted in with dividers using relative scale.

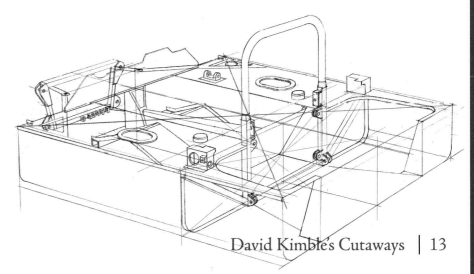

important to know what not to show, and I left the lower portion of the cockpit center divider from my original drawing out because it didn't contribute anything, and as a painting the illustration would look better without it.

I have always done small spot layouts of areas with a lot of detail, but the one of the McLaren engine and transaxle from 1968 was little more than a sketch. I also didn't get it right with the aluminum big-block Chevy's exhaust ports not equally spaced and exhaust header primary tubes that were too small in diameter. One important detail I did get right was the triangular strut that supported the cylinder block, which was otherwise cantilevered from the firewall bulkhead with the rear suspension mounted to the transaxle. This setup was inspired by the 1966 Lotus 49 Formula One car whose Cosworth DFV engine was designed to be a structural member. The Chevy needed a little help.

Fortunately I illustrated a 1969 ZL-1 aluminum 427 for GM Powertrain and still have the engineering drawings, allowing me to do a convincing layout even though it isn't exactly the same engine. I like to cut away the engines in see-through cars, but to make this work the crankshaft centerline needs to be above the closest tire, and here it's down on the sidewall, so I left it solid. The transaxle was upgraded from photos in books, and the engine was redone from the intake manifold and magneto down, including the exhaust system. Construction was again done in red pencil with the block's vertical and cylinder bank centerlines showing through the bellhousing. Taking advantage of the grid position, marks for precise alignment are in blue.

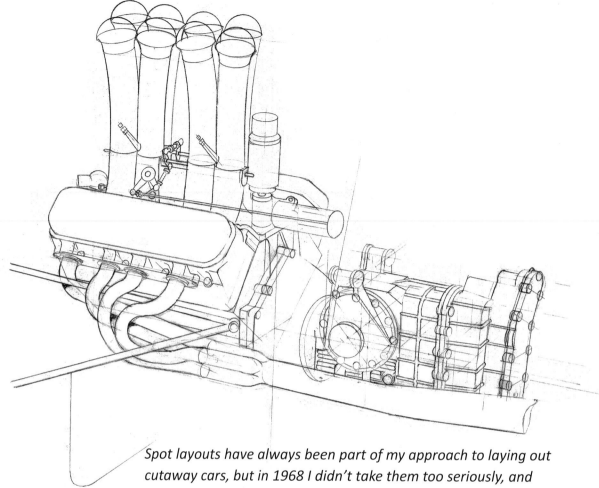

Spot layouts have always been part of my approach to laying out cutaway cars, but in 1968 I didn't take them too seriously, and this one is little more than a sketch. I was around these big-block Chevys every day at Bartz, but I must not have been paying much attention, because I drew the center exhaust ports close together as on a small-block.

In addition to the preliminary powertrain layout, I also did a separate drawing of the M8A with a solid body, which unfortunately was just dropped on rather than attached to the chassis, for my photo. This quickie move came back to bite me, because my perspective grid revealed that the rear bodywork wasn't sitting level, even though it looked okay in the line drawing. If this hadn't been corrected, the

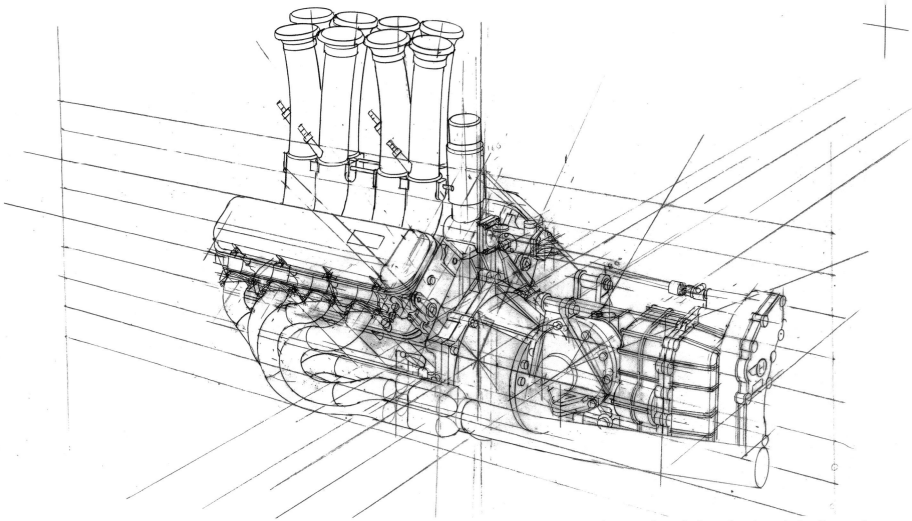

For this go-round I got serious about the McLaren's engine and transaxle spot illustration, with everything below the throttle bodies and magneto completely redone. I used engineering drawings of the aluminum ZL-1 big-block to upgrade the engine with improvements to the fuel injection pump, bellhousing, and Hewland transaxle.

large rear spoiler would have appeared twisted when the new drawing was airbrushed, which adds both form and clarity. Racing car graphics are typically too large to be solid, and making them transparent wasn't possible with my early technique, so I always left them off. Today, transparent graphics aren't a problem, and I had a little help from the past in adding them, because I had traced the lower portion of the car

number on the side of the tub, which made it easy to complete.

As the top layer of the final layout, the body drawing is not entirely solid with both near-side tires showing through to separate their tread from detail underneath. Positioned by registration marks from the base layer grid, the car looks as it did at the 1968 *Los Angeles Times* Grand Prix, the event it was being prepared for when I took my photos.

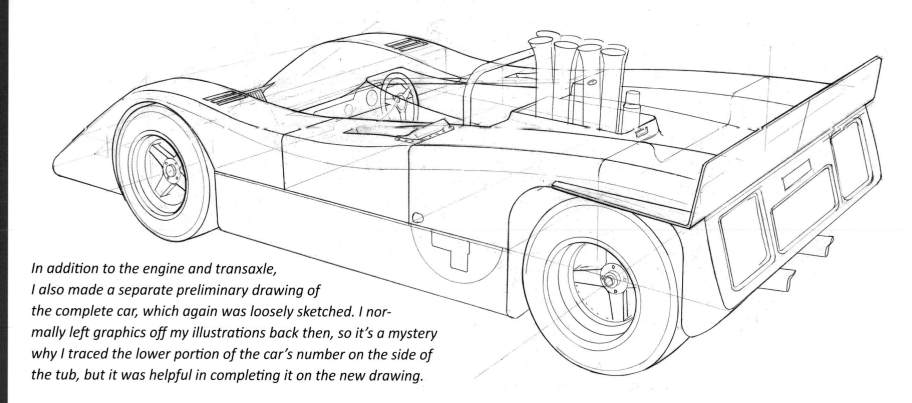

In addition to the engine and transaxle,
I also made a separate preliminary drawing of
the complete car, which again was loosely sketched. I nor-
mally left graphics off my illustrations back then, so it's a mystery
why I traced the lower portion of the car's number on the side of
the tub, but it was helpful in completing it on the new drawing.

Fortunately, as a lifelong, full-time professional car freako, I have a lot of automotive books, and period photos of the M8As were in five of them, of which Pete Lyon's were the most important. Between *Can-Am* and *Can-Am Photo History* I found what was needed to get the No. 4 McLaren's decal package and windshield tint correct for Riverside from the author's photography.

I'm not the least bit shy about using a lot of preliminary layers to keep final layouts clean, especially when they involve tire tread and lettering, which is not one of my strong points. After refining and detailing the body up to the point that more construction was needed, I started a full-sized supplemental layout that was intended to work out all of the loose ends. As it turned out, the tire tread and some of the lettering took two more passes on smaller spot layouts to get them ready for tracing into the final drawing, which unfortunately wasn't a surprise. There were also a few missing details from the chassis that I

took care of, including the far-side tire lettering, tread grid, rear brake caliper, and the screens over the intake trumpets.

I detailed one of these hemispherical screens before deciding to leave them off, because even though they were on the engine when I photographed the car, it raced without them. This was for historical accuracy, but I also used my artistic license to lose a diamond-shaped Goodyear decal that would have obscured some engine detail and two strips of unsightly black tape. This tape secured a Dzus button and the top edge of a scoop that wasn't on the car when I saw it, with my original illustration only showing the opening for it. The McLaren cars and tire lettering turned out well enough to transfer to the final, but Bruce McLaren's name and the Gulf decal with the checkered flag needed more work.

The overlap between the lettering that needed help and the near-side front tire worked out just wrong with Bruce's name in script cutting

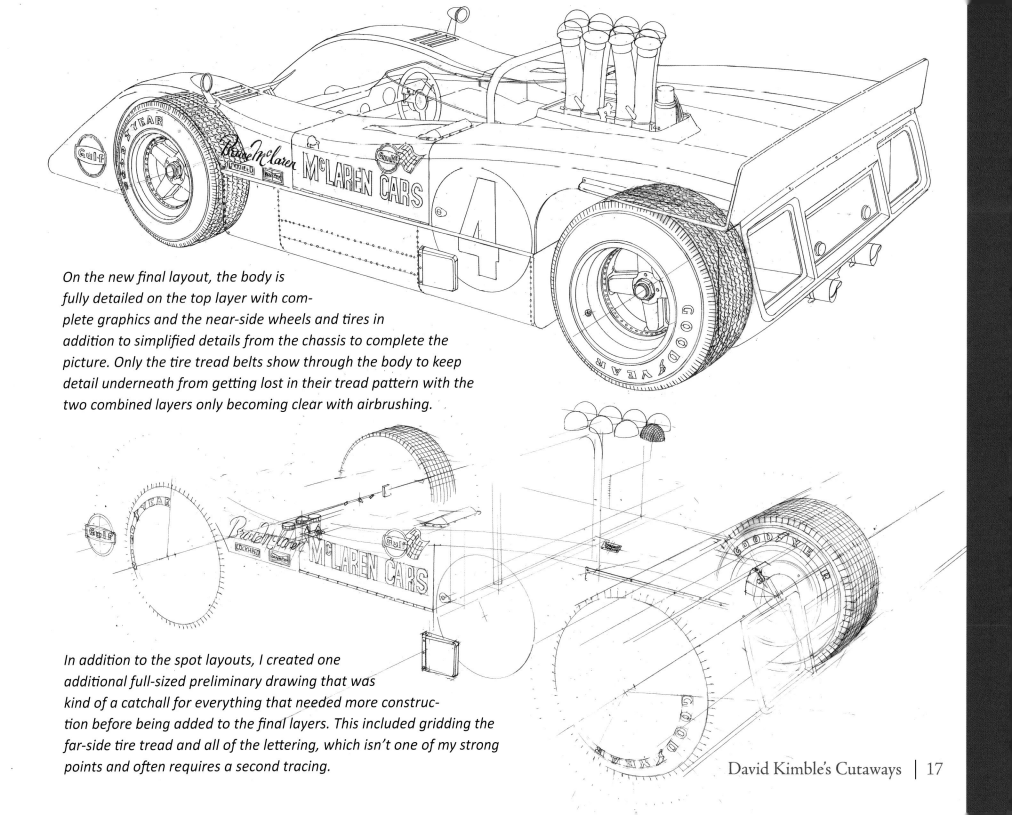

On the new final layout, the body is
fully detailed on the top layer with complete graphics and the near-side wheels and tires in
addition to simplified details from the chassis to complete the
picture. Only the tire tread belts show through the body to keep
detail underneath from getting lost in their tread pattern with the
two combined layers only becoming clear with airbrushing.

In addition to the spot layouts, I created one
additional full-sized preliminary drawing that was
kind of a catchall for everything that needed more construction before being added to the final layers. This included gridding the
far-side tire tread and all of the lettering, which isn't one of my strong
points and often requires a second tracing.

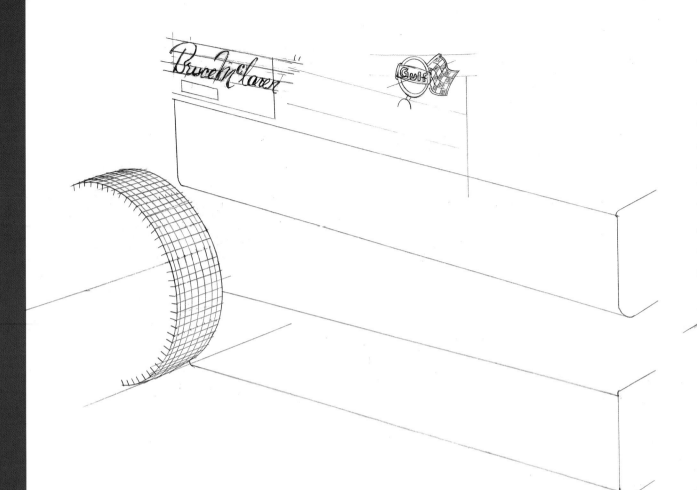

Block lettering isn't difficult, and the McLaren turned out fine, but Bruce's name in script and the Gulf decal with the checkered flag, which is on a curved surface, took some more work. The overlap between the McLaren script and the front tire tread made it necessary to put it on a separate layer with the outline of the monocoque tub added to both drawings for location.

into the front tire tread. This meant that these elements had to be separated on two spot layouts, without much on either one of them, that were too short to reach the registration marks with the side of the tub added for alignment. The Goodyear Blue Streak Sports Car Specials were all but slick with a fine tread pattern that was more like fine engraving than tread grooves, which wasn't difficult but very tedious to draw. All four tires were gridded with transverse lines and the correct number of circumferential grooves, with only a small section of the pattern detailed as a guide for completing all of the tread on the final layout.

Submission Prep

Living in a small town in Texas has a lot of advantages, but services aren't among them. With the closest Kinko's 200 miles away, I have to lease my own Xerox, which only has an 11 x 17–inch scan. The final step in getting a drawing ready for approval by the client and then inking is to make a copy small enough to email, which can only be done by reducing it in sections. It took five scans on the copier spliced together on my light table to get the McLaren down to 11 x 17 inches with another reduction to 8½ x 11 inches for the computer's scanner. There is a lot of scanning and splicing involved

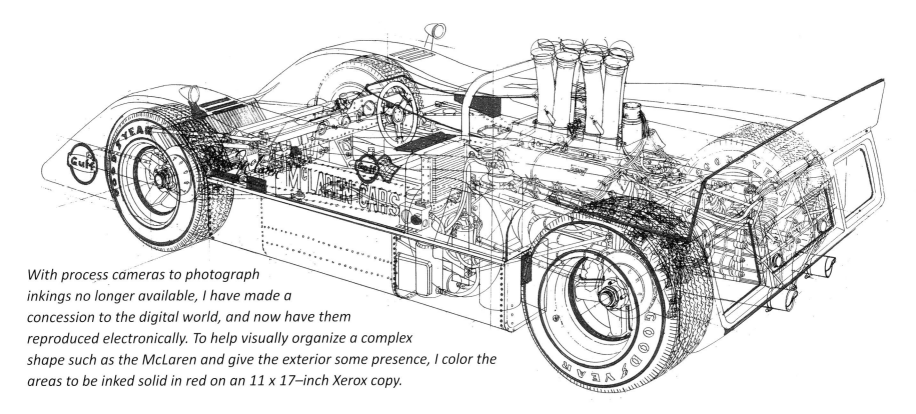

With process cameras to photograph inkings no longer available, I have made a concession to the digital world, and now have them reproduced electronically. To help visually organize a complex shape such as the McLaren and give the exterior some presence, I color the areas to be inked solid in red on an 11 x 17–inch Xerox copy.

in copying a two-layer see-through car, with the body and chassis needing to be copied together, along with individual copies of both layers to get a complete picture. This complete first look at the car appears overly complicated and confusing, but with selective edges and small details to be made solid marked in red to organize it visually, the M8A will paint just fine.

Low Angle

In addition to its small size, the reincarnated McLaren illustration isn't entirely representative of my current work because the only cutaway is one rear brake cooling duct hose. Today, my preferred approach is to show the engine and, where possible, transmission and other important components cut away inside a transparent skin. The only other Can-Am car I have illustrated, the 1966 Chaparral 2E done 33 years later, shows a good mix of internal cutaway and see-through.

The Chaparral's cutaway engine, transaxle, exhaust system, and near-side radiator are seen through a transparent body, allowing the complete car to be viewed along with its technical details.

The McLaren looked best at a low angle because it was slab sided and seemed too rectangular in a higher view, which was a good thing because all I had to stand on for my photos was the car's open trailer. Except for its straight-sided tub, the Chaparral was rounded with deeply sculpted contours making it more suitable for getting up high with my camera, and fortunately there was a handy stepladder. Looking down into a car is always more revealing, but in the tradeoff between art and information, both high and low points of view have their advantages, with angles closer to eye level easier to relate to. Even though it's a bird's-eye view, the Chaparral 2E has special significance for me, so I was motivated to do a solid exterior version along with a see-through illustration for two separate paintings.

Can-Am Mystique

So what was the Can-Am, and why is it such a big deal to me that I have illustrated two of the cars from a racing series that only lasted nine years, with the last event run in 1974? Outrageous is the only word to describe the Canadian-American Challenge Cup organized by the SCCA as an experiment to encourage technical development without any performance-limiting restrictions. These were the most exciting sports racing cars of all time and the fastest for decades to come. They were even quicker than For-

mula One cars of their era. The hairs still stand up on the back of my neck remembering the ground-pounding bass rumble of the aluminum big-block Chevys that dominated the series from 1968 through 1971, eventually producing more than 800 hp. For its first three years the Can-Am was a short, six-event fall series of 200-mile races held between September and November and then expanding to eleven events in 1969. It ended with five in 1974.

The McLaren was my eighth see-through car and the first to be inked. The Chaparral 2E, drawn 33 years later, was also based on an inking even though it was a full-color airbrush painting. Whether an inking is done by hand, as this one is, or electronically, the body contour lines that show so prominently in the drawings are left off and only used as a guide in painting.

The *Los Angeles Times* Grand Prix for sports racing cars, run in late October at Riverside International Raceway, became something of a must after my father took me in 1960. In 1966 this event was part of the new Can-Am series, and I saw something there that would change the direction of my life a few years later. Most of the starting field was made up of conventional Lolas and McLarens except for the gleaming white, high-winged Chaparral 2Es that stood out like a pair of UFOs. This really put the hook into me, and after working on the design of a car that made the Indy 500 that year, I wanted to be involved with the mysterious Chaparrals. This seemed highly improbable at the time, but it did happen in 1969 through contacts I made at Bartz Engine Development while designing cylinder heads and intake manifolds for a Pontiac Trans-Am project.

Al Bartz was one of the best Chevrolet-based road racing engine builders, and his shop was the right place at the right time for me, leading to some exciting opportunities. Two Can-Am races were in California. After Laguna Seca, the McLaren team prepared their M8As for Riverside, in Van Nuys, close to Bartz's shop, where they could use the machine tools. Teddy Mayer, the team manager, was aware of my cutaway illustrations and asked me to do one of Bruce McLaren's car, which was partially disassembled at the time only a couple of miles away. There was no way I was turning this down, even though I was working long hours on the engine that Pontiac had contracted Al to develop. In retrospect, I'm glad I squeezed it in.

After moving back to Texas late in 1992, it wasn't long before I visited Chaparral Cars, which looked just like it had 23 years earlier when I worked there. Even Troy Rogers, the shop foreman, was still there, but instead of a crew building new cars, the fabrication shop was jammed full of historic Chaparrals restored by Troy in the 1980s. Near the back wall, a pair of wings on struts standing above the other cars caught my attention. It was the 2E parked next to the 2F endurance-racing coupe, and illustrating it would be the realization of a dream. It was 2000 before I could find the time to take it on and it took almost a year to complete what turned out to be three illustrations, but it was worth it!

I have occasionally been asked to do a solid exterior version of a see-through car.
The first was a series of two-channel holographic covers for Motor Trend *in the 1990s. My memories of the 2Es in the 1966 Los Angeles Times Grand Prix compelled me to do a separate painting of Jim Hall's car the way it appeared on the track all those years ago, even though no one was asking.*

2

FROM INK TO AIRBRUSH

A signature feature of my full-color airbrush illustrations is their unusually high definition, which comes from painting on both sides of a film positive. I use two airbrushes: an Iwata Custom Micron SB for cool colors and small details, with an Iwata HP-SB for warm ground reflections and large areas; I have paint in both airbrushes at the same time. This allows me to switch back and forth during a pass without any interruption, using the brush that is best sized to the area being painted for maximum control and the smoothest possible tones. Air pressure comes from an Iwata Power Jet compressor equipped with a "T" fitting to supply compressed air to both airbrushes. I use this setup for everything except backgrounds. For these I use an Iwata "Wider 88" based on an automotive touch-up gun that the Power Jet can't keep up with. It requires a large dual-pump compressor to do these jobs.

INK AND FILM

I use Winsor & Newton designers' gouache, which is a semi-opaque watercolor that comes in an ideal palette of colors for my work. In addition, this paint sticks to the film positives as if it were illustration board. The gouache is thinned with distilled water in a watercolor tray and mixed with nylon-bristle brushes. I then use these same brushes to load the paint into the airbrush side cups for spray-

I have painted everything from cars to cruise liners with these well-used Iwata airbrushes and ones like them that I have worn out through the years. The airbrush in the foreground is an HP SB used for large areas and warm colors; the Custom micron behind it is for small details and cool colors. (Photo Courtesy Chris Endres)

ing. Adhesive-backed vinyl masking film called frisket is placed over areas to be painted, and the shapes are cut out and removed with a craft knife using No. 11 blades. Even though I do most frisket cutting freehand, I use old worn ellipse templates, curves, and triangles

Some other important tools I use while airbrushing are these Peterson Briar bent-stem pipes that I smoke in rotation so they don't overheat. Next to the pipe stand is one of the 12-compartment water-color trays and some nylon-bristle brushes that I use to thin paint with distilled water and to mix colors. (Photo Courtesy Chris Endres)

to cut critical areas. I also use these guides to spray over for uniform soft edges. This approach is handy for long tubular shapes and tire sidewalls, along with body contours that would look unrealistic with a sharp frisket-cut edge.

Neil Nissing, a professional photographer with whom I later shared a studio, introduced me to film positives in 1975. A film positive is a negative of a negative so it is actually black lines on clear film. At that time they were being used primarily in the making of offset printing plates. However, what was then mainstream is now a rarity in this digital world. Fortunately, enough people still have a use for film positives that they are still made, although on a very limited basis. My source is Designer Imaging in Ohio. With most of the remaining process cameras that used to shoot the line negatives now gathering dust, Tom Kirk puts positive lines directly on the film using a digital process in his Designer Imaging studio. This means that inkings done by hand have to be scanned before being sent to him. I work with computer artist Rick Terrell in Michigan, who inks my pencil drawings electronically and emails them straight to Tom.

My film positives are made with the emulsion side up, so that the lines are on the front. As with an animation cell I paint them on the back. Only the highlights, see-through effects, and value adjustments vare on the front side.

Gouache sprayed on untreated acetate wipes right off, but it sticks to photographic emulsion and also to the opposite side of the film, which has a non-photoreactive coating. This means I am working

Airbrushing can be messy and the pile of Winsor & Newton Designer Gouache tubes I use isn't pretty, but when the paint is sprayed onto the film it can be beautiful. This semi-opaque water-color comes in an ideal palette of colors for my work and sticks to film positives as though they were illustration board. (Photo Courtesy Chris Endres)

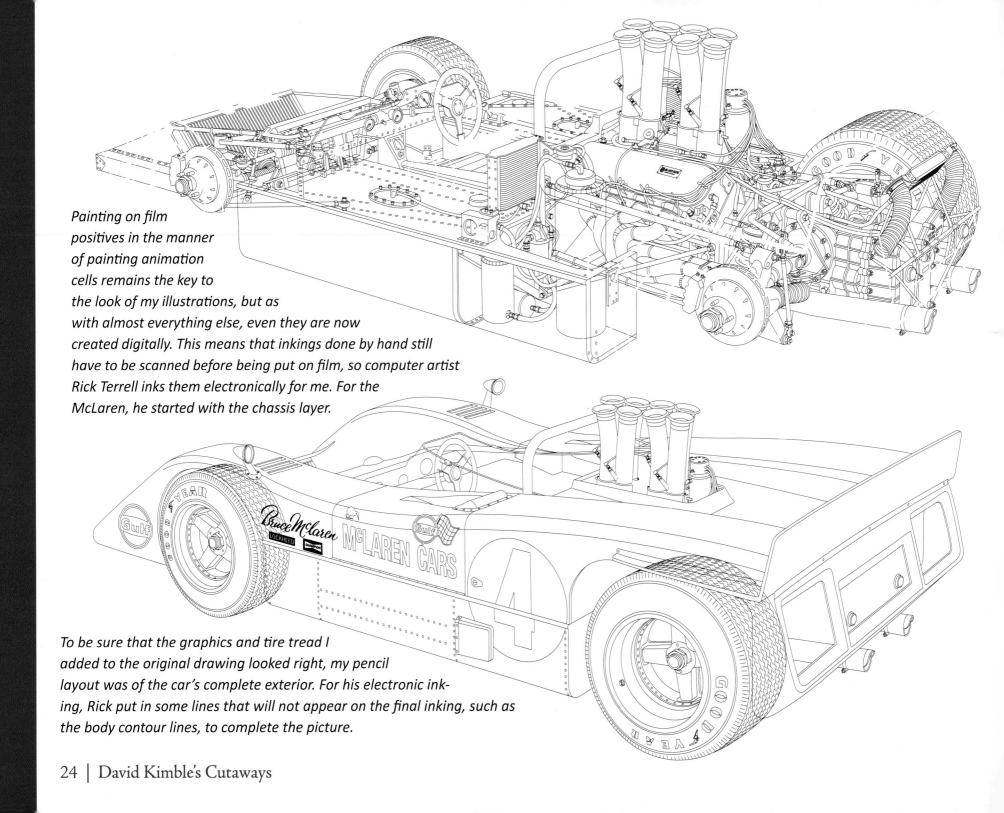

Painting on film
positives in the manner
of painting animation
cells remains the key to
the look of my illustrations, but as
with almost everything else, even they are now
created digitally. This means that inkings done by hand still
have to be scanned before being put on film, so computer artist
Rick Terrell inks them electronically for me. For the
McLaren, he started with the chassis layer.

To be sure that the graphics and tire tread I
added to the original drawing looked right, my pencil
layout was of the car's complete exterior. For his electronic inking, Rick put in some lines that will not appear on the final inking, such as
the body contour lines, to complete the picture.

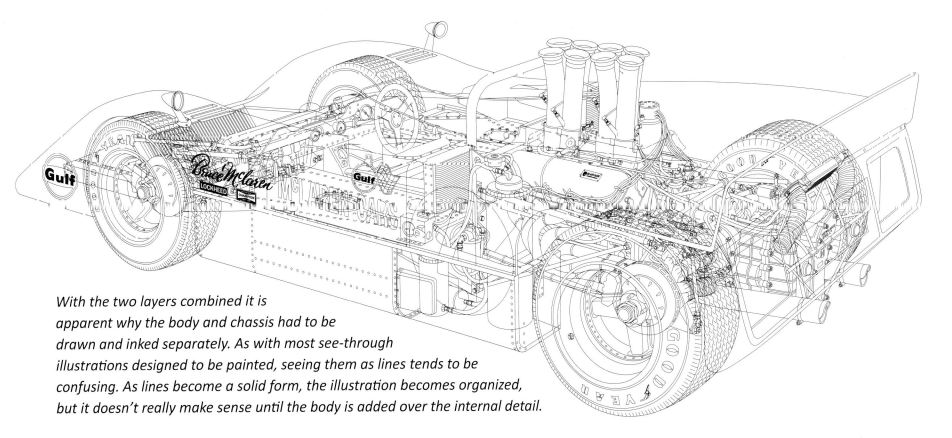

With the two layers combined it is apparent why the body and chassis had to be drawn and inked separately. As with most see-through illustrations designed to be painted, seeing them as lines tends to be confusing. As lines become a solid form, the illustration becomes organized, but it doesn't really make sense until the body is added over the internal detail.

backward until the final phase of the painting. The film positive is taped to a foam core board backside up and covered with sheets of vellum from a tracing pad to prevent overspray. Holes cut in the vellum expose the areas to be painted; they are then masked with clear adhesive-backed frisket film.

BODY COLOR

I always start by painting the blacks, working toward aluminum, and then finally white. This establishes a painting's range of values, beginning with the sidewalls of the tires. The portions of the tires showing through the body are painted with a little less intensity and fade as they reach the wheelwells to define the wheelwell openings. After spraying the sidewalls, new frisket is put down for the tire tread

belts, followed by new sheets of vellum for the next pass. This process is repeated until the entire car is filled in. To give the blacks some color, I primarily use cool jet black, with ivory black for warm tones, and Chinese Orange to suggest ground reflections.

If a car's body is a dominant color, the areas without internal details showing through come next, and the McLaren is painted in the team's unique orange. Normally I use gouache transparently with tones becoming darker as more paint is added, but a solid body color looks more convincing if it is opaque. With this approach the white board under the film doesn't show through. Highlights are then added to the front side; the darkest values are painted first and covered by the lighter ones on the back. Because I am working backward this makes the body look flat, requiring a test before spraying it on the final art to avoid a rude surprise when the film is turned over.

The vellum is replaced after the tire tread belts are added, with more holes cut and covered over as areas are painted. This protects the painted areas from scratches and overspray. This is how it looks during a typical pass. The painting is surrounded by some of the "high-tech" tools I use, including a scrap piece of copy paper to start the airbrush.

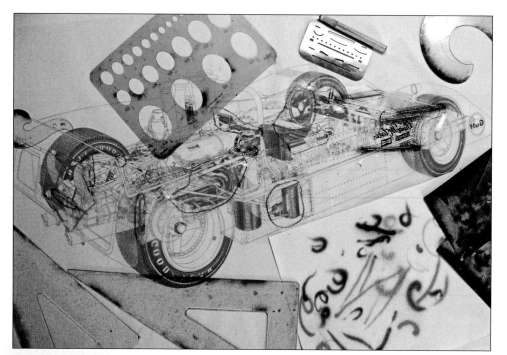

Painting begins by turning over the film positive so that the emulsion side (with the lines) faces down. It is covered with sheets of vellum from a tracing pad and openings are cut in the vellum to expose the areas to be painted. These areas are then covered with frisket masking film. I always start with the blacks, working toward aluminum to establish a painting's range of values. The tires come first beginning with the sidewalls, using a photo from a book for accuracy. At this point, the first frisket is ready to be peeled off after being cut with ellipse guides. It is also used as an aid in spraying the contours.

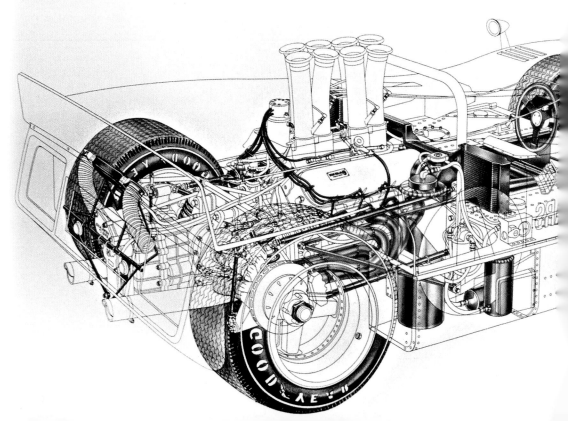

McLaren Orange is a very elusive color, so it had to be mixed in a large-enough quantity to ensure that it wouldn't run out before the project was completed. Fortunately cadmium orange was a good starting point for this color. After mixing it in a medication cup, both darker and lighter shades were mixed in additional cups; a scrap piece of film was then taped down over a body contour drawing for a test. The test revealed that the dark tone needed more black but the color match was good so I went ahead for real, cutting frisket only for sharp edges and airbrushing over a ship's curves for softer contours. The moment of truth comes when the film is turned over for the first time and I see what I have. Mercifully, I haven't blown one of these in years, and the McLaren looks good.

This painting sequence is about context. The blacks look darker by themselves than they do surrounded by McLaren Orange, which is brought out by the red-orange portions of the Gulf decals and the big-block Chevy's rocker arm covers, along with the other small bits of bright color. There is a lot of aluminum, and the final step in putting it into context is painting the cast-iron brake rotors and the magnesium castings, which were boiled in a chemical solution to prevent oxidation of this volatile material. This gives the wheel centers, brake calipers, transaxle, and intake throttle bodies a color that varies from dark warm gray to a golden brown.

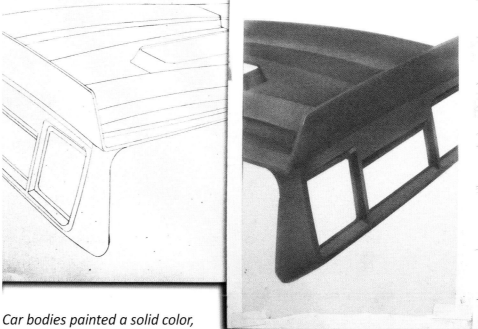

The first phase is completed. All the black areas without detail are showing through, filled in with transparent jet black. To keep the blacks from appearing monochromatic, a little Chinese Orange has been added to suggest ground reflections, with the tone fading to define the see-throughs.

Car bodies painted a solid color, such as the McLaren, look best if the gouache is used opaquely on the back of the film. This requires a test, so I tape a piece of scrap film over a reverse photocopy of the body contour drawing, spray the color, and turn it over. This prevents what could be an unpleasant surprise; this test shows that my color is good, although the darkest tones need more black.

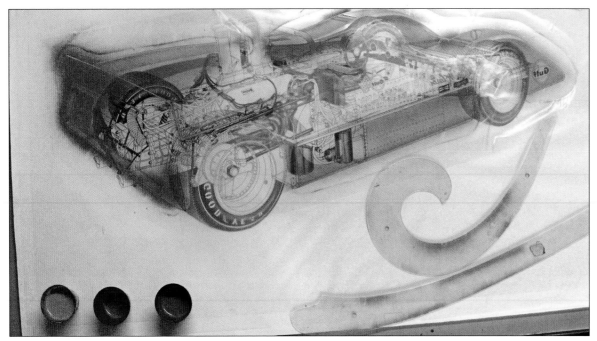

Because McLaren Orange is an elusive color, a large quantity was mixed in three medication cups in light, middle, and dark values to ensure that I wouldn't run out. The body was sprayed in a single pass with the frisket pulled progressively. Only the sharp edges were cut; softer edges were sprayed over ship's curves, following the contour drawing.

The moment of truth comes when the film is turned over for the first time, and even though I haven't blown one of these in years, there is still a lot of anxiety. My main concern this time was getting the orange right. The painting is a good match to this 1:18-scale diecast model of the M8A, which is an accurate color, so it's off to a good start.

STEEL AND ALUMINUM

I almost forgot the unpainted steel in the chassis, which is a little darker than the surrounding aluminum. This includes the bulkheads, which are fabricated from square tubing. Even though the headers are finished with black heat-paint, the exhaust pipes are also left unpainted and have a dark patina from the heat of 650 hp. When I painted the aluminum, I started with the intake velocity stacks, wheel rims, and brake rotor mounting hats; however, the rims were later polished by my artistic license before the painting was finished. With chrome all but disappearing from production cars, I haven't had many opportunities to render any of it in recent years, and even though I usually wait until a painting is more filled in, I just couldn't wait this time.

After getting sidetracked by the chrome, the remaining aluminum was filled in starting with the 427 Chevy's block, heads, and magneto, followed by the remaining small aluminum parts all over the car. The large unpainted portion of the reflective aluminum monocoque chassis tub is now surrounded so it can be rendered in context, leaving only the nuts, bolts, and braided stainless steel–sleeved hoses unpainted. The small hardware and stainless hoses are filled in next, but they are not the last things to get painted on the back of the

Continuing on the back side of the film positive, all the spots of bright color have been filled in, along with the golden brown magnesium castings. Simple geometric construction is done on the frisket to find the centers of the brake discs for rendering the radial cores that result from scoring by the brake pads.

film; this follows a strategy that keeps the illustration from getting too dark. Because of its large openings, the last paint to go on the back of the film is a little McLaren Orange over the detail showing through the rear fascia to give it more presence.

I usually turn the film over for the first time in a state of high anxiety to find out how I've done painting the body, but it is exciting to turn it over for the last time. I get a high-voltage charge seeing the car all filled in, even though it is painted a little light, which makes it look flat (so there's plenty of room for value adjustments). Before going any further, I add a shadow under the car so it has something to sit on. This is projected using parallel light rays, because the sun is 93 million miles away. Jet black adds transparency to the shadow and is added to all the openings in the body, including the wheelwell flanges. A lot of the blacks on the back of the film look washed out after this and they

Next is to surround the aluminum with color to put it in context so that it will shine, starting with the wheel rims and intake velocity stacks. Before turning the film over for another look, I couldn't resist also painting the chrome, even though I usually wait until the car is almost completely filled in before I do this step.

I usually don't look at the front side of the film this often. But with the aluminum cylinder block, heads, magneto, and radiator completed, the most stressful area came next. Only the sides of the aluminum chassis structure were painted, leaving a lot of flat reflective panels that had to be rendered in just the right way to tie the illustration together.

Small details such as nuts, bolts, and the spherical rod ends are among the last to be painted, ensuring that they stand out as bright spots. On this pass, value adjustments have also been made to a few areas, leaving only the braided stainless steel hose sleeves and white tire lettering to be finished.

With the McLaren completely filled in on the back, painting moves to the front side of the film. I usually start with a shadow under the car, but this time I painted the transparent graphics on the door first. The body openings and the area under the M8A that will be in shadow are exposed; an outline of the car's shadow on the ground is plotted using parallel light rays drawn on the frisket.

One of the biggest challenges in painting a see-through car is that it can easily become too dark when all of the layers are added, so it starts out a little light and flat. This leaves a lot of room for adjustment of values. The exterior is complete here except for the transparent portions of the orange body over the interior detail.

The most gratifying part of a transparent car rendering is the final one, which begins by adding almost-opaque permanent white edge highlights to sharp corners. These thin white lines are painted over the film positive's black lines, except for the doors, where they are painted next to them to look like a panel gap.

The body was built up selectively in a series of vignettes while looking at my 1:18-scale diecast model and color photocopies of period photos to give the look of outside light. Above the car number I used the middle-value McLaren Orange and permanent white to bring out the left oil cooler's NACA duct and give its scoop a surface to sit on.

are pumped up at this time. I follow this by painting the transparent lettering and the car number, which also gets its disc fogged in with permanent white.

Highlights

The most gratifying phase of a transparent car rendering is the final one, which begins by adding highlights to the sharp edges with almost-opaque permanent white, because it is a light color. These thin white lines are right up against the film positive's black lines. They are then covered with frisket and the body contours are built up by spraying over ship's curves. I used the middle-value McLaren Orange with white highlights, following the body contour drawing and looking at my 1:18-scale M8A diecast model along with period color photographs. My see-through cars are created as a series of vignettes; their bodies go from almost solid (to define contours) and fade away to nothing (over important internal details).

Art Imitating Reality

Beyond making the car look good, my objective is to find a balance between art and information that allows the viewer to clearly see the car's exterior along with its anatomy in the same illustration. This is exactly how Bruce McLaren's M8A looked when it won the 1968 *Los Angeles Times* Grand Prix; well almost, because you couldn't really see through its body and I used my artistic license again to lose a diamond-shaped Goodyear decal. This would have been positioned over the engine's rocker arm cover so it had to go, and I couldn't resist polishing the wheel rims. (Besides, the M8B had polished rims in 1969.) To satisfy anyone who looks at photos of this car, it had wire mesh stone guards on the intake trumpets until the last two races of the season at Riverside and Las Vegas.

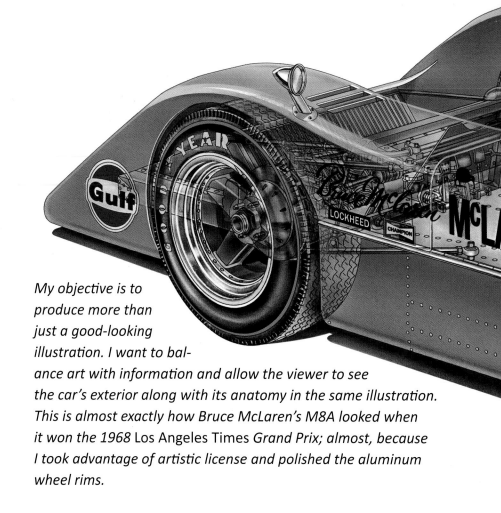

My objective is to produce more than just a good-looking illustration. I want to balance art with information and allow the viewer to see the car's exterior along with its anatomy in the same illustration. This is almost exactly how Bruce McLaren's M8A looked when it won the 1968 Los Angeles Times *Grand Prix; almost, because I took advantage of artistic license and polished the aluminum wheel rims.*

Even though this is the first time my McLaren M8A has been seen in print, it is not the first time it has been redone. The Reynolds Aluminum Corporation had me do a "high wing" M8B version for a poster in 1969. It was said at the time that the M8A was an ordinary race car done extraordinarily well, but the M8A's performance was also extraordinary; it won all six rounds of the 1968 Can-Am championship. Driving the No. 5 car to the Can-Am championship after winning the Formula One championship earlier that year, Denny Hulme was

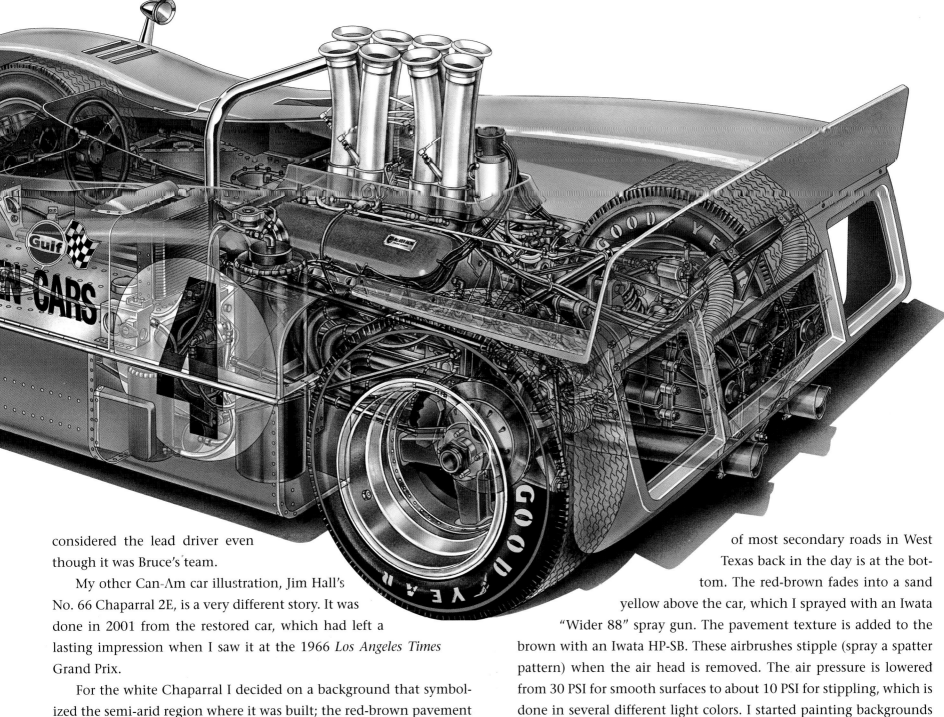

considered the lead driver even though it was Bruce's team.

My other Can-Am car illustration, Jim Hall's No. 66 Chaparral 2E, is a very different story. It was done in 2001 from the restored car, which had left a lasting impression when I saw it at the 1966 *Los Angeles Times* Grand Prix.

For the white Chaparral I decided on a background that symbolized the semi-arid region where it was built; the red-brown pavement

of most secondary roads in West Texas back in the day is at the bottom. The red-brown fades into a sand yellow above the car, which I sprayed with an Iwata "Wider 88" spray gun. The pavement texture is added to the brown with an Iwata HP-SB. These airbrushes stipple (spray a spatter pattern) when the air head is removed. The air pressure is lowered from 30 PSI for smooth surfaces to about 10 PSI for stippling, which is done in several different light colors. I started painting backgrounds on my car illustrations in the mid-1980s, but art directors frequently left them off or added one of their own, making the car look too light or too dark. This is because the value range of the painting changes with the background, so for the past few years, I have painted my cars on white.

Even though these cars are separated by two years, they did race against each other in a way. In 1967, the Chaparral 2E was modified to run aluminum 427-ci big-block Chevys, which made it the 2G. The McLaren M6As were powered by 6-liter cast-iron small-block Chevys that year, but in 1968 the new M8A had a similar 7-liter aluminum big-block. Jim Hall continued to race against the McLarens with the 2G. Jim had become famous for his Chaparral 2's groundbreaking

aerodynamics, fiberglass chassis, and automatic transmissions, which dominated the United States Road Racing Championship in 1964 and 1965. In 1966, he inadvertently traded racing success for innovation with the radical 2E; he won only one Can-Am race, and the successor, the 2G, was unable to win in two more seasons.

Here is a closer look at the M8A's aluminum big-block 427 Chevy and Hewland transaxle, dominated by the Lucas fuel injection system's velocity stacks. A wobble plate pump under the magneto provides high-pressure fuel for the injectors with exhaust exiting through the headers' huge 2 1/8-inch-diameter primary pipes.

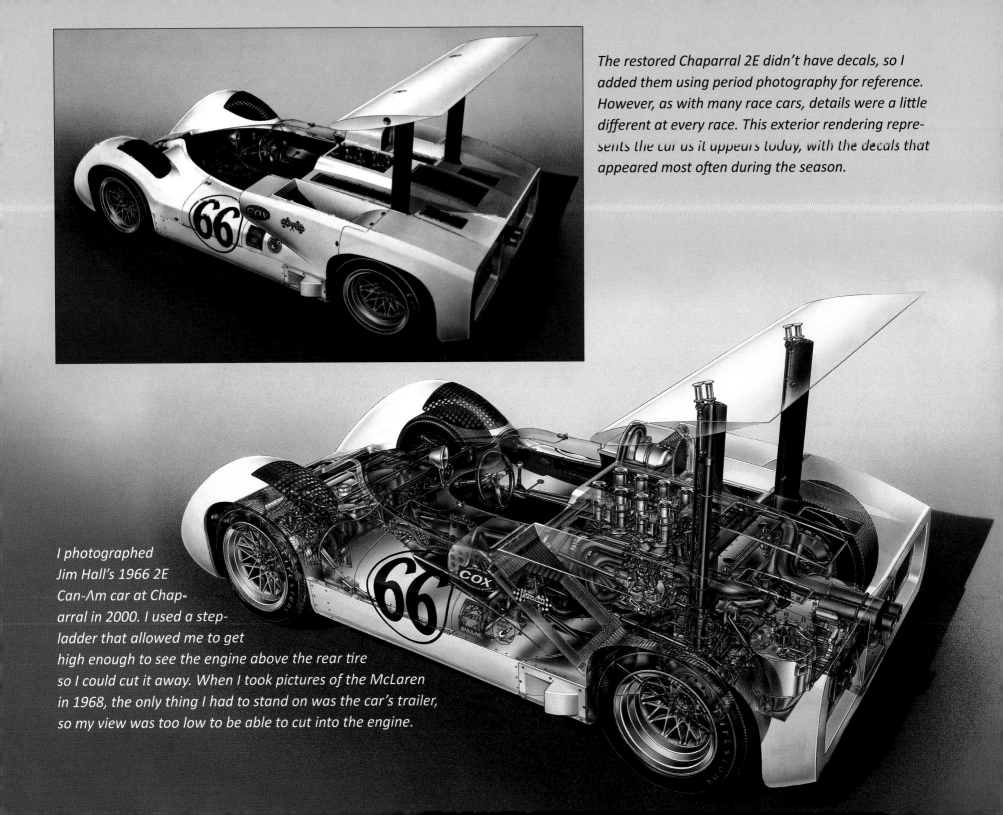

The restored Chaparral 2E didn't have decals, so I added them using period photography for reference. However, as with many race cars, details were a little different at every race. This exterior rendering represents the car as it appears today, with the decals that appeared most often during the season.

I photographed Jim Hall's 1966 2E Can-Am car at Chaparral in 2000. I used a stepladder that allowed me to get high enough to see the engine above the rear tire so I could cut it away. When I took pictures of the McLaren in 1968, the only thing I had to stand on was the car's trailer, so my view was too low to be able to cut into the engine.

HIGHLIGHTS AND REFLECTIONS

Can-Am cars from the 1960s are exciting and fairly simple, making them good subjects for showing basic painting techniques. However, they don't offer many opportunities for advanced rendering. Even though I am best known for illustrating cars, my first full-color airbrush painting was a cutaway of a 1947 Indian Chief motorcycle done in 1977. I realize that this book is primarily about illustrating cars, but 1940s-era American motorcycles are real eye candy, which makes them ideal for demonstrating how I render a variety of reflective surfaces, including chrome. In 1987 I had a deal to do three vintage Harley-Davidson cutaways, starting with a 1949 Hydra-Glide, which was drawn but never completed, leaving it to be finished just for this chapter.

1947 INDIAN CHIEF MOTORCYCLE

The Indian's story began not long after I left engineering to become a full-time professional artist in January 1976. I had to choose between making an illustration deadline for *Road & Track* magazine and completing a prototype irrigation valve on schedule for my then current employer. I made the *Road & Track* deadline. I had steady work from the Willis Oil Tool Company, but doing one oil field valve cutaway after another was less than fulfilling and it led me to look for something fun to do between their projects. I had always been intrigued by

the 1940 and later Indian motorcycles with their outrageous streamline-deco skirted fenders, and I decided that doing a cutaway of one of these jukebox bikes was just what I needed.

Indian had gone out of business in the mid-1950s but lived on in many places, including American Indian Parts in Monrovia, California, which was an easy ride from our house. My wife and I were on my Norton 850 Commando when we visited American Indian Parts with Neil Nissing who did my reference photography riding with us on his Yamaha 500-cc twin. The company's new owner, Charlie, seemed put out by our showing up on a "Limey bike" and a "rice burner" when the post-war Indian I wanted to illustrate was his everyday transportation. "Indian Charlie" was eyeing our foreign bikes when I asked him what the big Chief was like to ride. He responded, "Mister, this here is the smoothest, fastest, safest motorcycle ever built. Any man that tells you different is a goddamn liar!"

I assumed that this bike was a factory-correct 1947 Chief and illustrated it exactly as it was, except for losing the huge modern windshield. Blinded as I was by faith, it didn't occur to me that the 30-year-old Indian was on modern motorcycle tires (with an oval cross-section)

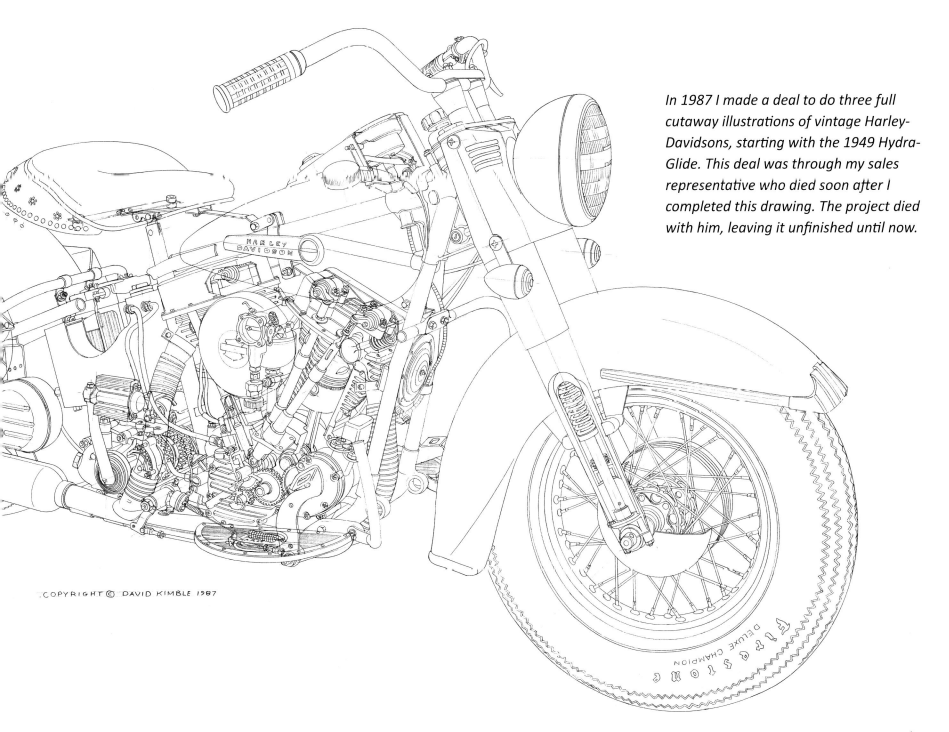

In 1987 I made a deal to do three full cutaway illustrations of vintage Harley-Davidsons, starting with the 1949 Hydra-Glide. This deal was through my sales representative who died soon after I completed this drawing. The project died with him, leaving it unfinished until now.

COPYRIGHT © DAVID KIMBLE 1987

Road & Track was the holy grail of car magazines in 1976 when they asked me to illustrate this sprint car, and I gave up my day job to meet their schedule. This is a Pantone rendering done by cutting out multiple layers of colored adhesive-backed film and applying them in steps on a sheet of acetate.

and had an equally modern oil filter between its frame's down tubes. After the painting was finished I also discovered that this Indian had been assembled from 1946 through 1948 parts and its chrome-plated forks should have been painted black. The gas tanks had the most dramatic custom touch with the factory chrome Indian script replaced by a fanciful hand-painted chief's head reminiscent of Indian's 1930s tank decals. My intent had been to illustrate an authentic 1947 Indian, so I learned a valuable lesson and would never start another historical illustration without thoroughly researching the subject.

In May 1976 John Steinberg contacted me; he was the best artist sales agent in Los Angeles, and he offered to represent me. Seemingly overnight I was working for the biggest advertising agencies in the country. John was an amazing salesman and every project he brought in was a new challenge, stretching my limited abilities and keeping me in a constant state of high anxiety. The approach I used to render both the *Road & Track* and Willis illustrations made use of Pantone's adhesive-backed sheets of translucent color in stepped layers to create a

It was a steady flow of freelance work from the Willis Oil Tool Company that made it possible to leave my engineering position at Tyme Valve. This pig ball launcher is typical of the Pantone-rendered cutaway illustrations I did for Willis. This would later transition into airbrush.

graduated tone. Steinberg was able to sell the unconventional look of these Pantone renderings but encouraged me to add some airbrushed paint over their hard-edged stepped tones.

I learned to use an airbrush by watching Dick Bruton, who taught airbrush classes at the Los Angeles City Colleges. He painted some oil field valve sections that I had drawn for Willis in 1975. My Pantone renderings were done on acetate taped over a film positive that was placed on top after they were completed, and I found that the Winsor & Newton gouache Dick was using worked well right on the film.

I started airbrushing the highlights, and by May 1977 I was rendering with more paint than Pantone, leading to a complete full-color airbrush painting without any Pantone backing it up.

I didn't have any idea how long this Indian painting might take, which made it too risky for a commercial project with a deadline, but I had finished the drawing and was waiting for an opportunity to complete it. John Steinberg was talking to Gray Advertising about my doing the technical illustrations for their Honda Motorcycle account and he thought the Indian would be an ideal demonstration of what

What started as an experiment turned into a career after my first airbrush painting of this 1947 Indian Chief was shown to prospective clients by my sales rep. After starting to use an airbrush for adding highlights to Pantone renderings in 1975, my illustrations became more paint than Pantone by 1977 when I did the Indian.

With the Indian, John Steinberg convinced Gray Advertising to have me create the technical illustrations for their Honda Motorcycle account, but mostly all I illustrated were parts. The only complete bike cutaway I did for Honda was of a 6-cylinder CBX, making the Harley only my third motorcycle cutaway, but I'd like to do more.

I painted the Indian on the front side of a film positive as though it was on illustration board and when I turned the film over for a look, I made an amazing discovery. Seeing the lines on top of the painting improved its resolution, and looking at the paint through the film increased contrast and made the colors appear brighter. This was in spite of spraying the lighter colors first; the effect was even more dramatic the next time when I started with the darks. Now the backward Indian would have to be flopped for reproduction, so I removed the Indian logotype from the chief's head on the tank to allow the image to be reversed. This, however, didn't help the framed original, which now had its shift lever on the wrong side, giving people in the know a lot of laughs.

I could do with a bike. John turned down some minor projects to give me time, which paid big dividends. The wild Indian went over really big at Gray and with Honda, leading to a two-year contract. Even though this painting is a little heavy-handed and basic, it still looks pretty good today and was the starting point for the approach to painting I have used ever since. Fortunately, this bike was photographed in good outdoor light so I could copy the photos' cores, reflections, and highlights, which was a big help at the time but is no longer necessary.

1949 HARLEY-DAVIDSON HYDRA-GLIDE

The Harley's story is very different and starts 10 years later in 1987, following up a cutaway illustration of the starship *Enterprise* that John Steinberg and I did under license from Paramount Studios. John obtained a license from Harley-Davidson, along with factory support, for me to illustrate and for him to sell cutaway posters of the 1936 Knucklehead, 1939 UHL Flathead, and 1949 FL Panhead Hydra-Glide. Examples of these bikes were in Harley's historical collection in the small museum at the York, Pennsylvania, assembly plant. Upon returning from a trip to France to visit the Renault Alpine plant in Dieppe, I flew into Baltimore and then drove out to the plant to photograph the bikes. Harley-Davidson's licensing trademark department then sent the material on these bikes to me from their archives.

I started with the 1949 Hydra-Glide because it was the inspiration for the Heritage models that were currently in the showrooms and prints of my illustrations were going to be available at Harley dealers. When the pencil layout was finished it had to be submitted to Harley-Davidson for approval and I received a letter back from no less a luminary than Willie G. Davidson. I was blown away by Willie G.'s response; he really liked my drawing and was very enthusiastic about the other bikes I planned to illustrate. This was in April 1987. Tragically, John Steinberg died in May and the entire Harley deal died with him, leaving the Hydra-Glide unfinished for the next 27 years.

Even though the Harley was drawn 10 years into my career, it was a long time and a lot of illustrations ago; my skill and perception continued to develop through the years. Unlike with the McLaren, which was done in the 1960s and drawn for an entirely different finishing approach, I was able to rework the original Harley drawing to bring it up to my current standards.

At the museum, I was told that the bikes I was photographing had all rolled off the assembly line and directly into their collection, mak-

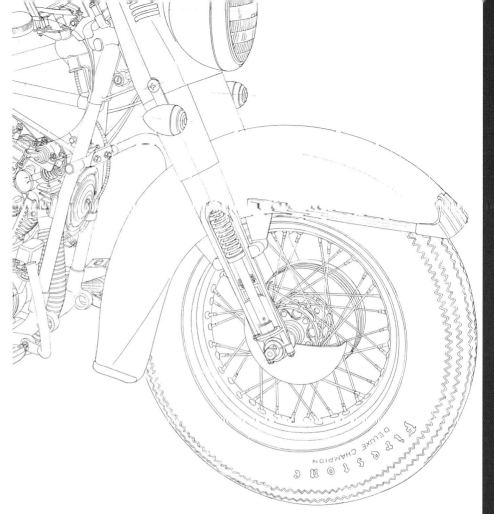

After 27 years of doing cutaway illustrations I went over the entire Harley drawing, but the only significant changes I made were to the tires. I don't know how I missed it in 1987, but after studying the factory photos again, the 1970s (or later) tires on the bike looked completely out of place.

ing them 100-percent original. However, this proved to be only partly true. I had equipped my 1949 Hydra-Glide drawing to match the factory studio photography. When I compared it again to these photos, I realized that, like the Indian, this bike was on modern tires. Mercifully,

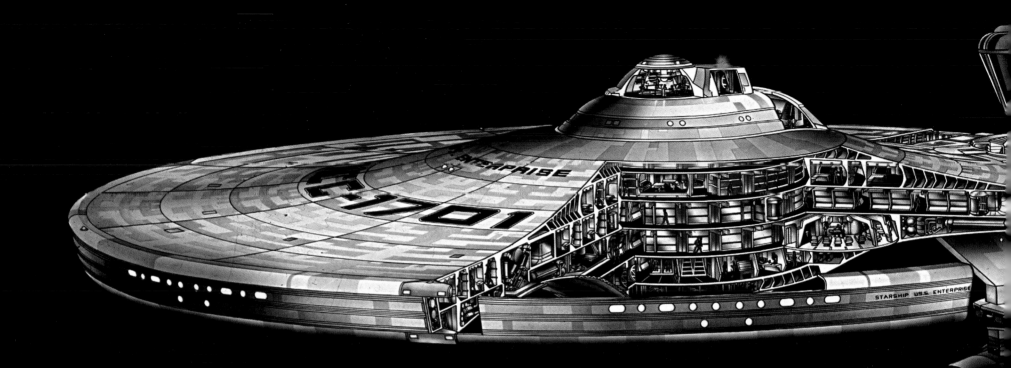

Improbable as it seems, my involvement with the production of Star Trek: The Motion Picture *and a cutaway illustration of the starship Enterprise led to the Harley-Davidson illustration. John Steinberg got me this gig and we partnered on the second printing of this poster as we were planning to do with the vintage Harleys.*

STARSHIP U.S.S. ENTERPRISE

SPECIFICATIONS:
LENGTH OVERALL — 1000 FT.
LENGTH OF SECONDARY HULL — 397 FT.
HEIGHT OVERALL — 234 FT.
DIAMETER OF PRIMARY HULL — 450 FT.
DIAMETER OF SECONDARY HULL — 108 FT.
SPEED — WARP 12
COMPLIMENT OF MEN — OFFICERS:72
ENLISTED PERSONNEL:420

1. DEFLECTOR
2. PRIMARY HU
3. FORWARD P
4. BRIDGE
5. NAVIGATION
6. CAPTAIN KIF
7. BRIDGE TUF
8. PRIMARY DC
   STAGING AF
9. V.I.P. (OFFIC
10. OFFICER'S S
11. REC. ROOM
12. CONNECTIN
13. TURBO ELE\
14. IMPULSE EN
    CRYSTAL

ABOUT THE ARTIST.

DAVID KIMBLE IS A NATIONALLY KNOWN
COMMERCIAL ILLUSTRATOR LIVING IN LOS ANGELES,
SPECIALIZING IN CUTAWAY ILLUSTRATION. HIS
BACKGROUND AS A MECHANICAL ENGINEER/ARTIST
LED TO HIS INVOLVEMENT IN STAR TREK® THE
MOTION PICTURE; CREATING THE WORKING
DRAWINGS AND PLANS FROM WHICH MOST OF THE
MODELS WERE CONSTRUCTED. HIS INVOLVEMENT
INSPIRED THIS COMPREHENSIVE ILLUSTRATION
THAT SHOWS IN DETAIL THE RELATIONSHIP OF ALL
THE INTERIOR SCENES FROM THE MOTION PICTURE TO
THE EXTERIOR OF THE STARSHIP U.S.S. ENTERPRISE.™

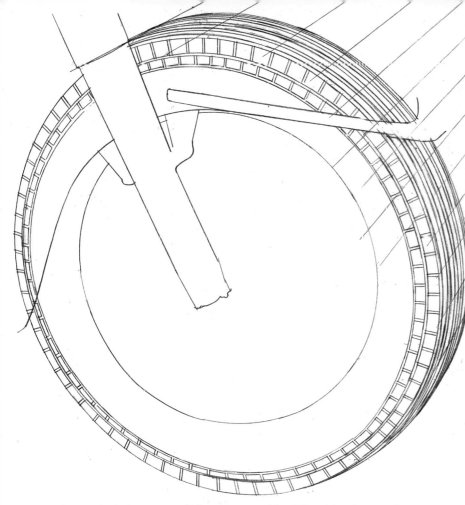

To make period tires out of the ones on the bike, I had to reshape them with a flatter tread that had a more pronounced shoulder. The real challenge was laying out the sidewalls' two rows of staggered blocks that had to be consistent enough to show through the front fender.

everything else checked out and the tires were the only major revision. But, while I was at it, I redesigned and upgraded most of the engine and transmission sections also.

It takes a lot of information to do a cutaway illustration, and in addition to my photos, I worked from the 1949 Glide's service man-ual, a parts catalog, and the archival material that Harley sent to me. All of this was very helpful, but there is nothing like seeing and photographing the actual disassembled parts to make a cutaway real. David Hanson, who restores vintage Harleys and Indians and sells parts for them, made it possible. Neil Nissing and I made several trips to Hanson's shop in Ventura, California, while I was doing the original drawing in 1987, and I recently called David before starting to paint. Even though he was overwhelmed with customers, he took the time to answer my questions. Having this exciting drawing lying around for so many years was frustrating, but the final results benefitted from this wait. Rick Terrell electronically inked my upgraded drawing.

I was lucky to be able to have the Indian photographed outside, but in later years, illustrating pre-production cars outside that were "still under wraps" was usually not possible. I like to render vehicles in outside light regardless of the lighting conditions of the reference photography. Such light is often plain lousy, with big fluorescent lights reflected across the car or bike to be illustrated.

The lighting of the rendering can be done convincingly by following a few simple principles. You start with thinking of the vehicle as a contoured mirror with varying degrees of reflectivity. Visualize the sun behind and slightly to the rear of the subject so that the front is darker than the side. The upward surfaces reflect the sky, the lower surfaces reflect the ground, and the horizon is reflected somewhere in between.

The colors of the painted surfaces are only slightly influenced by the sky and ground reflections, although chrome reflects them almost like a mirror with brighter highlights and a darker, sharp-edged

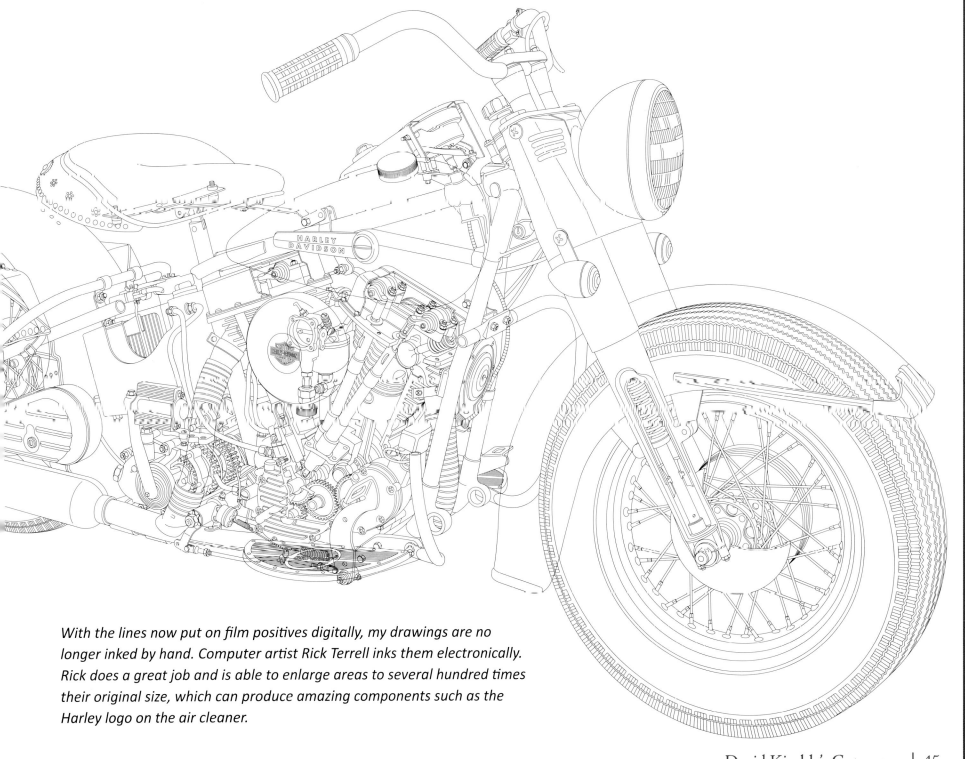

With the lines now put on film positives digitally, my drawings are no longer inked by hand. Computer artist Rick Terrell inks them electronically. Rick does a great job and is able to enlarge areas to several hundred times their original size, which can produce amazing components such as the Harley logo on the air cleaner.

These bars show how the different metals in the Harley illustration were rendered. From left to right: The first bar is chrome, with sharp-edged jet-black cores and fades overlaid with Cerulean Blue for sky and Chinese Orange for ground reflections. Next, aluminum is done the same way except that Cerulean Blue is mixed into the jet black for the cores, which have softer edges. The brass, which I've shown in the third bar, doesn't appear in the Harley illustration, but uses jet black for cores and fades overlaid with brilliant yellow and Chinese Orange. On the Harley, the yellow metal is bronze, which is copper alloyed with tin, making it grayer than brass, which is alloyed with zinc. The final bar shows pure copper, rendered by mixing Havana Lake with jet black for the cores and fades overlaid with Chinese Orange.

horizon. Without a background the horizon needs to be very simple, although reflections within the image can be highly detailed and sharp-edged on shiny surfaces. Matte finishes are rendered with soft-edged tones that get a little harder-edged for semi-gloss surfaces such as the Harley's tires, leather saddlebags, and cast-aluminum timing gear cover. When I taught advanced rendering for *Airbrush Action* magazine, I used to demonstrate how to render different surface materials with a series of cylinders like the ones I've done here.

The McLaren drawing is small for a car at 26½ inches long, limiting me to basic rendering. The 29-inch-long Harley is a good size for a bike and allows for detailed highlights and reflections. The Harley's black components were painted first to put the lighter colors in context, working toward aluminum and finally chrome; this bike has just enough of it to not cancel itself out. With the engine, transmission, and suspension out in the open (unlike a car), only a few isolated parts need to be transparent; the most prominent are the front fender and right gas tank. The portions of the front tire and frame showing through these parts are rendered with a lot of contrast to allow the color surrounding them to be added into their highlights without making them too dark.

As always, the tires were painted first, but before getting started, I had to correct one of the few problems in the electronic inking. The sidewall tread blocks did not line up correctly, so I had to color in the grooves between them with a Stabilo pencil to realign them radially before cutting the frisket.

American motorcycle tires in the 1940s had an almost automotive look except for the tread on their sidewalls. With their narrow-crowned tread I was able to paint them in one pass, pulling frisket progressively. The Harley museum collection's 1948 Panhead, unlike the 1949, has original-style tires, and I used this photo from a book for reference while painting.

If I had completed the 1949 Hydra-Glide in 1987, it would have been red on a black background, but I now feel this bike's Peacock Blue has a great vintage look, so I stayed with it. Also, unless the client requests a background, I no longer do them. On this painting I am the client, so the Harley is on white, which makes a better comparison with the Indian, showing my progress over the past 37 years. A car's shadow on the ground gives it a surface to sit on, but none of my bikes have a shadow under them because they are open between their wheels on the bottom, which makes a shadow look awkward. Harley's Peacock Blue is as elusive to match as McLaren Orange and also needs to be painted with opaque color, and like with the McLaren, body color follows the black areas.

Continuing with the same strategy as with the McLaren, small spots of bright color come next, with the scarlet red gas tank badge graphics having a visual impact far greater than their size. Even though the bronze carburetor and rocker arm shaft bearing caps along with the copper-plated rocker arms are relatively subdued, they also stand out because they are surrounded by aluminum. It's all about context, and small spots of contrasting color can make much larger areas look brighter. Note the amber marker lights mounted to the chrome fork legs, and even the orange wire sleeves.

The 1949 model was the first Harley that had a lot of chrome, which is essentially a mirror reflecting everything

I thought everything black was filled in at this point. Then I discovered that the chain and sprocket should show through the saddlebag; I had left them off the drawing, and as more line becomes form, additional small black parts, such as the battery cover, continued to show up. But at least I didn't have to add anything else.

Everything bolts to the frame, which comes with its intriguing combination of steel tubing welded to iron castings, including the fork head. It is painted high-gloss black so it offers some great rendering opportunities, and fades at the edges where it goes behind the gas tank.

Continuing to follow my cutaway painting playbook, the sharp-edged contours and reflections were drawn with a blue Stabilo on the frisket over the solid portions of the bodywork. I also added a little shading because if I don't like the way the body turns out it is a real mess to wash off this much paint.

As with the McLaren, the Harley's bodywork needed to be painted opaquely, and even though I used Winsor & Newton Derwent Blue as a starting point, Harley's version was difficult to match. This color didn't flatten out as much as McLaren Orange (with the lighter shade sprayed on top), so it looks better on the back of the film.

step in rendering chrome. Before cutting the frisket, I usually do a little shading with black, or if it is a complex shape also red and blue Stabilo pencils, to simulate how it is going to look. With almost solid jet black sprayed on the cores, another frisket is cut and a thin fog of black is airbrushed at the top, followed by a Cerulean Blue fade that stops short of the lower core, leaving a white horizon. A denser black fog is added under the lower core and then painted over with Chinese Orange for the ground reflection, and when I get it right, this combination of black, blue, and orange paint looks like chrome.

With the chrome painted backward, that is, with black going down first and then painted over with blue and orange, it looks subdued but comes to life when the film is turned over. Painting moves onto the front of the film at this point, with the rendering on the back airbrushed a little light to leave room for density to be added with shadows and value adjustments without the illustration becoming too dark. This is the first look at the bike completely filled in. Before going any further, it needs to be evaluated and a list made of what it needs to reach completion. A side benefit of painting on the back of the film

around it, so it had to be painted last after everything else was filled in. This left a nagging problem that had to be fixed, along with the internal detail in the cutaway sections, the external cast aluminum, and the cad-plated steel to be dealt with before taking on the chrome. When the seat was airbrushed along with the other black components I realized my original contour line was way off, but I decided to live with it for a while. Fortunately gouache painted on film can be washed off and another frisket cut, but the photo eradicator I used is no longer available so the bogus line had to be scraped off and retouched.

Stabilo pencils will even draw on actual chrome and they are used to lay out the black sharp-edged cores on the frisket, which is the first

Almost all of the unpainted white areas are bare metal, which includes a lot of chrome, and it will be a real treat to render. The painting is looking good so far except for the seat, which needs its upper contour line moved down to look as though someone can sit in it.

Opposite: Even though all of the small spots of contrasting color are concentrated around the engine, they add a lot to the entire illustration. Shown here from the back side of the film, the recessed scarlet red gas-tank-badge graphics in particular have a visual impact far greater than their size.

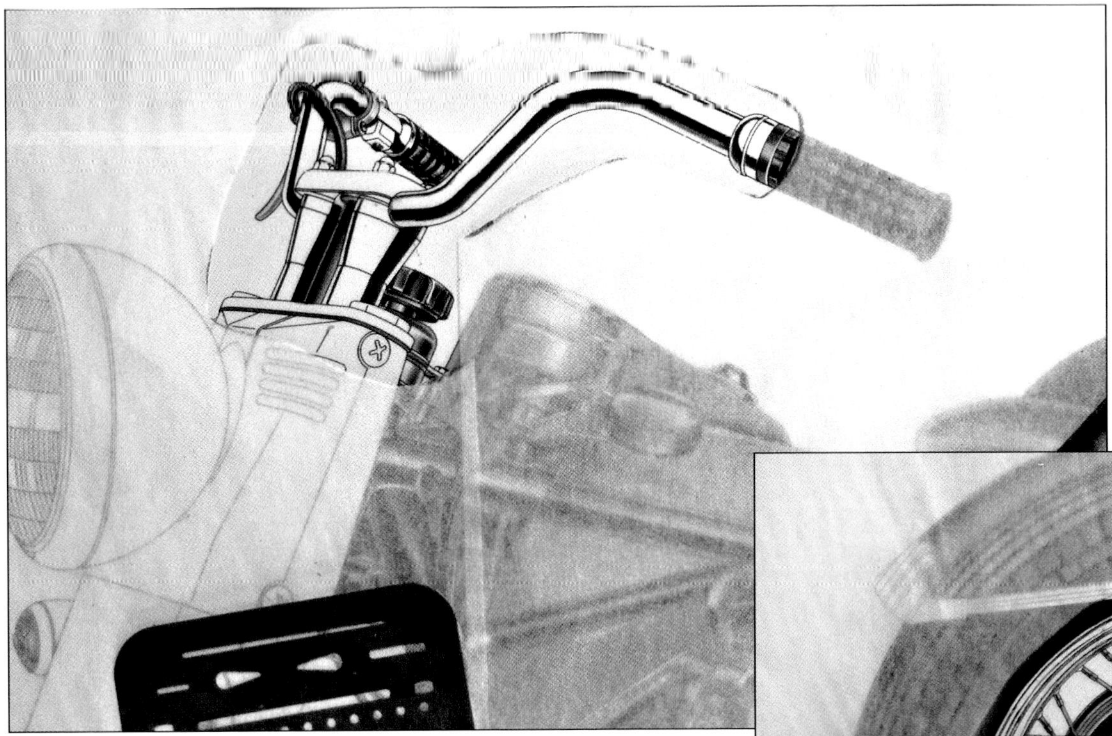

With chrome all but disappearing from current production cars, the McLaren's roll bar and rearview mirrors were the first chrome I've had the opportunity to do in years. Fortunately, the Harley has plenty of chrome, and the first step in rendering the shiny stuff is to draw its sharp, hard-edged horizon reflections and cores on the frisket with a black Stabilo pencil.

Wire wheels suck up a lot of time and if they have chrome rims they take even longer, but the cad plated spokes with a black hub saved a little time. Again, a black Stabilo was used to draw the hard-edged reflections on the frisket with a little shading added to the horizontal surfaces of the rims.

is that anything painted on the front that doesn't work out can be washed off for another try without wiping out days of work underneath it.

With shadowing and the first round of value adjustments completed, only the see-through effects remain before making the final adjustments to balance the illustration. Even though the Harley's transparent bodywork is far more limited than the McLaren painting, it is still the most gratifying part of the project. As with the chrome, Stabilo colored pencils are used to simulate airbrushing on the frisket over the gas tank and front fender; the solid rear fender is highlighted at the same time for a gratifying part. At this stage, with shadows under the tank and fender and the internal details fading toward the edges, they are already beginning to look slightly transparent without their outer skin being added. For a transparent surface to look pleasing, the combined density of it and the detail showing through cannot be much greater than either surface by itself or it looks too dark and filled in. Even if the values are well balanced, an uninterrupted see-through kills highlights and obscures details, which makes the illustration look dull. This is why I use vignettes. My approach is to dissolve the exterior into the interior detail with an unobstructed area in between the fades, so both layers remain bright in enough places that they do not look out of context with the solid portions. The Harley's frame and front tire fade near the edges of the gas tank and fender with the light area filled in with the exterior Peacock Blue, which also fades as the internal details get darker. With the addition of permanent white highlights, this technique allows bright transparent exterior contours to be painted over equally bright interior detail, but it is tricky.

Blue and white Stabilos used on the frisket simulate the transparent front fender, and even though I wasn't concerned about the gas tank, some white was added to it as well. This test revealed that the fender's highlight conflicted with the tire's ellipses, but with the tire protected by the film I decided to see what the see-through would look like painted.

The small see-throughs on the engine are very straightforward with only an edge highlight and simple cores needed to make the carburetor seem to be behind the chrome air cleaner cover. Also, a section of the rear cylinder's flexible chrome sleeve has been cut away so the transmission can be seen through the exposed exhaust pipe, again rendered with a simple white transparent core. Black is one of the easiest colors to look through without obscuring the detail underneath, and the seat mount, with its pendulum arm, comes through clearly even though

there is a lot of tone on top. Many different planes show through the right saddlebag, including the chain and sprocket on the other side of the bike, so a little transparent white has been fogged on in a few places to give its leather skin a presence before adding the black.

It took four rolls of frisket, dozens of sheets of vellum, and many tubes of paint to reach the final result. After cutting frisket and spraying paint for 18 days, a full-color cutaway illustration of a 1949 Harley Davidson FL Hydra-Glide emerged. Although this illustration is based on a bike I photographed in the company's museum, I added period-correct tires along with all of the accessories Harley used to equip one of these motorcycles for studio photography. One of the most challenging aspects of this project was that I intended to render

One of the advantages of painting on film is that both the hubcap on the back and the transparent fender on the front side could be washed off and redone. The problems were that the hubcap was cut below the horizon so its sky reflection had to be faked and the fender's highlight conflicted with the front tire, necessitating a vignette.

The gas tank see through wasn't a problem but the chrome upper fork leg cover worried me with its reflection in the headlight and the headlight's reflection back into the fork leg cover. As it turned out my concern was unnecessary; this area went down on the first try and turned out to be one of the most gratifying part of the painting.

the Harley in outside light even though I only had indoor reference photography to work from. Fortunately, the Indian Chief was photographed outside, and even though it was my first airbrush painting I had managed to follow the highlights and reflections reasonably well, so I could use it for reference while painting the Harley.

The focal point of any motorcycle is its engine, and the Panhead, which was named for the shape of its rocker arm covers, was arguably the most impressive-looking of Harley-Davidson's big 45-degree V-twins. I generally followed the factory cutaway illustration in this area, but detailed the internal components from photos of actual parts that were also used to do the transmission cutaway. These engines had a dry sump lubrication system with a U-shaped oil tank located under the seat. I cut that away to reveal the battery, which had to be drawn from a parts catalog illustration. I have always enjoyed rendering

chrome-plated flexible exhaust pipe sleeves on 1930s era classic cars, but this is a closer look so I could do more with them here, and I also had fun with the red graphics recessed into the chrome gas tank badge.

I watched a DVD of *Code Two*, a motion picture released by MGM in 1953, and re-watched it several times while redrawing and later painting the Harley, just to see these old bikes in action with the Los Angeles Police Department. All the motorcycles in the film are Harleys with Panhead engines and springer forks, making them 1948 models, except for the instructor's bike at the training school. It is a Glide, like the one in my illustration. My uncle, Glen Stone, who was a Los Angeles Police Department motorcycle cop and somewhat of a role model for me at the time, told us about the picture while it was being filmed, but I never saw it until it recently came out on DVD. I became interested in motorcycles because of Uncle Glen and can still see him and his partner, Jack Richardson, spinning a 180 side by side on his unpaved driveway and going through the gears in unison down the street.

David Kimble

All of the small transparent parts are around the engine; the carburetor shows the air cleaner and the transmission through the rear exhaust pipe. The right footboard is also transparent. The rear brake linkage shows through, and the frame, rear wheel, and tire are seen through the right saddlebag.

This is the final result of cutting four rolls of frisket, using dozens of sheets of vellum, and spraying many tubes of paint over 18 days. This cutaway is of the first 1949 Hydra-Glide to roll off the Harley-Davidson assembly line, equipped in the same manner as the bike they used for studio photography.

ENGINES AND TRANSMISSIONS

Engines are an important part of technical automotive illustration, and in recent years I have illustrated far more of them than complete cars, along with an occasional transmission, primarily for GM Powertrain.

255-ci OFFENHAUSER

My first engine cutaway illustration was of a 255-ci Offy, working with Leo Goossen, its designer at Meyer and Drake. This illustration would accompany an article I was writing for *Sports Car Graphic* magazine. These 4-cylinder double-overhead cam engines with four valves per cylinder had dominated the Indy 500 in the 1950s, and this is the last version of the 255, adapted for installation in the new rear-engine (actually mid-engine) "Funny Cars." The massive front engine mount wasn't needed and the integrated cylinder block and head was cast in

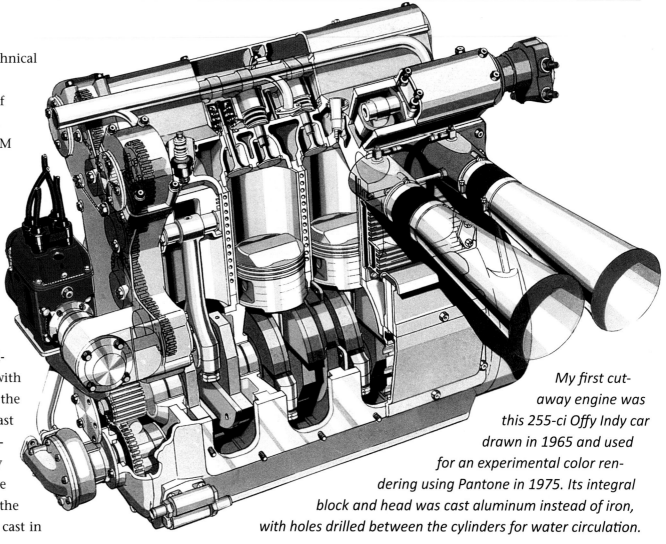

My first cutaway engine was this 255-ci Offy Indy car drawn in 1965 and used for an experimental color rendering using Pantone in 1975. Its integral block and head was cast aluminum instead of iron, with holes drilled between the cylinders for water circulation.

aluminum instead of iron, with the cylinders siamesed to make room for iron liners with holes drilled between them for water circulation.

This Offy was originally finished as a line drawing in pencil without shading, but when full color cutaways started appearing in the car magazines during the 1970s, I used it for an experiment with color. This engine became my first Pantone rendering in 1975 and appeared in numerous magazines in color. The most important thing, though, was that the Willis Oil Tool Company's art director, John Ackerman, liked it, and I used this technique for rendering cutaways of many of their products. Even though the fully airbrushed Indian cutaway had landed me the Honda Motorcycle account, there were art directors who liked the unique look of my Pantone ren-

derings, and I used a mix of the two techniques for Gray Advertising. Honda had gone BMW's flat twins one better with their horizontally opposed 4-cylinder Gold Wing engine, and Gray had me use Pantone to render my cutaway of it, which included the Honda's BMW style shaft drive.

Honda Engines

Even before John Steinberg asked me to join the stable of artists he represented, I had done a little work for Honda through Asbury, Rome, and Word, a small ad agency in Signal Hill, California, near Willis.

Even after I started airbrushing, my Pantone renderings remained popular, and this 4-cylinder Honda Gold Wing engine and driveline were done for Gray Advertising. This was Honda's take on BMW's horizontally opposed twins with shaft drive, but Honda went one better with an additional pair of cylinders.

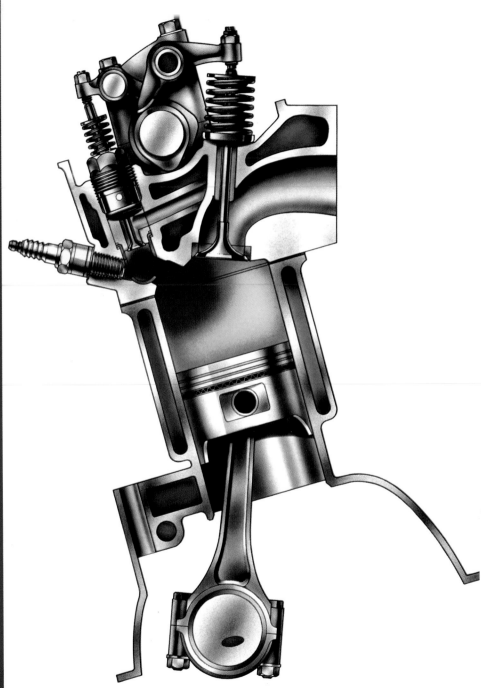

Because it is just a section through a single cylinder of a Honda 4-cylinder car engine and not a complete vehicle, I don't count this as my first airbrush illustration even though it was drawn a year before the Indian. This illustration features Honda's CVCC cylinder head with a pre-combustion chamber that gave them an advantage in both emissions and fuel economy.

They had a small piece of the Honda Automotive account, and I did very simple basic see-through illustrations for them of the Civic, Civic Wagon, and Accord in Pantone with airbrushed highlights. I also did a full-color airbrush illustration of Honda's CVCC engine that was cut through a single cylinder more than a year before painting the Indian, but I don't count it as my first because it was just an orthographic (straight-on flat plane) section. Honda's controlled-vortex combustion chamber head design gave them an advantage in both emissions and fuel economy, and they gave me an actual sectioned head to work from, which I still have.

Acura Brochure

My career really took off in the 1980s with Steinberg bringing in work from the advertising agencies, while I dealt directly with the car magazines and through them with the manufacturers. Even with these contacts, it was John who brought me the biggest automotive deal to date, an assignment to do every illustration for Acura's first brochure, which included two engine cutaways. I was disappointed to find out that Acura's inline 4-cylinder and V-6 engines had already been drawn in Japan, and all they wanted me to do was Ink and airbrush them for the brochure. I was able to get creative with the rendering, however, because they only wanted the internal components painted at full intensity with the exterior fading into line, like the Yamaha motorcycle illustrations done by Richard Leach, for whom I had been hired to sub.

An assignment to illustrate Acura's first brochure included a 4-cylinder and a V-6 engine cutaway, but unfortunately, they had to be created from Japanese drawings. Only the internal components were to be painted at full intensity; the exterior faded into line, a popular approach at the time.

PETERSEN PUBLISHING PROJECT

The first cutaway illustration of a GM engine I did was the result of working for the car magazines with Leonard Emanuelson, who had been editor-in-chief of *Hot Rod*, arranging for an early production quad-4 to be delivered to the studio I shared with Neil Nissing. This was The General's first domestic double-overhead-cam, four-valve-per-cylinder production car engine. I came through a mechanic who disassemble it, with Neil photographing the teardown in stages. This was the only way to approach this project because even though my illustration was for a GM advertising insert, it was a Petersen Publishing project and General Motors wouldn't release any engineering drawings. I made my own rough orthographic assembly drawings to plot the internal components into the illustration, and although the water jacketing and other passages were only speculation, there were never any complaints from The General.

From the beginning of our association in 1976, John Steinberg and I had an understanding that he would manage and receive a commission only on the projects he brought in, while my existing clients were mine alone. This created some friction when my work for the car magazines started progressively taking more time in the 1980s, but John saw that his sales were benefitting from my increased visibility. One project John brought in that clearly came out of our compromise was a catalog cover illustration for Edelbrock, featuring a small-block Chevy engine equipped with their various products. The concept came from Edelbrock's ad agency Dancer Fitzgerald Sample, and I met with Vic Edelbrock in one of the agency's conference rooms to discuss how much to exaggerate the size of the engine in a stylized Camaro.

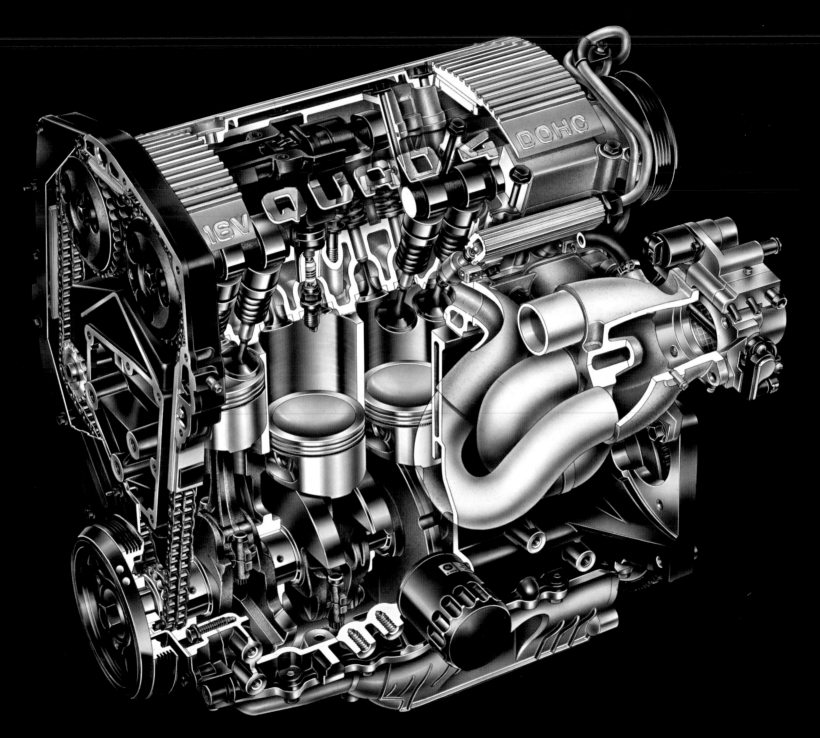

Opposite: The quad-4 was my first cutaway of a GM engine, and The General's first double-overhead cam, four-valve-per-cylinder dome-stroke production engine. This illustration was done for a Petersen Publishing advertising insert, they were not able to obtain the engineering drawings, so they had an engine disassembled for me to work from.

Edelbrock's ad agency, Dancer Fitzgerald Sample, hired me for this catalog cover illustration of a cutaway small-block Chevy equipped with their products in a stylized Camaro. I made copies of the engine drawing in different sizes for a meeting with Vic Edelbrock; he chose the 900-ci version.

By the late 1980s I still hadn't done a cutaway illustration directly for a manufacturer, but with General Motors coming out with their first two double-overhead cam four-valve-per-cylinder V-8s that was about to change. I was fortunate enough to illustrate both of these engines starting with Chevrolet's 5.7-liter LT5 for the ZR-1 super Corvette, but with a cutaway already done internally at General Motors, mine was commissioned by *Automobile* magazine. General Motors owned Lotus at the time, which designed the LT5 working with GM's Chevrolet Pontiac Canada (CPC) Engine Group, based on the stillborn Lotus Etna 4.0-liter V-8 architecture. Following the same architectural approach, Cadillac designed the second V-8. This was the 4.6-liter Northstar, and I worked directly with Cadillac's engine group to illustrate it and its 4-speed automatic front-wheel-drive transaxle. So I did my first factory engine and transmission cutaways at the same time.

After the disappointment of missing out on the factory cutaway of the LT5 in 1988, I was much better known in 1991 when the first partial redesign of the small-block Chevy since its introduction came along. Tom Hoxie, Chevrolet's deputy director of public relations, asked me to illustrate the Gen II small-block-designated LT1, which was a Corvette exclusive for 1992. It brought back a 300-hp base engine to the Y-body for the first time since 1970. The CPC's Powertrain Product Information Group liked my LT1 illustration better than the ones it was having done in-house, and it wasn't

The Northstar's 4-speed front-wheel-drive transaxle was another first for my career: a cutaway illustration of an automatic transmission. Hydromatic was still a separate entity at this time and was located in the former Ford World War II B-24 bomber plant, so this project took me to Willow Run.

long before I was illustrating all of GM's engines, working with Jack Underwood. The next year Jack had me illustrate the Camaro-Firebird 275-hp version of the LT1, which had to be an entirely new drawing from the opposite side to prevent the F-Body's accessories from being cut off.

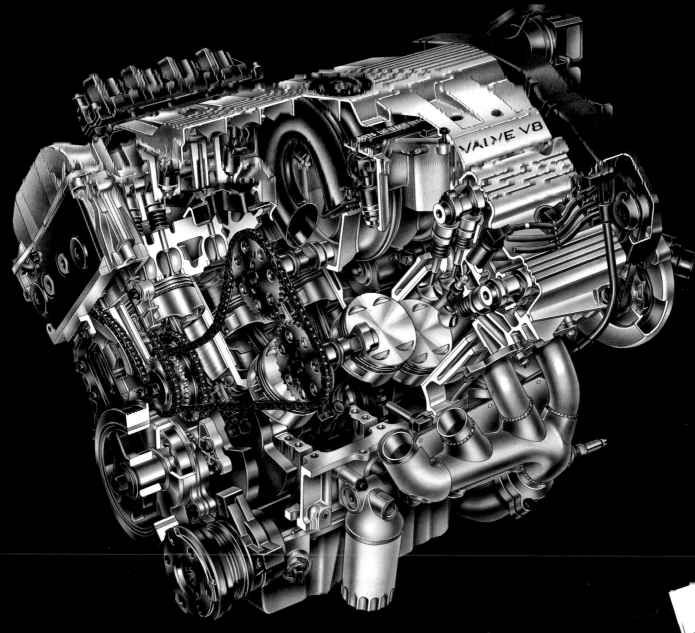

The Cadillac Northstar 4.6-liter double-overhead cam four-valve-per-cylinder V-8 was my first cutaway engine illustration done directly for a manufacturer. Cadillac still had their own powertrain group in 1990, and I worked with them at the GM division's old Clark Street plant near downtown Detroit.

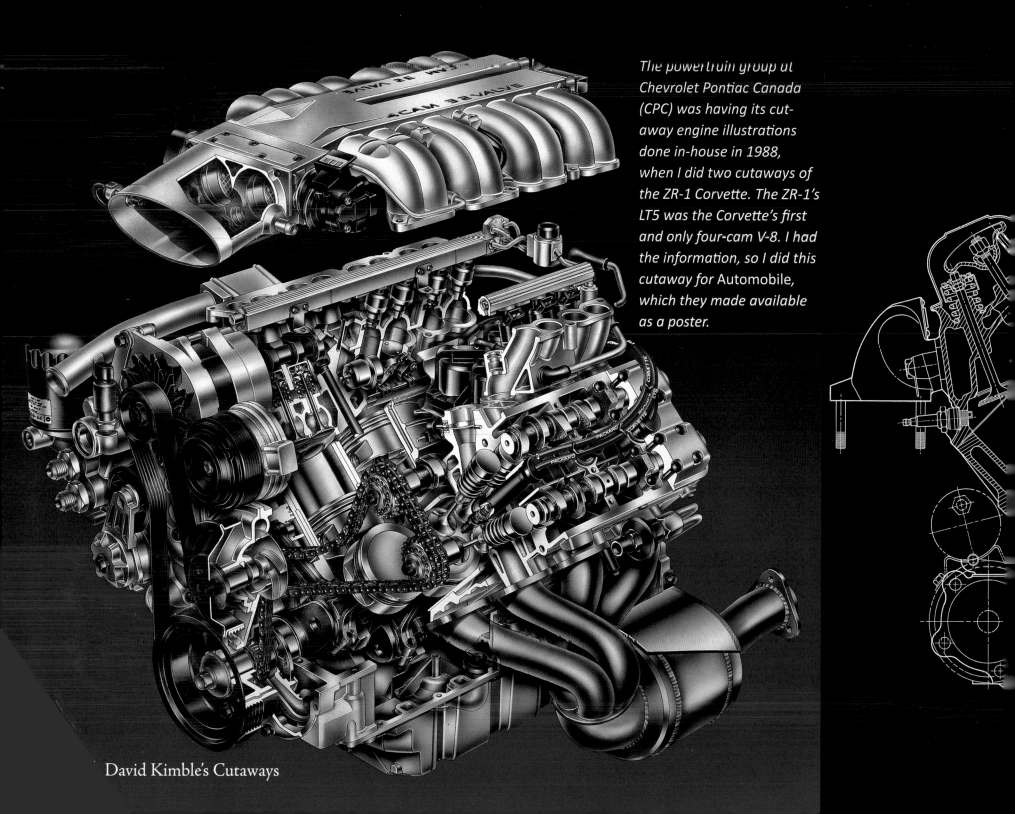

The powertrain group at Chevrolet Pontiac Canada (CPC) was having its cutaway engine illustrations done in-house in 1988, when I did two cutaways of the ZR-1 Corvette. The ZR-1's LT5 was the Corvette's first and only four-cam V-8. I had the information, so I did this cutaway for Automobile, which they made available as a poster.

David Kimble's Cutaways

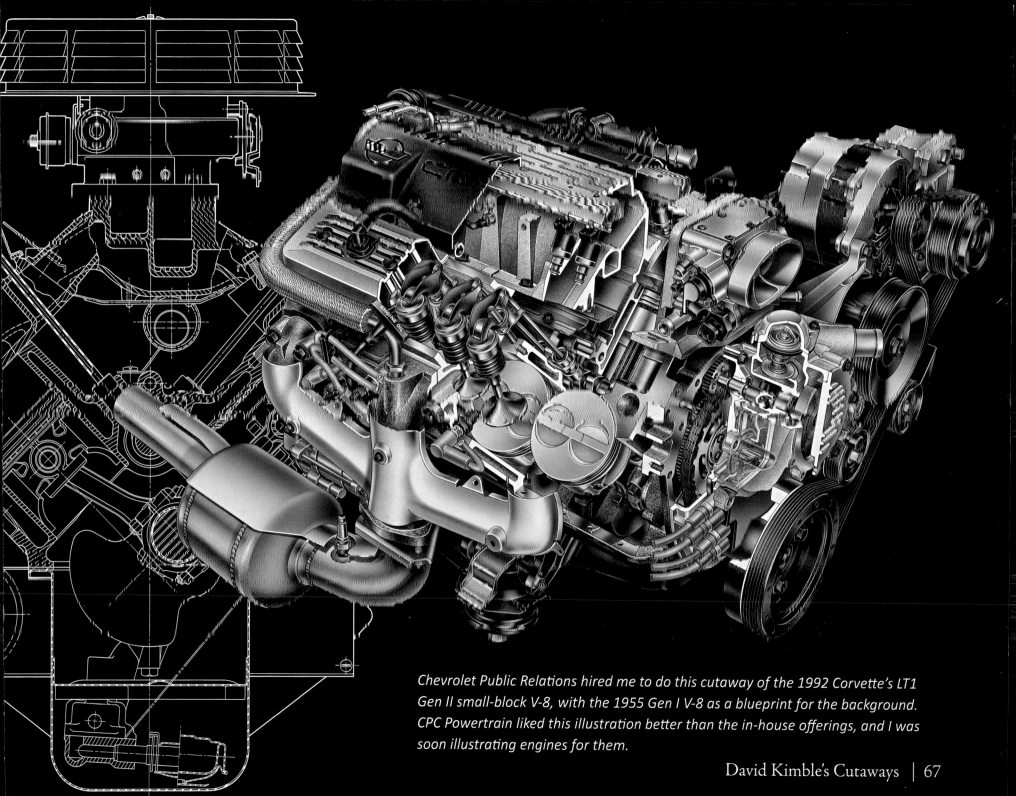

Chevrolet Public Relations hired me to do this cutaway of the 1992 Corvette's LT1 Gen II small-block V-8, with the 1955 Gen I V-8 as a blueprint for the background. CPC Powertrain liked this illustration better than the in-house offerings, and I was soon illustrating engines for them.

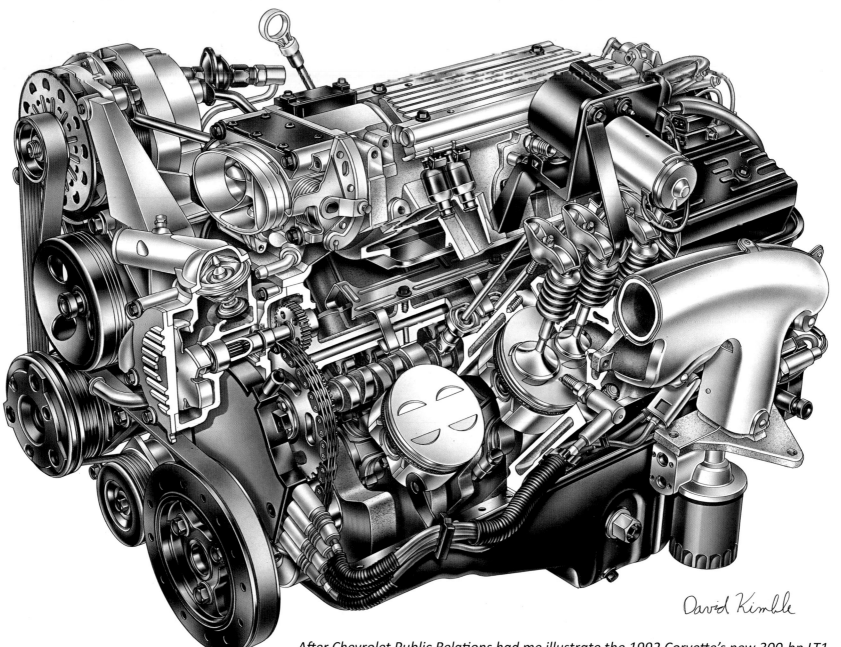

After Chevrolet Public Relations had me illustrate the 1992 Corvette's new 300-hp LT1 pushrod V-8, CPC Powertrain commissioned this illustration of the 275-hp Camaro-Firebird version the next year. This was early in my long-term relationship with them that continues today.

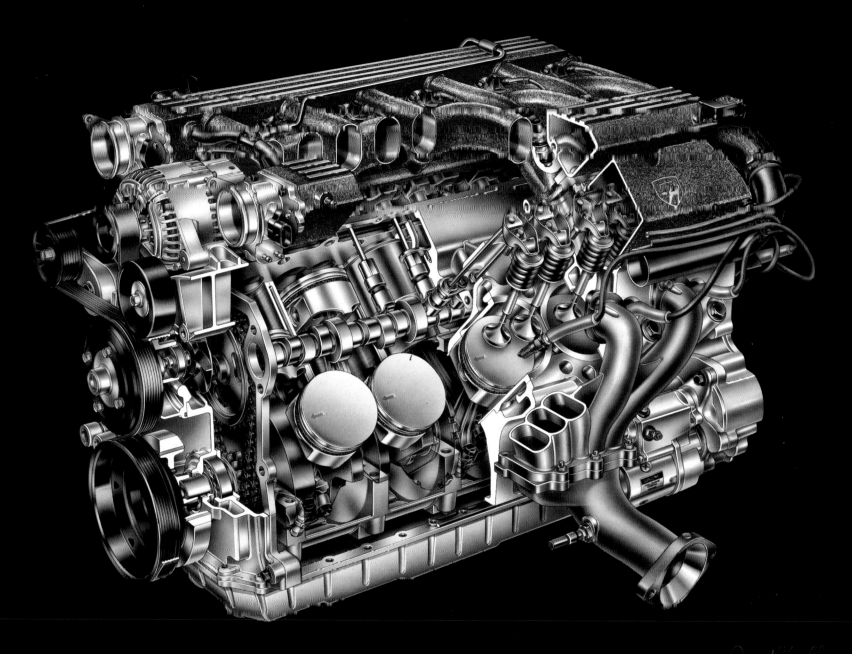

The 1992 Corvette was not a new platform so I didn't illustrate it along with the LT1, but the Dodge Viper
RT/10 was a new car and I drew cutaways of it and its 8.0-liter V-10 engine. This monster engine was developed from the Dodge cast-iron V-10 truck engine, only cast in aluminum. With a twin throttle body cross-ram
induction system it made 400 hp and 465 ft-lbs of torque.

FORD V-12

This sounds as though I had started working almost exclusively for General Motors, but actually there were projects for automakers all over the world until I moved from Southern California in December 1992. With more work than I could handle from the Detroit Three, I decided to concentrate on their projects from the Palace, my old movie theater in the remote West Texas outback. At this time I was Ford's recommended outside source for cutaway illustrations, and one exciting project that came out of this position was illustrating the only V-12 I have done out of a car. This was for their advanced powertrain engineering group, who had hooked two Duratec 60-degree double-overhead cam four-valve-per-cylinder 3.0-liter V-6s together to make a 6-liter V-12. This engine produced 460 hp with minimal development, and first appeared in Ford's Indygo Technology demonstrator, which was essentially a Raynard Indy car with side-by-side seating, but would eventually go into production for Aston Martin.

I don't get many opportunities to illustrate experimental engines, but Ford Advanced Powertrain Engineering had me do the only V-12 I have ever illustrated out of a car. This engine was made from two Duratec 60-degree double-overhead cam four-valve-per-cylinder 3.0-liter V-6s cooked together with a specially cast V-12 cylinder block and heads that (despite their humble origin) went into production for Aston Martin.

GENERAL MOTORS PROJECTS

Even though there were years that Ford or Chrysler were my best clients, General Motors was the most consistent. In 1996 Jack Underwood asked me to illustrate the first completely new small-block V-8 since its introduction in 1955. This engine was the LS1 and the only thing it shared with the original small-block Chevy was its 4.40-inch cylinder bore center spacing. It was a one-model-year Corvette exclusive, as was the LT1. Many Corvette enthusiasts were expecting double-overhead cams with four valves per cylinder as with the LT5, but the LS1 stayed with a pushrod valvetrain, which is lighter weight and gives the engine a lower center of gravity. The third-generation small-block was over 100 pounds lighter than the LT5, and in 2002 the LS6 version matched its 405 hp at a fraction of the cost.

Another series of illustrations I did for General Motors in the 1990s was for their Advanced Vehicle Technology Group, and even though it would seem that electric vehicles would put off an extreme performance junkie such as me, it was fascinating. Dick Thompson, the group's communications director, liked my work and wanted to use cutaways to illustrate almost every aspect of their new technology. He also let me drive the electric cars as it was developing. I started by doing a cutaway of the Impact, of which 50 were built. Along with many of its components, including the electric motor, I later redid these illustrations for the production EV1, which was not sold but leased to customers.

My 1997 LS1 cutaway has appeared many times through the years, with its Corvette engine covers, which are on an overlay, but it's never been seen before without them. Unlike the Gen II LT1, which shared a lot of parts with the original small-block, the Gen III LS1 shared nothing with the past but its 4.40-inch bore centers.

David Kimble

My last project for Dick was the Precept in 1999. This was a parallel hybrid technology demonstrator built for a U.S. Department of Energy initiative and again I illustrated the complete car along with the individual components including its diesel motor–generator.

Late in 1999 I was working for Ford again on one of the biggest projects I would ever do for the Blue Oval. This was a series of cutaway illustrations of the sporty Lincoln LS, their BMW-fighter. I worked for Glen Ray, who had come over from Ford's

radio station to manage the launch and he made sure I had everything I needed to do the best job possible. The LS was available with either a V-6 or a V-8 engine. In addition to illustrating both versions of the car, part of the deal was to do individual cutaways of both engines with their transmissions attached, something I had always wanted to try. Both the 3.0-liter 60-degree V-6 and 4.0-liter 90-degree V-8 had four valves per cylinder, actuated by double-overhead cams, and were shared with Jaguar, which along with Aston Martin was part of Ford's Premium Car Group.

This is how my 1997 Corvette LS1 illustration has appeared in dozens of publications, with the transparent engine covers overlaid on the base art. For anyone not blinded by its pushrod valvetrain, there was a lot of innovation to see and the 345 hp with 350 ft-lbs of torque was just the beginning.

David Kimble

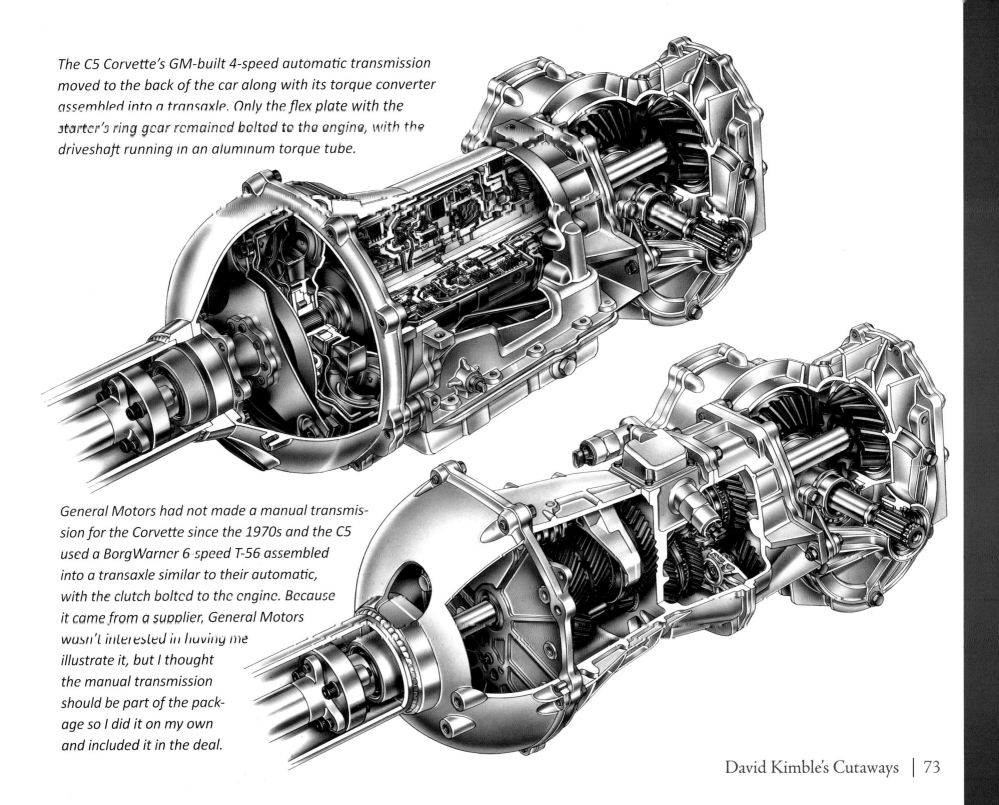

The C5 Corvette's GM-built 4-speed automatic transmission moved to the back of the car along with its torque converter assembled into a transaxle. Only the flex plate with the starter's ring gear remained bolted to the engine, with the driveshaft running in an aluminum torque tube.

General Motors had not made a manual transmission for the Corvette since the 1970s and the C5 used a BorgWarner 6-speed T-56 assembled into a transaxle similar to their automatic, with the clutch bolted to the engine. Because it came from a supplier, General Motors wasn't interested in having me illustrate it, but I thought the manual transmission should be part of the package so I did it on my own and included it in the deal.

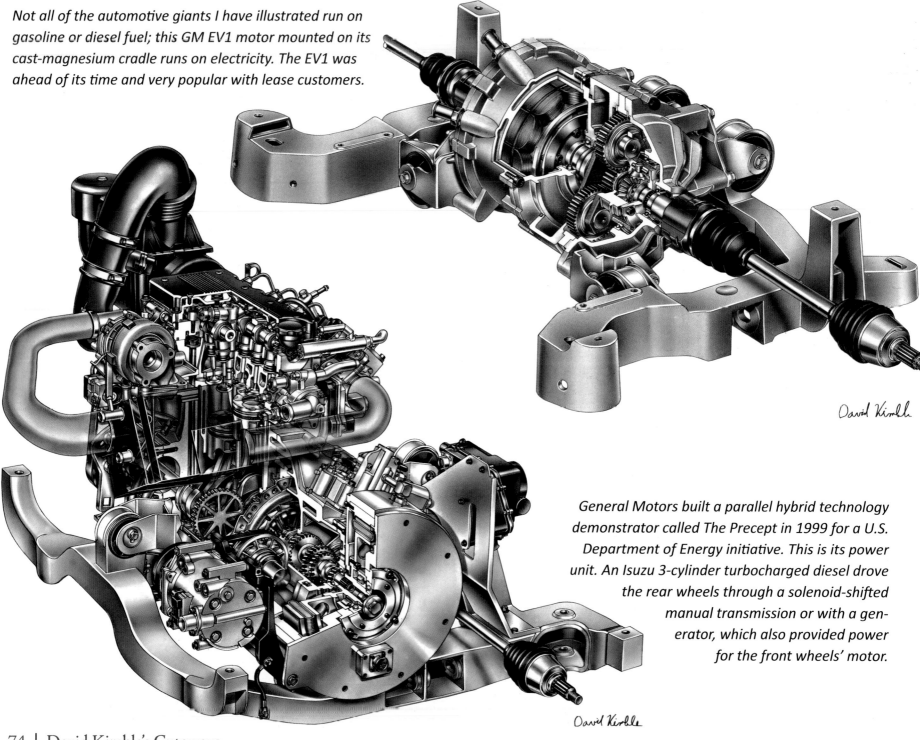

Not all of the automotive giants I have illustrated run on gasoline or diesel fuel; this GM EV1 motor mounted on its cast-magnesium cradle runs on electricity. The EV1 was ahead of its time and very popular with lease customers.

General Motors built a parallel hybrid technology demonstrator called The Precept in 1999 for a U.S. Department of Energy initiative. This is its power unit. An Isuzu 3-cylinder turbocharged diesel drove the rear wheels through a solenoid-shifted manual transmission or with a generator, which also provided power for the front wheels' motor.

David Kimble

David Kimble

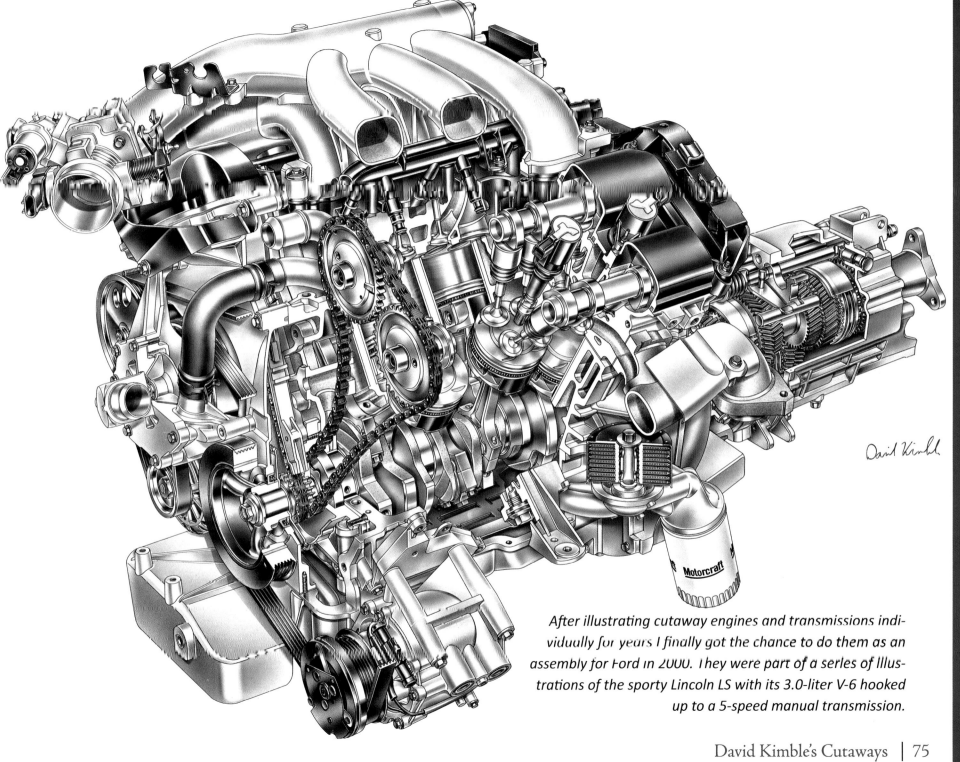

After illustrating cutaway engines and transmissions individually for years I finally got the chance to do them as an
assembly for Ford in 2000. They were part of a series of illustrations of the sporty Lincoln LS with its 3.0-liter V-6 hooked
up to a 5-speed manual transmission.

David Kimble's Cutaways | 75

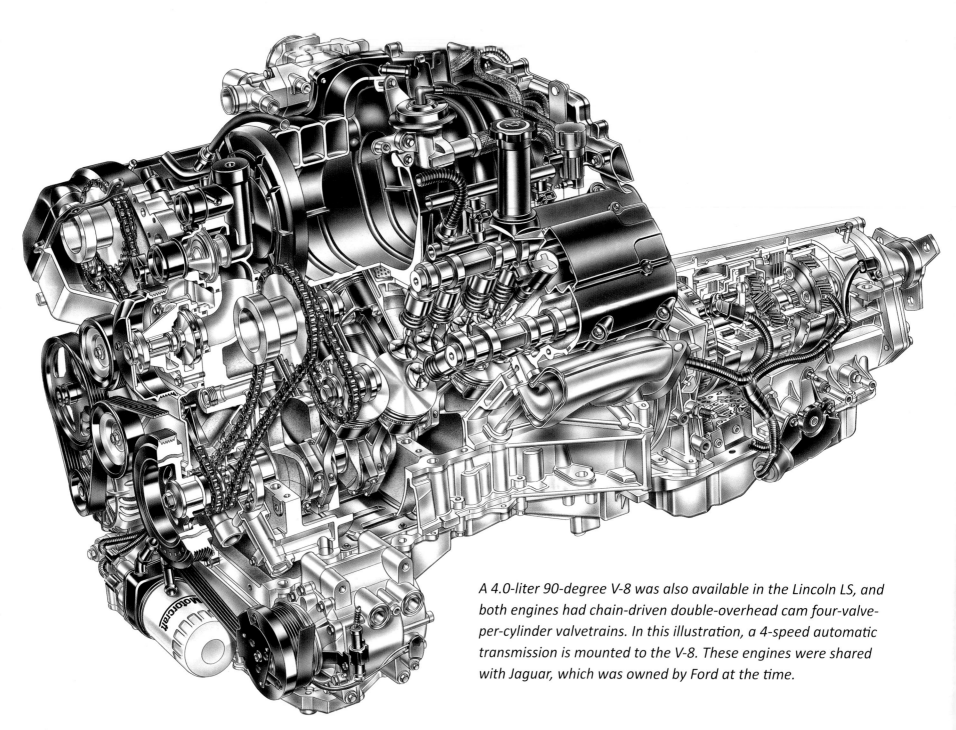

A 4.0-liter 90-degree V-8 was also available in the Lincoln LS, and both engines had chain-driven double-overhead cam four-valve-per-cylinder valvetrains. In this illustration, a 4-speed automatic transmission is mounted to the V-8. These engines were shared with Jaguar, which was owned by Ford at the time.

CHAPARRAL 2E

After years of being offered more projects than I could possibly do and wondering how I was going to get the ones I accepted completed on time, I hit a flat spot with nothing to work on in 2000. For an obsessive-compulsive workaholic such as I, this is a serious situation, and one night while walking my rottweiler around the Presidio County Courthouse it came to me to do a cutaway illustration of a Chaparral race car. I decided on the 2E Can-Am car along with a cutaway of its secret automatic transmission. That transmission had motivated me to accept a job offer from owner Jim Hall and move

to West Texas for the first time in 1969. While I was photographing the car and transmission at Chaparral for my illustrations, I made a deal with *Road & Track* on my cell phone, giving my hobby projects a place to be seen but also a deadline.

Business picked up soon after I started the Chaparral drawings, but by then I was on a mission and squeezing them in between commercial projects. I completed the illustrations in time for them to appear in the November 2001 issue of *Road & Track*. After Tom Hoxie retired, Bob Tripolsky at Chevrolet communications became a

Chevrolet Communications requested a gradated dark blue background for my cutaway of Chevy's 2003 Indy Racing League engine, which was a change of pace. This was the first year the organization didn't require engines to be production-based; this one looked very racy, with a flat-plane crank and spur gear-driven camshafts.

regular client, and in 2002 when the Aurora Indy Racing League (IRL) engine was rebadged as a Chevrolet, he had me do a cutaway of it. The IRL's rules changed for 2003, no longer requiring their engines to be production-based, giving GM Racing's Roger Allen a chance to design a dedicated racing engine and giving me a chance to illustrate one. I have done very few engines without also illustrating the car they go in and not having done an Indy car since 1984, I was hoping there might be a chance here but it didn't happen.

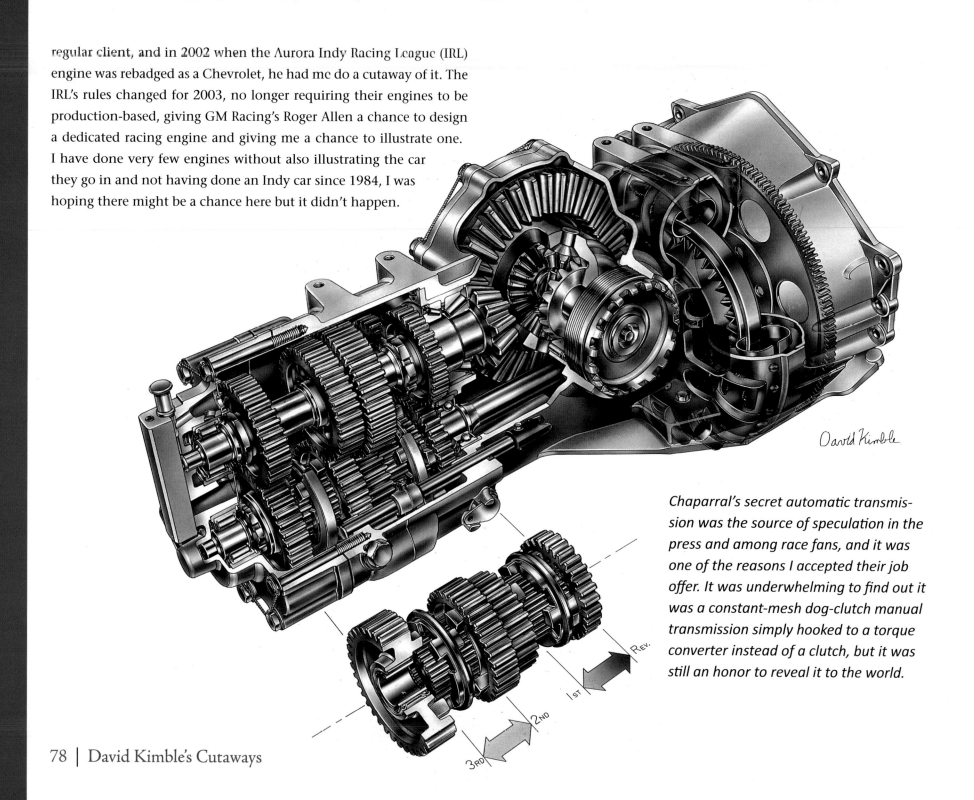

David Kimble

Chaparral's secret automatic transmission was the source of speculation in the press and among race fans, and it was one of the reasons I accepted their job offer. It was underwhelming to find out it was a constant-mesh dog-clutch manual transmission simply hooked to a torque converter instead of a clutch, but it was still an honor to reveal it to the world.

REV.

1ST

2ND

3RD

CHRYSLER HEMI

I started illustrating engines for Chrysler in 1991, usually but not always accompanying cars, and getting the opportunity to do a cutaway of their third-generation Hemi in 2002 was the realization of a dream. I could still remember lying in bed in my room at my parents' house in 1965, looking at a factory cutaway of the upcoming 426 street Hemi in *Hot Rod* magazine and wishing I had done it. Now I was illustrating the next new hemi and even though it was a pickup truck engine then, it would later evolve into the 707 HP Dodge Challenger Hellcat engine for 2015.

Chrysler's reborn Hemi started out at 350 ci. The only engine that could match it for raw power in the 1960s, the Chevy MK IV big-block, had stayed in production since 1965 and displaced 492 ci when the new Hemi came out. Unfortunately, Chevy's MK IV had only been available as a truck engine since 1976, but when I illustrated the final version in 2000 the MK VI L18 had all the latest technical features. Similar to GM's third-generation small-block, this engine was equipped with throttle-by-wire, electronic port fuel injection, and individual ignition coils that were mounted on the rocker arm covers above each spark plug. This was one of the last projects I did working with Jack Underwood, who retired soon after the L18 illustration was completed for GM Powertrain.

Working on this illustration of Chrysler's third-generation Hemi, I remembered looking at a factory cutaway of the second-generation engine in Hot Rod and wishing I had done it. That was in 1965. Now, in 2002, I was the one doing the factory cutaway of the new Hemi. Even though it was a light truck engine, it was the realization of a dream.

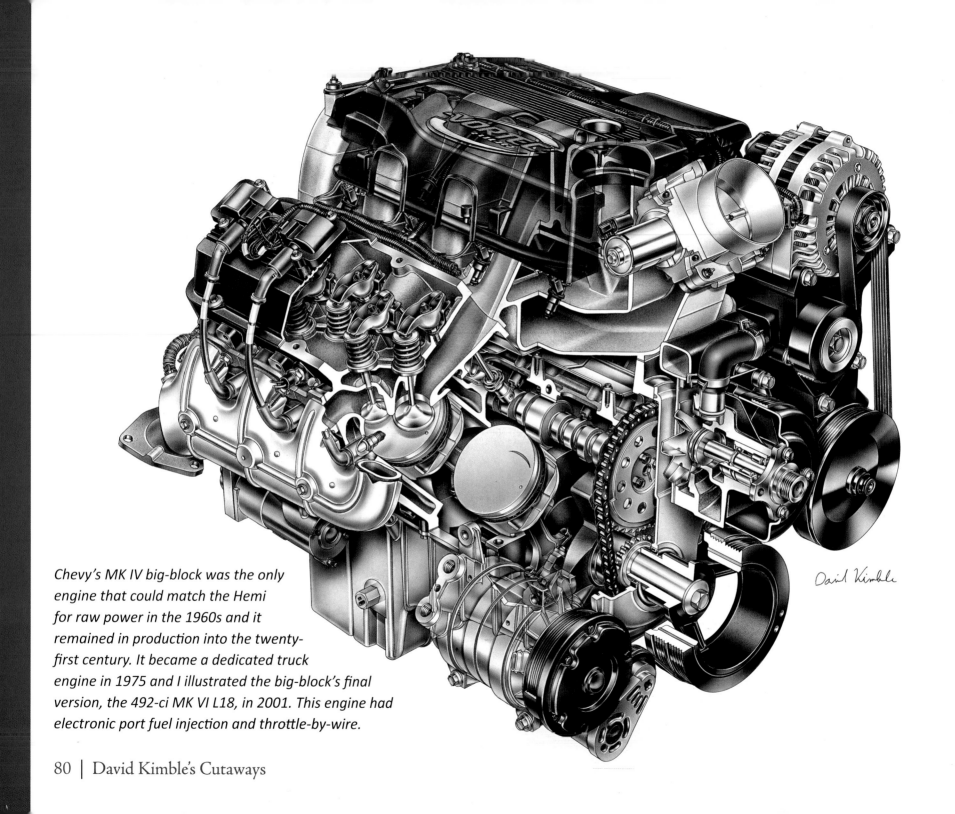

Chevy's MK IV big-block was the only engine that could match the Hemi for raw power in the 1960s and it remained in production into the twenty-first century. It became a dedicated truck engine in 1975 and I illustrated the big-block's final version, the 492-ci MK VI L18, in 2001. This engine had electronic port fuel injection and throttle-by-wire.

L-84 FUEL-INJECTED 327

By 2005 I felt the need to do another historic illustration. A friend of mine, Bill Haggie, was collecting parts to build a 327 fuelie for the 1965 Corvette convertible he was restoring. Bill had been the service manager at Jack Sherman Chevrolet in Midland, Texas, where I had my ZR-1 Corvette maintained, and we agreed that the L-84 fuel-injected 327 would make a great subject for a cutaway illustration. In addition to the appeal of looking inside a port fuel injection system controlled by manifold vacuum instead of a computer, the L-84 offered a relief from my steady diet of monochromatic modern engines. Bill didn't have enough parts to mock up a complete engine for photography, but he did have a complete 1965 fuel injection unit, which he loaned to me with permission to disassemble it.

To start the drawing I enlarged a 4 x 4-inch photograph of a prototype 1963 L-84 from the service manual to 400 percent on my copier, traced the enlargement, and then enlarged it again to 22 inches for my layout. The engine's castings stayed pretty much the same, but a lot of changes to the plumbing had been made between this prototype and a production 1965 model L-84, so I updated my drawing before going any further. The service manual also gave me what I needed to lay out the L-84's internal architecture with longitudinal and transverse orthographic sections of a base small-block used to diagram the lubrication system. I made my own rough orthographic drawings from the borrowed fuel injection unit and copied drawings from books for the rotating group and valve-train to complete my layout.

In 2005 a friend of mine was collecting parts to build a 327 fuelie for a 1965 Corvette he was restoring, and I decided to do a cutaway illustration of this legendary engine. He didn't have enough parts to mock up a complete engine for me to photograph, so I enlarged a small photo from the service manual to 400 percent and traced it as a starting point.

Working with this material I was able to piece together the basic engine, but there were details that eluded me and I needed to find someone who lived and breathed the L-84. I was fortunate enough to locate Andy Cannizzo, who was restoring his own 1963 Z06 Corvette, along with collecting and selling parts for the L-84 and other vintage engines. Andy was quite enthusiastic about this project and reviewed my drawing, as well as taking photos of parts and sketching the correct bolt head and other markings for me. I also showed the L-84 drawing to Ron Bluhm, who was in charge of GM Powertrain's collection of historic engines and accompanied them to events such as the Woodward Dream Cruise. Ron had been my contact at Powertrain for some time, and we worked out a deal that would make this illustration the first in a series of historic GM engines with support from The General.

It was a lot of fun airbrushing the Corvette's last engine equipped with Ramjet mechanical fuel injection, with Chevrolet engine orange reflecting in the chrome ignition shielding. Neil Nissing reproduced most of the illustrations in this book from 8 x 10–inch transparencies that he shot; this was the last one he did for me. I wasn't happy with my painting when I saw the trannies, and after I reworked it, Neil was not available to reshoot the L-84. Steve Constable had it scanned and digitally enhanced in the same manner as my regular GM illustrations. With 8 x 10-inch sheet film becoming rare and Steve's studio, Idea Design Technique, doing all the digital photography for Powertrain anyway, this was the end of an era.

GM Powertrain's support and the help of some of The General's engineers, both retired and still working, opened a lot of doors for me and I no longer had to piece together my historical cutaways. I obtained copies of the original engineering drawings that had been preserved on microfilm. Not everything I needed was available, however, and I still received some outside help. This included experts on a particular engine or family of engines and collectors including, Delmer McAfee, who is an oil tool manufacturer in Odessa, Texas. Delmer, who has a huge collection of 1950s and 1960s American performance cars and parts, was very generous with his time and loaned me many parts for reference.

After enlarging the 12¾-inch-long tracing to 22 inches, the sections and internal components that were revealed were plotted in. The starter, which was missing from the photo, and the ignition coil along with the distributor, which were hidden from view by the ignition shielding, were also added.

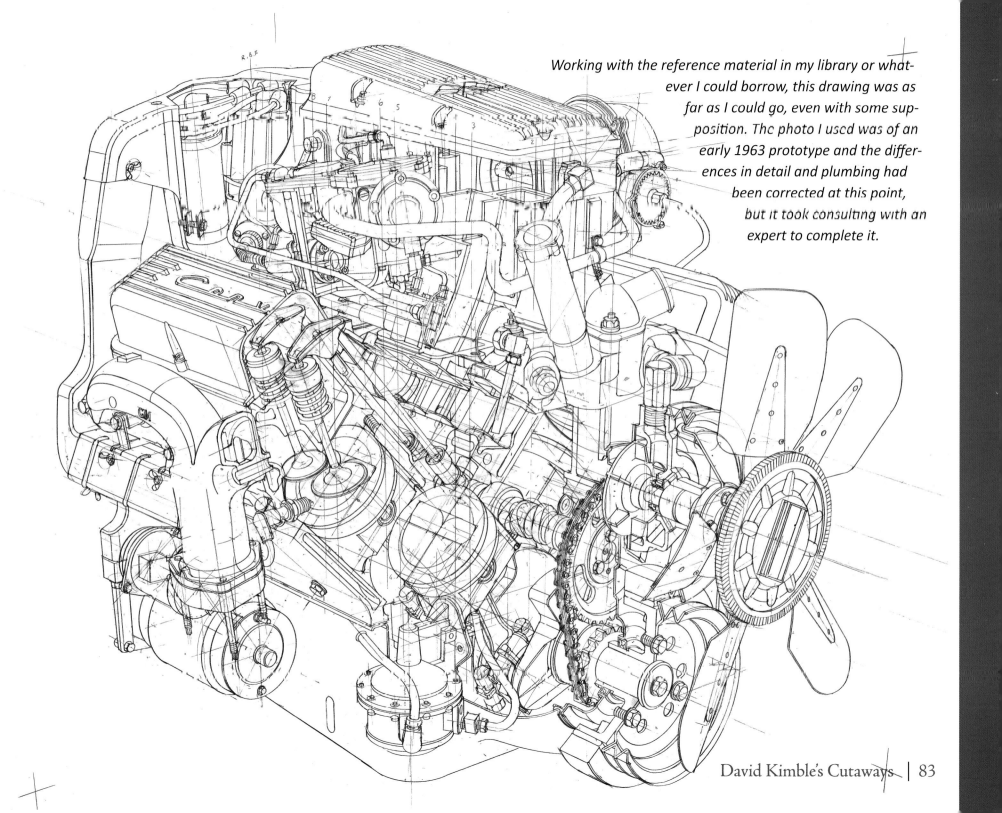

Working with the reference material in my library or whatever I could borrow, this drawing was as far as I could go, even with some supposition. The photo I used was of an early 1963 prototype and the differences in detail and plumbing had been corrected at this point, but it took consulting with an expert to complete it.

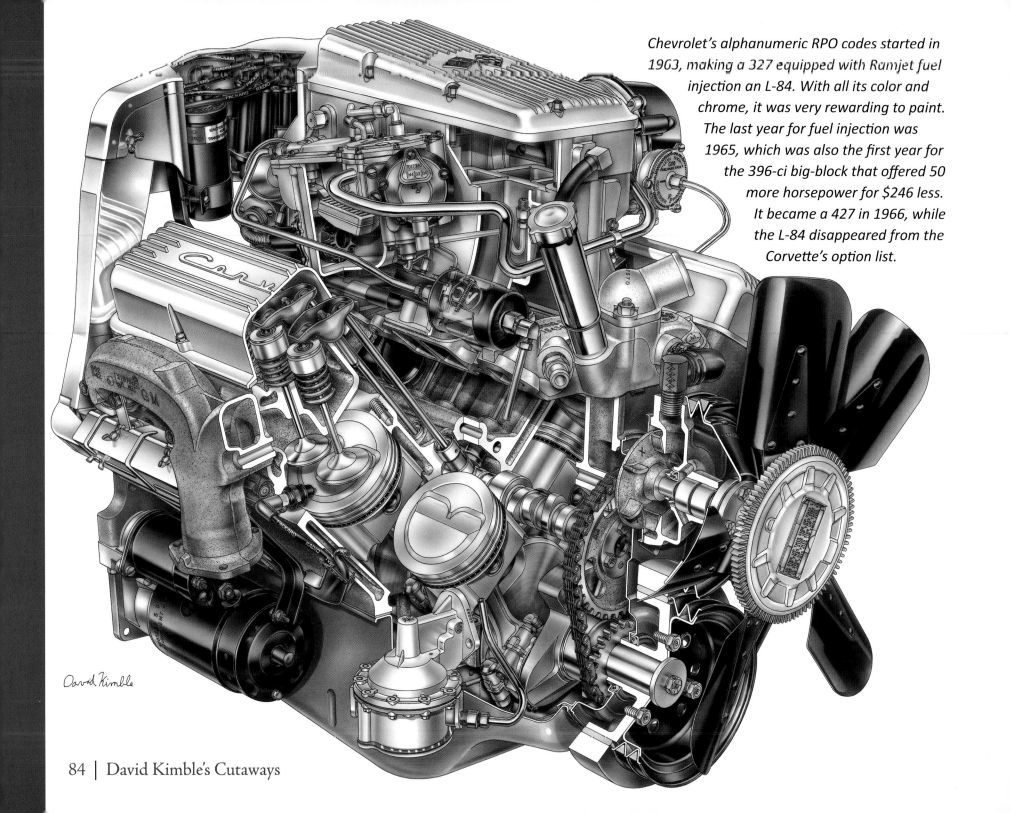

Chevrolet's alphanumeric RPO codes started in 1963, making a 327 equipped with Ramjet fuel injection an L-84. With all its color and chrome, it was very rewarding to paint. The last year for fuel injection was 1965, which was also the first year for the 396-ci big-block that offered 50 more horsepower for $246 less. It became a 427 in 1966, while the L-84 disappeared from the Corvette's option list.

1956 CHEVY 265

I illustrated only one Pontiac, the original GTO 389. All the others were Chevrolet V-8s starting with the small-block, and the first cutaway from each family of engines was used as a starting point for the others. Next to the 1965 L-84, my favorite small-block illustration is the 1956 265 equipped with Chevy's first optional speed equipment, a pair of Carter WCFB 4-barrels on an aluminum intake manifold. Delmer McAfee loaned me one of those manifolds, complete with the carburetors and throttle linkage, and I got carried away making an orthographic assembly drawing of it to plot from. There also

Plotting something as complex as a pair of Carter WCFB 4-barrel carburetors and their throttle linkages can be confusing so I use red and blue pencils for construction lines to keep from getting lost. I had already drawn the 1955 Corvette 265 and a lot of the early parts came from it, but this was the first year for the ram's horn exhaust manifolds, and it and all the other parts that were different are on this drawing.

weren't drawings of the correct harmonic balancer available from the microfilm archive, so I bought one and tore it apart to get the section right in my illustration.

Order Code 469 put a pair of dual quads on 1956 265s, which were painted Chevrolet engine red the same as the little V-8s had been in 1955, except the truck version

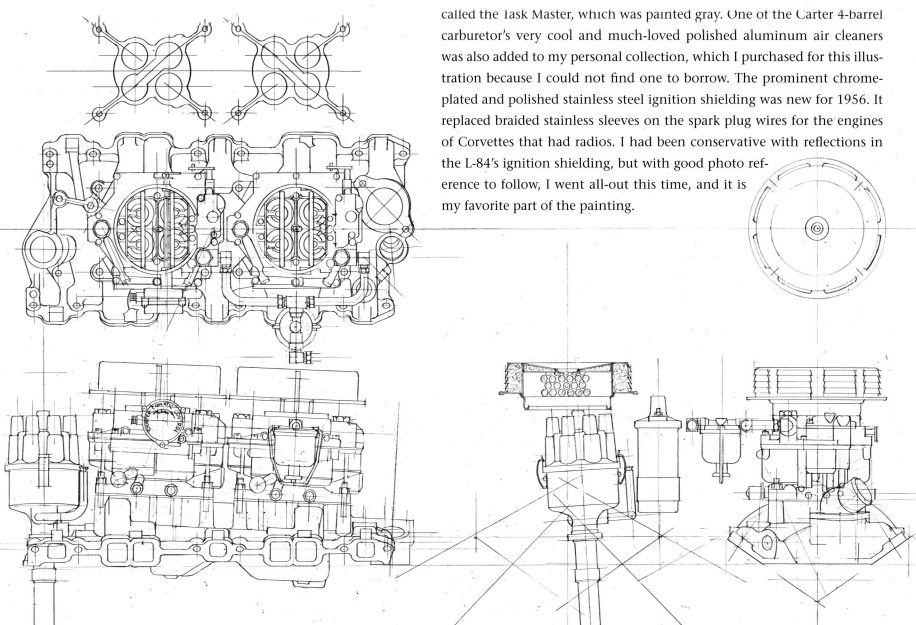

called the Task Master, which was painted gray. One of the Carter 4-barrel carburetor's very cool and much-loved polished aluminum air cleaners was also added to my personal collection, which I purchased for this illustration because I could not find one to borrow. The prominent chrome-plated and polished stainless steel ignition shielding was new for 1956. It replaced braided stainless sleeves on the spark plug wires for the engines of Corvettes that had radios. I had been conservative with reflections in the L-84's ignition shielding, but with good photo reference to follow, I went all-out this time, and it is my favorite part of the painting.

As with all of my 1950s and 1960s small-block illustrations, the 1956 265 was based on the 1965 L-84 with the new parts plotted geometrically from orthographic assembly drawings. I couldn't find an assembly drawing of Order Code 469, so I made my own from a borrowed dual-quad setup, adding the distributor because it is quite different from a 1965.

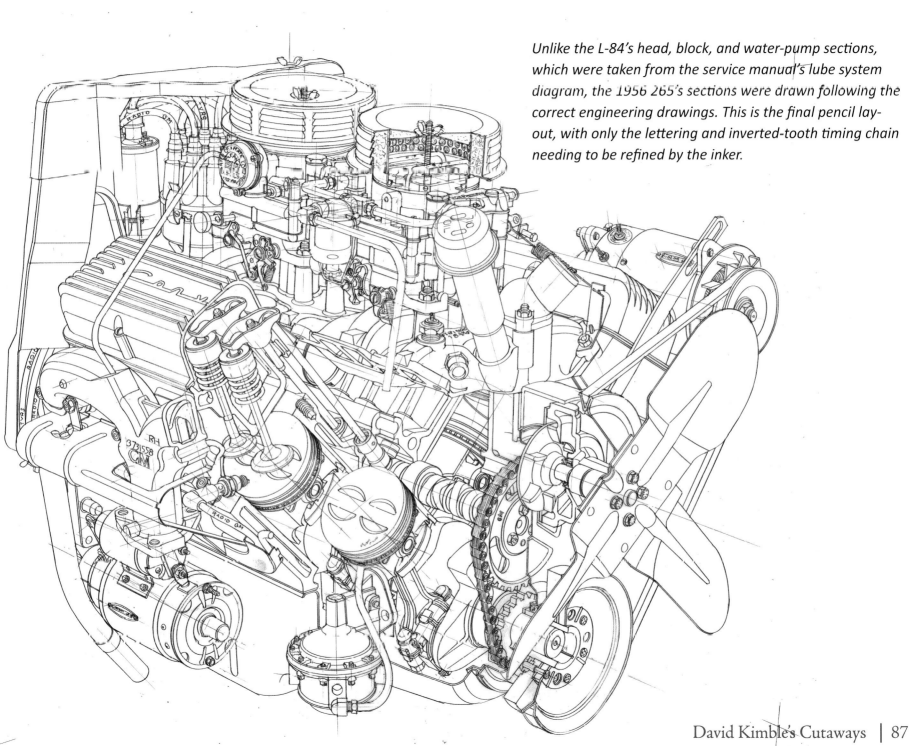

Unlike the L-84's head, block, and water-pump sections, which were taken from the service manual's lube system diagram, the 1956 265's sections were drawn following the correct engineering drawings. This is the final pencil layout, with only the lettering and inverted-tooth timing chain needing to be refined by the inker.

Next to the 1965 327-ci L-84, my favorite small-block illustration is this 1956 265 equipped with the Order Code 469 dual Carter 4-barrels with its deep Chevrolet engine red paint. I was conservative with the engine reflection in the ignition shielding on the L-84, but let it all hang out on the 1956 with detailed reflections of the rocker arm cover, carburetor, and air cleaner.

David Kimble

1969 427-ci ZL-1

It wasn't necessary to improvise or scrounge around for reference material to start the MK IV big-block series of illustrations with Steve Constable making a print to my working size of Powertrain's 1969 427-ci ZL-1. Except for the ZL-1's aluminum block and hotter cam it was almost identical to that year's L-88, and I used my tracing of Steve's photo for both engines, with the rest of the series of MK IV illustrations based on them. I had engineering drawings of all the major castings including both the aluminum and cast-iron blocks, but still plotted in the internal detail from Chevy's service manual lube system diagrams. My library was also helpful, along with parts borrowed from Delmer McAfee and from Kevin McKay of Corvette Repair on Long Island, New York, for the big-block illustrations.

Despite the unassuming name, Kevin McKay's Corvette Repair is one of the most respected Corvette restoration services, and he was my expert consultant on all the big-blocks, including the Chevelle LS6 454. Kevin was also a big help in sorting out Powertrain's ZL-1, which had been built as a Camaro engine and had later been converted into the Corvette version using a lot of similar-looking common parts. Vince Piggins had been instrumental in the ZL-1's reaching limited production, and this engine was an occupant of his office for many years until he retired in 1982. He then had it shipped to GM's Tonawanda, New York, engine plant. This was the only way Vince could keep it from being scrapped at the

General Motors had an original ZL-1 427-ci MK IV big-block in their collection and I used a photo of it as a starting point for my series of big block cutaways. This ZL-1 had been converted from a Camaro engine into the Corvette version using some common parts that looked similar but weren't really the right ones, and I didn't bother to change them on this tracing.

time, but in the 1990s GM Creative Services started collecting historic engines for display and brought his ZL-1 back to Michigan.

With two almost identical engines to illustrate, it only made sense to combine the ZL-1 and L-88 with one drawn as a complete illustration and the parts that were different drawn on an overlay and substituted electronically. Except for its orange spark plugs wires, the ZL-1 was almost all black and silver, as are GM's current engines, so I chose the L-88 for the complete illustration with its orange block, water pump, and sheet metal. The ZL-1 water pump and sheet metal were identical to the L-88 except for being painted black, but its unpainted aluminum block was redesigned with additional webs, gussets, and core support plugs. Its more aggressive camshaft didn't look any different, and a splash shield under the intake manifold's plenum was the only other item on the ZL-1 conversion overlay.

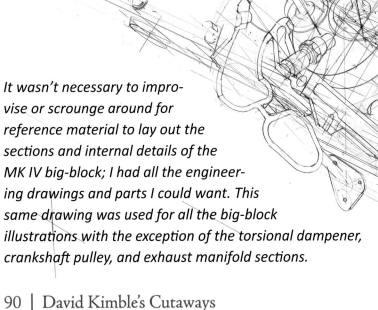

It wasn't necessary to improvise or scrounge around for reference material to lay out the sections and internal details of the MK IV big-block; I had all the engineering drawings and parts I could want. This same drawing was used for all the big-block illustrations with the exception of the torsional dampener, crankshaft pulley, and exhaust manifold sections.

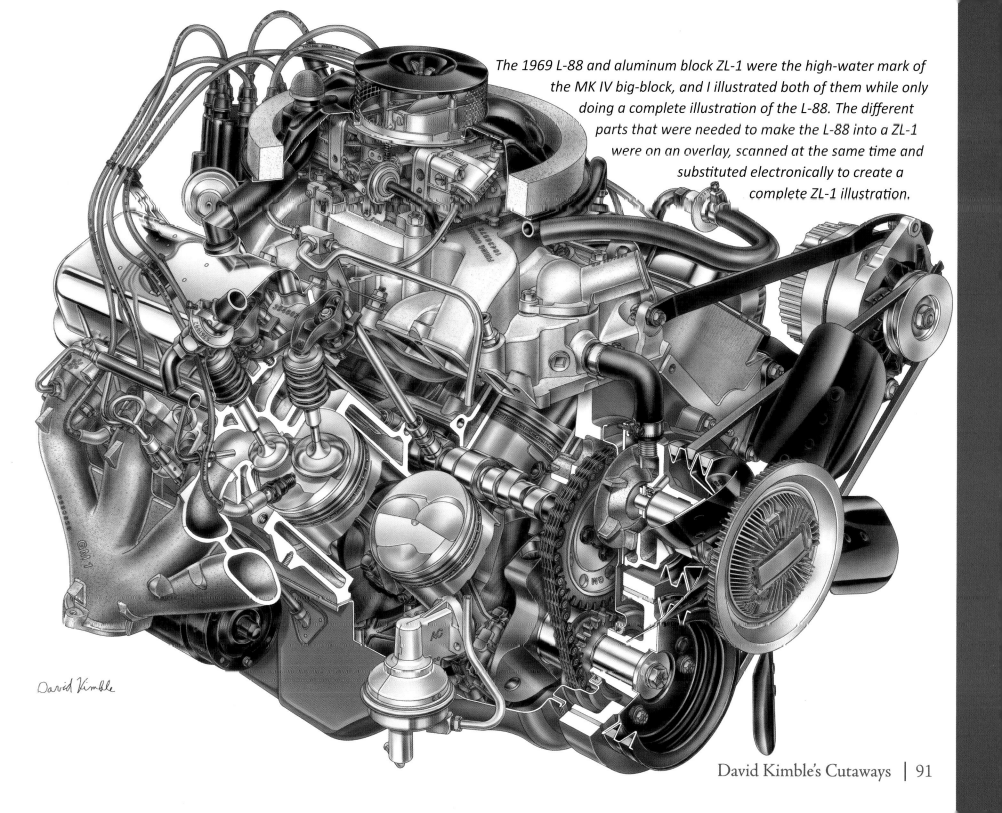

The 1969 L-88 and aluminum block ZL-1 were the high-water mark of the MK IV big-block, and I illustrated both of them while only doing a complete illustration of the L-88. The different parts that were needed to make the L-88 into a ZL-1 were on an overlay, scanned at the same time and substituted electronically to create a complete ZL-1 illustration.

David Kimble

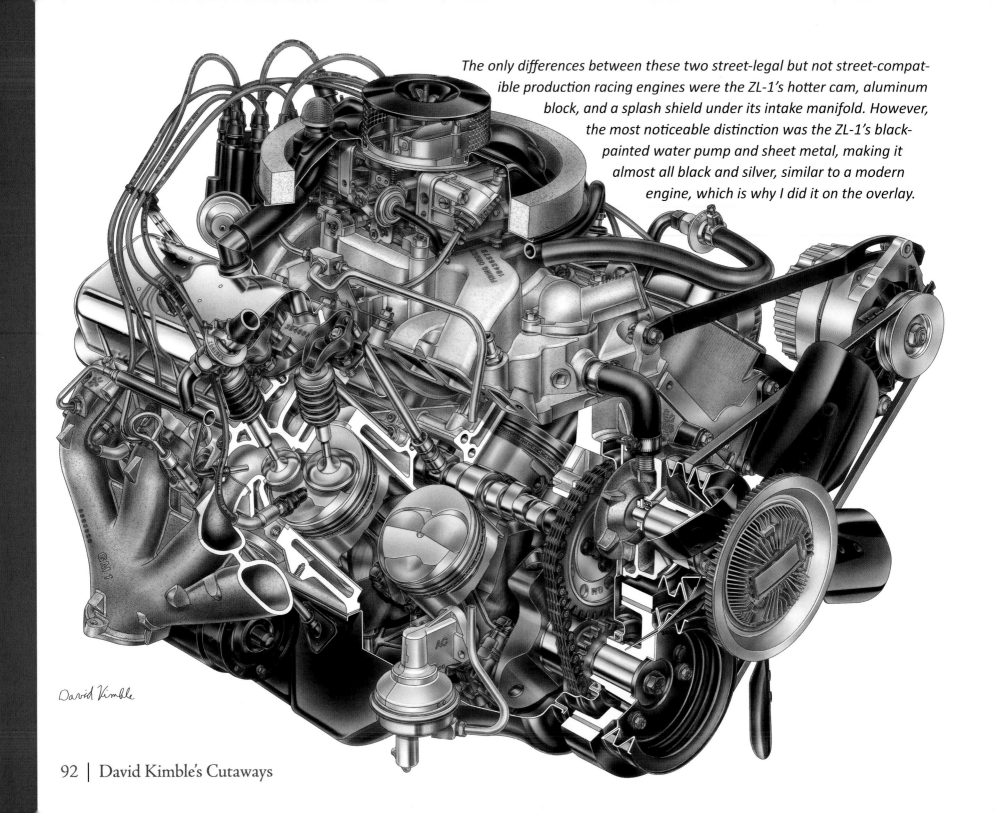

The only differences between these two street-legal but not street-compatible production racing engines were the ZL-1's hotter cam, aluminum block, and a splash shield under its intake manifold. However, the most noticeable distinction was the ZL-1's black-painted water pump and sheet metal, making it almost all black and silver, similar to a modern engine, which is why I did it on the overlay.

David Kimble

1964 GTO 389

Pontiac's iconic 1964 GTO 389 equipped with the optional trio of 2-barrel Rochester carburetors was a must for my historical series and Powertrain had an example in its collection. However, once I got into this project it turned out to be quite a challenge with this engine having been put together at a time when any part that looked close was considered good enough.

My intention was to make these cutaway illustrations so accurate that they could be used for restoration guides in the future, and that was going to be tough because I could not find any help at General Motors. There also was very little published technical information, but I did manage to find Ed Centofante, who restored and sold parts for 1960s

Pontiac GTOs and their engines, and thus the project was saved. The finished illustration isn't quite as accurate as the Chevy V-8s but it looks good, and Pontiac's Robin's Egg Blue engine paint makes a great counterpoint to Chevrolet engine red and orange.

Pontiac's GTO was the first of what are now called muscle cars: intermediate size cars with a full-size car's engine. That engine was the 389-ci V-8. The optional Tri-Power was also part of the legend that transformed the A-Body Tempest into a GTO wide-track Tiger, the terror of the streets.

MYSTERY MOTOR

Even though my last vintage GM V-8 had no chrome, for me it was the most gratifying because it was an opportunity to reveal the internal details of Chevrolet's Mystery Motor. It was designated the MK IIS, but neither this nor any other information about it was dis-closed when five Impalas powered by these engines dominated the qualifying races for the 1963 Daytona 500. I had numerous conver-sations with the designer, Dick Keinath, and worked from an actual disassembled engine because with only minimal drawings having been made and none surviving, this was the only way to get inside the MK IIS.

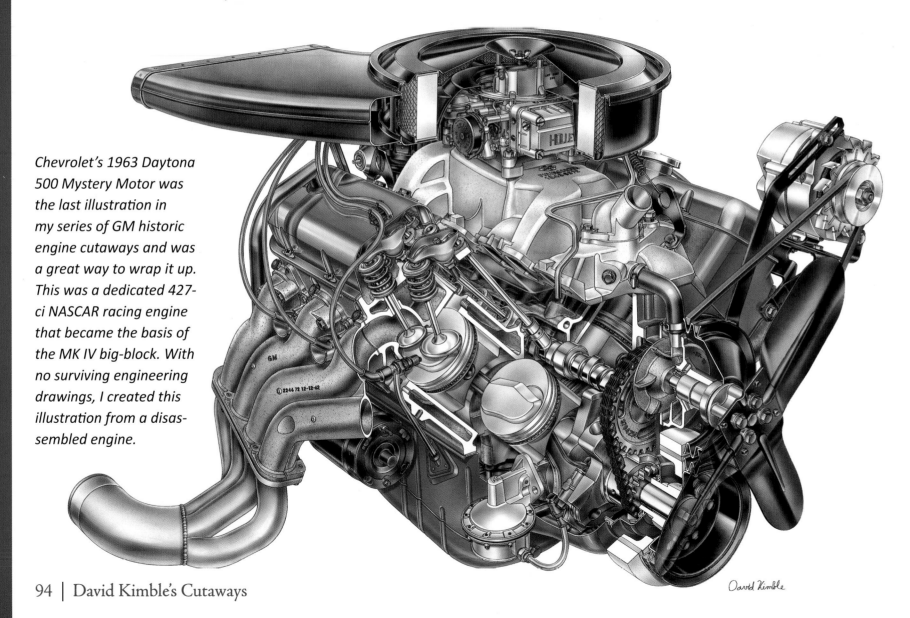

Chevrolet's 1963 Daytona 500 Mystery Motor was the last illustration in my series of GM historic engine cutaways and was a great way to wrap it up. This was a dedicated 427-ci NASCAR racing engine that became the basis of the MK IV big-block. With no surviving engineering drawings, I created this illustration from a disas-sembled engine.

David Kimble

Z06 CORVETTE

My most exciting recent GM Powertrain project is a cutaway illustration of the new Z06 Corvette's supercharged 650-hp LT4 Gen V 6.2-liter V-8, in which I lit up the number-5 cylinder. I use diagrammatic color to show the temperature changes as air is heated while being compressed by the supercharger rotors and cooled by the intercooler cores before reaching the intake ports. In addition, fuel is shown being injected directly into the number-4 cylinder, making my latest Gen V illustration educational as well as colorful.

The LT4 wasn't ready for photography when I drew this cutaway, but I had illustrated the naturally aspirated Gen V LT1, so as with the families of historic engines I used it as a starting point and added the blower geometrically.

The most exciting illustration I have done recently for GM Powertrain is this cutaway of the 2015 Z06 Corvette's supercharged 650-hp LT4 6.2-liter V-8. I lit up the number-5 cylinder and used diagrammatic color to show temperature changes in the intake air as it is compressed by the supercharger and goes through the intercoolers before reaching the intake ports.

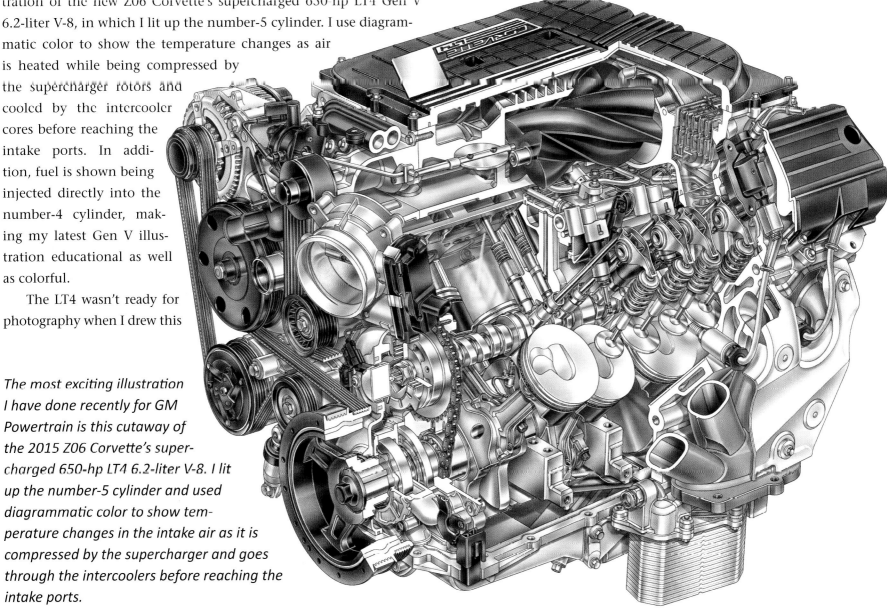

High-end European sports cars currently favor double-clutch automatic transmissions. General Motors developed one for the Z06 to keep pace and broaden its appeal, but it is conventional with a torque converter for smoother shifting. I had thought the 6L80 automatic transmission was incredibly complex when I illustrated it, but my cutaway of the 8L90 with eight speeds crammed into the same amount of space as a six makes it look simple. The Z06 version is designed to handle the LT4's 650 ft-lbs of torque and I showed it assembled into a Corvette transaxle, but its use in GM pickups and SUVs is what will pay for the tooling.

The Z06 is also available with a 7-speed manual transmission. I would have liked to do a cutaway illustration of it as well, but unfortunately Tremec makes it, not General Motors.

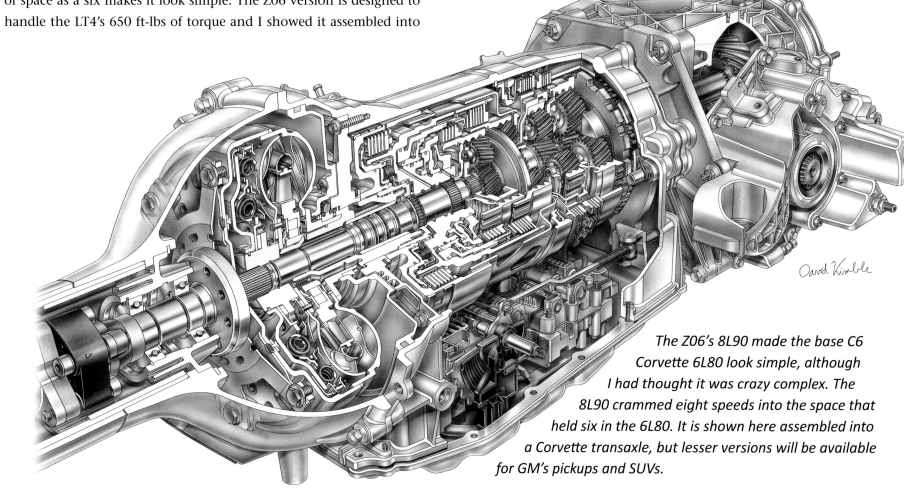

The Z06's 8L90 made the base C6 Corvette 6L80 look simple, although I had thought it was crazy complex. The 8L90 crammed eight speeds into the space that held six in the 6L80. It is shown here assembled into a Corvette transaxle, but lesser versions will be available for GM's pickups and SUVs.

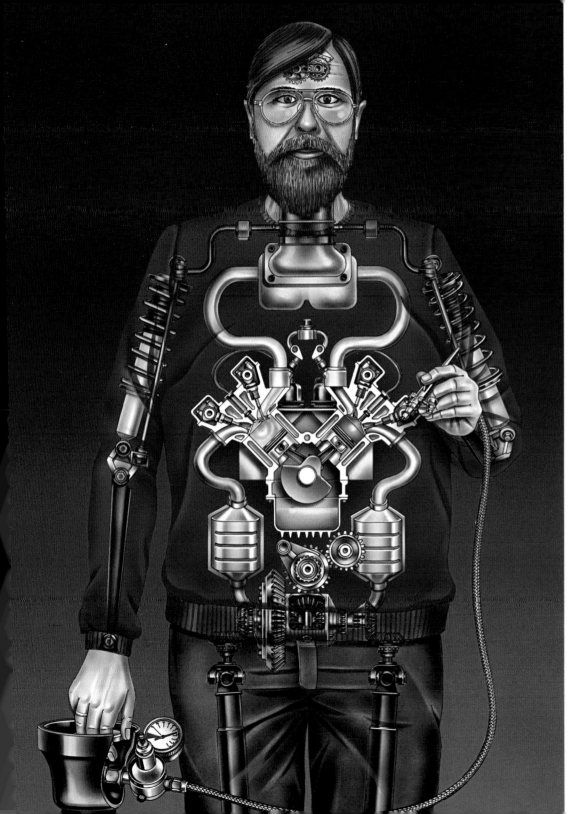

FINAL THOUGHTS

It is my sense of humor that keeps me going, as I turn out back-to-back exacting illustrations such as the engines and transmissions in this chapter. When challenged by stress I now watch a funny movie to keep going. In high school I did humorous caricatures of famous people, and thanks to Kevin Smith I did one of myself with an LT5 engine for my heart and lungs as a foldout center spread in *Car and Driver*.

I first worked with Kevin when he was an editor at *Motor Trend* and they always ran a headline of the cover saying "David Kimble Cutaway Inside" whenever I did an illustration for them. The joke was that this same headline appeared on the cover of the 1995 April Fool's issue of *Car and Driver*, and the cutaway inside was of me, done in the same style as my cars.

I drew this caricature of myself for the 1995 April Fool's issue of Car and Driver *with an LT5 engine for my heart and lungs and a headline on the cover reading "David Kimble Cutaway Inside." The joke was that* Motor Trend *used to run this headline when one of my cutaway cars appeared in the magazine.*

CARS FROM THE GOLDEN AGE OF CLASSICS

During the formative years of my career before "Kimble" became synonymous with "cutaway illustration" in Detroit, I had time to illustrate some vintage cars, beginning with a Duesenberg-powered Indy car for *Road & Track* in 1980. This car was owned by Briggs Cunningham and was on display in his museum at the urging of his curator, John Burgess. John remembered it from back in the day when he was racing sprint cars on the Midwest Fairground circuit. He was also a good friend of mine and a fellow artist who painted scenes of sprint cars, including his own Fronty Ford in action during the 1930s, and he wrote the article that my Duesenberg illustration accompanied. Fred Frame, who John said could "swear the paint off a race car," had this car built from an unusual combination of parts including a Bugatti Type 35 rear axle and Maserati brakes.

After competing in eight Indy 500s and winning the 1932 event with a Miller, Fred had two top-10 finishes in Duesenbergs, and this one was powered by a straight-8 Sidewinder Duesey, so called because its centrifugal supercharger was mounted sideways. This engine was originally built for the 91-ci formula of the late 1920s and probably did not make enough power to be competitive. In his last attempt Fred failed to qualify for the 1939 Indy race with the Duesey, but John remembered him winning a lot of dirt-track races behind its wheel.

One of these races was the Oakland Mile before the United States was drawn into World War II. I think John Burgess had a lot to do with

my assignment from *Road & Track*. He showed me a sectional assembly drawing of a similar Duesenberg engine and suggested that I cut it away in my illustration, but I just wasn't ready to try that yet.

When I proudly walked into the offices of the magazine with the finished painting I was met by the technical editor, John Dinkle, who was known for his sarcastic but good-natured wit. He said I got the color wrong. Mercifully the art director, Bill Motta, a fine automotive artist himself, was all smiles, and his only negative comment was that he felt my highlight on the nose was too sharp-edged; looking at it now, I agree.

I believe this was my first fully airbrushed cutaway to appear in a car magazine. The areas that look the best to me now are the upholstery and the engine-turned gold leaf 34 on the tail. This is a true cutaway with detail showing only through the near-side tires, which along with the wheels would have benefitted from near-opaque edge highlights, but I was only vaguely aware of the significance of these highlights at the time.

It was during the Duesenberg Indy car project that Gordon Schroeder, whom I had met through Ted Halibrand in 1965, and I discovered that we were now neighbors; both his shop and my studio were located on Flower Street in Burbank. Schroeder Steering made worm-and-gear cross-shaft steering boxes for midgets and sprint cars, along with quick-disconnect steering wheel hubs that were also used by

In 1980 Road & Track *asked me to illustrate Fred Frame's 1939 Due-senberg-powered Indy car in which he had failed to qualify for the 500, but did win some dirt-track races behind its wheel. With nothing to work from but the assembled car I was limited to cutting some holes in the body to expose the areas I could see into and making the tires transparent with the detail behind them show-ing through.*

A PAIR OF MILLERS

This motivated me to do another cutaway illustration of an old Indy car, and having read Griffith Borgeson's book *The Golden Age of the Ameri-can Racing Car*, I decided to paint one of the pair of Miller 91 front-drives he had recov-ered from France.

After the end of the 1929 U.S. racing sea-son, Leon Duray had taken these two Millers to Europe where he set an absolute closed-course speed record of 139.22 mph. This was at Montlhery near Paris, and a month later he entered his Millers in the Monza Grand Prix. When he returned to the pits after the last race, Ettore Bugatti was waiting for him and bought both cars on the spot.

The Millers were faster than any racing cars in Europe and Bugatti, whose engines all had single-overhead cams, introduced a copy of the Miller double-overhead cam head on his Type 50. In 1952 Griff saw a photo of the Millers taken at the shuttered Bugatti factory in Molsheim, France, and eventually managed to purchase the pair and have them shipped back home. At his hideaway in the Santa Monica Mountains of Southern California, Griff restored the front-drive No. 7, which had been driven by Ralph Hepburn in the 1929 Indy 500. Karl Kizer restored Job No. 6, the Duray car, for display in the Indianapolis Speedway Museum.

NASCAR. Gordon was the keeper of the flame of old-time oval-track racing lore, and he and his wife, Carmen, hosted the annual Gilmore Roars Again party that brought all the old racers together. It was through Gordon and John Burgess that I reconnected with the racing community in which I had grown up.

I decided on the Duray car for its significance of having set a qualifying lap record of 124.018 mph for the 1928 Indy 500 that stood for nine years, and a U.S. closed-course speed record of 148.17 mph at the Packard Proving Grounds. I was also a lot happier about painting a black car with white frame rails and wheels than I would have been painting the Hepburn car's Packard Cable livery of a purple body with yellow frame rails and wheels. By 1982, when I had time to get started, the Hepburn car was in Bill Harrah's collection in Reno, Nevada, which was a lot closer to Burbank, California, than the Speedway Museum in Indianapolis, Indiana, but the Duray car was the one I simply had to do.

To get the cooperation of the Speedway Museum and to give my illustration an appropriate place to appear in print, I contacted Scott Bailey, founder and publisher of *Automobile Quarterly (AQ)*, who was very receptive to the idea. Scott agreed to have Neil Nissing shoot my reference material along with the photos for the article, which was to

be written by Griff Borgeson, who was closely associated with *AQ* at the time. There was a lot of country between Burbank and Indianapolis that neither of us had seen, so we decided on a road trip, cramming luggage, all Neil's photographic equipment including a 4 x 5–inch–view camera, and my wife, Ellen, into Neil's Honda Accord along with the two of us and miscellaneous other items. It was an interesting trip.

I received a lot of enthusiastic support for this project. Gordon Schroeder loaned me a lot of original Miller 91 parts and John Burgess gave me access to the Miller engineering drawings that were being stored at the Cunningham Museum. The Speedway Museum also provided me with prints of Duray's Miller from negatives in their collection. These prints covered all three years that this car competed in the 500 and revealed developmental detail changes in 1928 and 1929.

When Karl Kizer restored the car it remained in its 1929 configuration except for its color scheme, which had been changed from purple

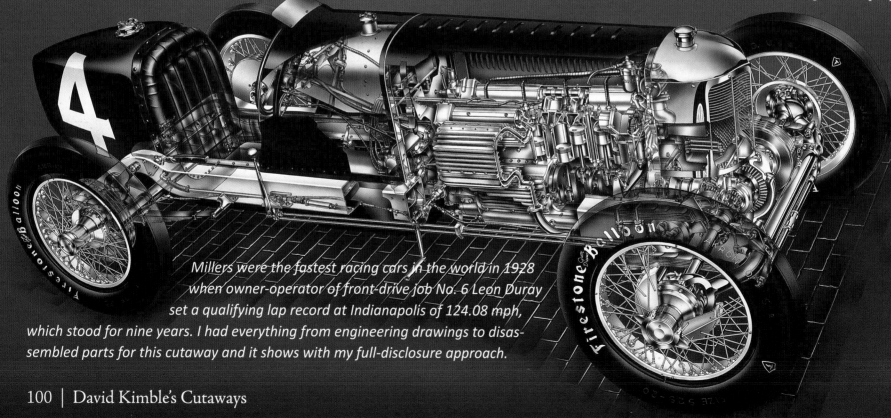

Millers were the fastest racing cars in the world in 1928 when owner-operator of front-drive Job No. 6 Leon Duray set a qualifying lap record at Indianapolis of 124.08 mph, which stood for nine years. I had everything from engineering drawings to disassembled parts for this cutaway and it shows with my full-disclosure approach.

and yellow back to the black and white of 1928, and I back-dated my illustration from these photos. The speedway is still known as The Brickyard, and to add some additional color I put the Miller on these bricks and faded them out into a brick-red background.

To my knowledge, Yoshihiro Inomoto was the first auto-motive cutaway artist to cut away engines and driveline components within complete car illustrations. He had made several trips from Japan to the Cunningham Museum by the time I did the Duesenberg. John had gotten to know Inomoto during these trips for reference photography, leading John to suggest that I cut away the Duesey's engine, but I told him I felt that engine cutaways should be separate illustrations. However, the truth was that the idea intimidated me.

The Miller was drawn two years later, and with all the reference material I could possibly want on the architecture of the engine and transaxle, it was time to cut away their castings and show the moving parts inside. This is still a cutaway like the Duesenberg, but with a lot more see-through; the frame rail, along with the hood, were cut away to showcase the supercharged double-overhead cam straight-8 and its finned intercooler. This painting was completed in 1983 and *AQ* entered it in the Los Angeles Society of Illustrators show in the technical category. *Road & Track* entered two of Inomoto's cutaways of 1930s German Grand Prix cars also, but the Miller won the gold medal.

The Miller's 91-ci double-overhead cam straight-8 was one of the first engines that I cut away in a complete car illustration, and I went inside its front-wheel-drive transaxle as well. Working from more information than I had had on any car before, I was also able to cut into the brass honeycomb radiator, centrifu-gal supercharger, and intercooler without any speculation.

Gordon Schroeder's shop was a gathering spot for racers and car collectors, and he often brought his visitors to my studio. While I was painting the Miller he came by with Jim Brucker to take a look. Jim had formerly owned the Movie World Cars of the Stars Museum and wanted Gordon to restore his two-man 1930s Indy car for an American auto racing museum he was planning to start. It was love at first sight when Brucker saw the Miller, and not only did he buy it on the spot even though it wasn't finished, he also told his car collector buddies about my work. This led to a number of private commissions to illustrate 1930s classic cars. I filled Scott Bailey in on this deal and he agreed, providing he liked the cars, to feature this series of cutaways in *AQ* with Neil doing the photography and either me or some notable expert writing the articles.

1931 Cadillac V-16

The first collector that Jim Brucker introduced me to was Bob Larivee, a car show promoter based in Pontiac, Michigan, who was having his 1931 V-16 Cadillac restored by Bill Harrah's restoration shop in Reno, Nevada. This wasn't long after Mr. Harrah's death, and the shop was taking in outside work from collectors, including Bob, when Neil and I visited it in 1984 to photograph the Caddy.

The car was finished except for the gas tank, as the original tank had blown up while they were trying to repair a leak and a new one was being fabricated while we were there. This complicated my problem of how to illustrate a complete car without any disassembled com-ponents, but fortunately Brucker came to the rescue by taking us to another friend's shop in Santa Paula, California. That building was jammed full with V-12 and V-16 Cadillacs in various stages of disassembly. This was close to the Brucker family's old lemon warehouse, a repository for their own collections and quite a story in itself.

Jim shared my passion for old engineering drawings and loaned me an original ink-on-drafting-linen sectional assembly drawing of a Cadillac 452-ci 45-degree V-16 engine from his collection. I also bought every book I could find that had any worthwhile technical

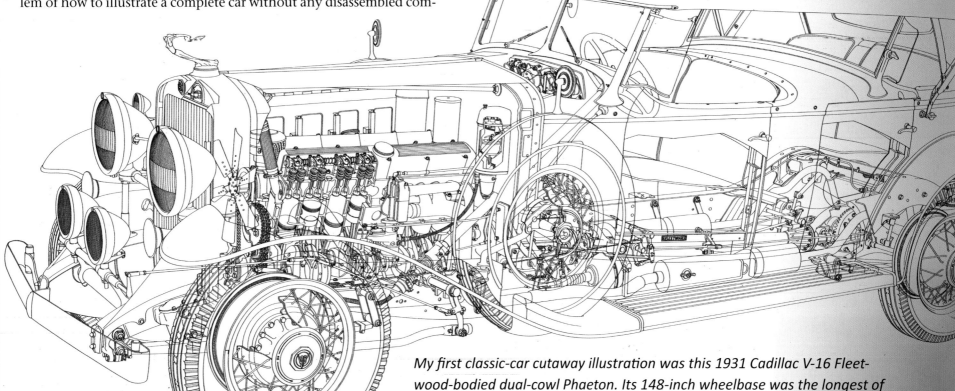

My first classic-car cutaway illustration was this 1931 Cadillac V-16 Fleetwood-bodied dual-cowl Phaeton. Its 148-inch wheelbase was the longest of any car I had ever done. In keeping with its size I made my drawing 42 inches long instead of the usual 36, which made it possible to put more detail into the 452-ci 45-degree V-16 that featured overhead valves.

content or info on this particular car's history to expand on what Bob Larivee was able to tell me, as I was writing the article this time. Cadillac's V-16 was a "modular engine" before the term existed, with a V-12 based on the same architecture and sharing all the same internal components except cams and crankshafts. It was intended to upstage Packard's V-12 and this was one of three dual-cowl Phaeton bodies built by Fleetwood for this chassis. To give Bob a heroic painting to frame, the drawing was 42 inches long instead of the usual 36.

When the 1931 dual-cowl Phaeton left Fleetwood's coach works it was painted Beechwood Tan, which Bob found unappealing, so with the help of Harrah's staff, he found an era-appropriate color he liked called India Red. This is when I started doing tests

on scraps of film before committing to painting an entire car body. I had to spray and wash off the India Red several times before getting it right, and that was a real mess.

I put this car on a cut flagstone driveway, which was popular in the early 1930s, and faded it into a Naples Yellow background that brought out the sky reflection in the chrome with a diffused shadow under it. I had also put a similar soft undefined tone under the Miller. Both cars would have benefitted from the detailed sharp-edged shadows I started doing a few years later.

Painted India Red, with no shortage of chrome, and sitting on a cut flagstone driveway, this Caddy makes a defiant statement of conspicuous consumption at a time when the national economy was going down the drain. The V-16 engine's monolithic styling carried the car's no-expense-spared elegance under the hood and could travel 8 miles on a 15-cent gallon of gasoline, producing 165 hp and 320 ft-lbs of torque.

Model J Duesenberg

I think Jim Brucker introduced Neil and me to John Mozart at the Quail Lodge during the 1984 Pebble Beach Concours d'Elegance when John was collecting classic cars and having them restored by his own shop in Reno. Mozart's restoration supervisor was Tom Bachelor, who had previously managed Bill Harrah's shop and was now in the middle of restoring John's 1930 Model J Duesenberg Murphy–bodied boat-tailed speedster. This was my next classic car cutaway project, and it was a Duesey without any reference material problems whatsoever.

Neil and I made two trips to Reno, the first to photograph the rolling chassis and a return visit for the fully assembled car. Murphy produced more bodies for the Duesenberg factory than any other coachbuilder, but this was the only boat-tailed speedster they built for the long-wheelbase chassis.

The V-16 Cadillacs were impressive but the ultimate of Depression-era power and prestige were the mighty Model J Duesenbergs with their 265-hp straight-8s. I stayed with the Caddy's 42-inch length so I could fully detail this Duesey's double-overhead cam four-valve-per-cylinder straight-8 with its triple-row inverted-tooth timing chain in my drawing.

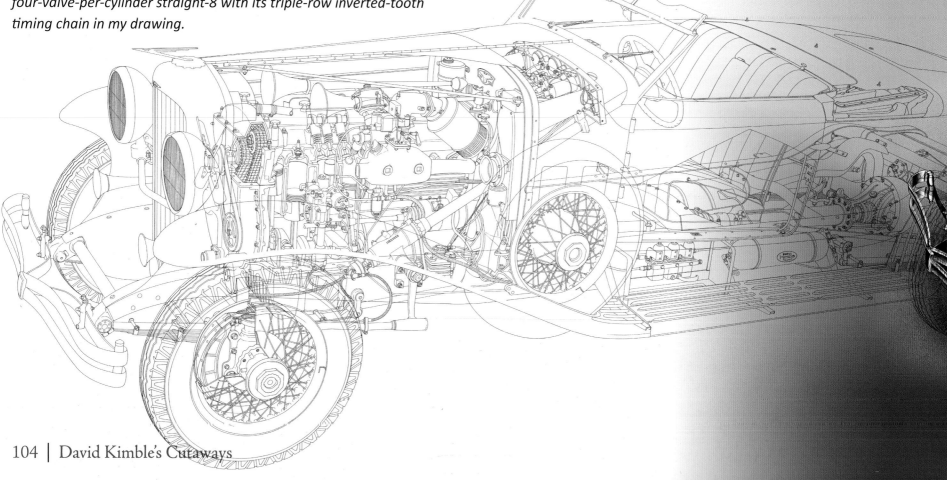

Again, my drawing was a longer-than-usual 42 inches, the same as the V-16 Cadillac.

The original owner of this car was George Whittell, the self-appointed commodore of Lake Tahoe. He had phoned Fred Duesenberg and told him he wanted to buy the fastest, most expensive car in the world. The Commodore eventually owned a fleet of seven Duesseys, including this one, which had a massive 1,400-pound double-overhead cam straight-8 with four valves per cylinder rated at 265 hp built by Lycoming. The fenders were black with the top surfaces of the aluminum body left unpainted and

highly polished, so I didn't have to do a test, as I should have before re-spraying the Cadillac's India Red several times.

Neil photographed Mozart's Model J on the Pebble Beach golf course, which inspired the grass-green background fade. Strother McMinn, who was an instructor at the Art Center College of Design in Pasadena, California, for almost 50 years knew this car well and wrote the article for AQ.

The original owner of this 1930 Murphy-bodied long-wheelbase Model J Duesenberg was George Whittell, the self-appointed commodore of Lake Tahoe. He had phoned Fred Duesenberg and told him he wanted to buy the fastest, most expensive car in the world, and he got it with this black and silver boat-tailed beauty that I put on a grass-green background.

David Kimble's Cutaways | 105

1936 Mercedes-Benz 540K

My next classic was also one owned by John Mozart, but unlike the Duesenberg he had bought this 1936 Mercedes-Benz 540K fully restored by Connie Bouchard, who had recently retired from General Motors. I tackled this project at Scott Bailey's urging in 1986 as part of *AQ*'s contribution to Mercedes-Benz's 100th Anniversary celebration of their co-founders' independent invention of the automobile.

John kept this car at his estate near Silicon Valley in Palo Alto so he could occasionally drive it on the street. We met Tom Bachelor there to photograph the 540K for my illustration. Later we drove it to a muffler shop to put it

up on a hoist. This sleek behemoth's engine weighed 1,200 pounds and made 140 hp, but with a clutch engaging its Roots type compressor it came up to 180 hp when the throttle pedal was floored. We could hear the legendary whine of its supercharger most of the time just keeping up with traffic.

As with the V-16 Cadillac, all we came away with from this trip were photos of a complete car. This time, however, Lowell Paddock, *AQ*'s editor, came to the rescue by putting me in touch with Tom Creed in San Diego. Tom collected and restored 500 and 540Ks, so Neil and I visited his shop with wife Ellen and son Jason in tow. Neil photographed everything from bare frames to complete engines and chassis. Meanwhile, Tom kept Jason amused by letting him drive an electric 540K kiddy car.

I flew to Stuttgart, Germany, in May that year to illustrate the Porsche 959. Lowell arranged for

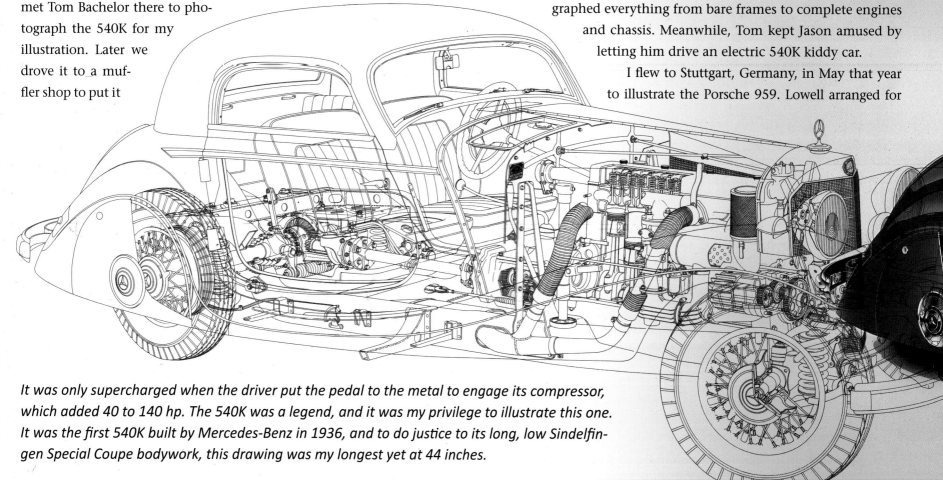

It was only supercharged when the driver put the pedal to the metal to engage its compressor, which added 40 to 140 hp. The 540K was a legend, and it was my privilege to illustrate this one. It was the first 540K built by Mercedes-Benz in 1936, and to do justice to its long, low Sindelfingen Special Coupe bodywork, this drawing was my longest yet at 44 inches.

me to meet with Max von Pine at the Mercedes-Benz Museum on the Untertürkheim campus. Max had copies made for me of the 540K engineering drawings from their microfilm archives, and included the frame, engine, driveline, brakes, and steering, giving me everything I needed to design my illustration without working around what I did not know.

I made this drawing an even more heroic 44 inches long.

Any 540K is something special, and this coupe with a streamlined deco body by Sindelfingen is an exceptional example because it was the first one built. It made its debut on the Mercedes-Benz stand at the 1936 Paris Auto Show.

I like to illustrate cars from the driver's side to show the controls, but the segmented chrome exhaust pipe sleeves were such a signature feature that I had to do this Mercedes from the passenger's side. By 1986 when this illustration was done, my style was maturing with more sophisticated rendering and less reliance on cutting away surfaces to see the detail underneath. This was more of a see-through, and the background was a subtly muted Naples Yellow dark-to-light fade with one of my first detailed cast shadows under the car. I sprayed this with a stencil cut from vellum to give it soft edges.

I usually illustrate cars from the driver's side, but I had to show the 1936 Mercedes-Benz 540K's segmented chrome exhaust pipe sleeves that were outside the body running from the side of the hood to the top of the front fender. Another of this streamlined deco Special Coupe's styling elements that I emphasized were its rear fender skirts with their simulated hubcaps.

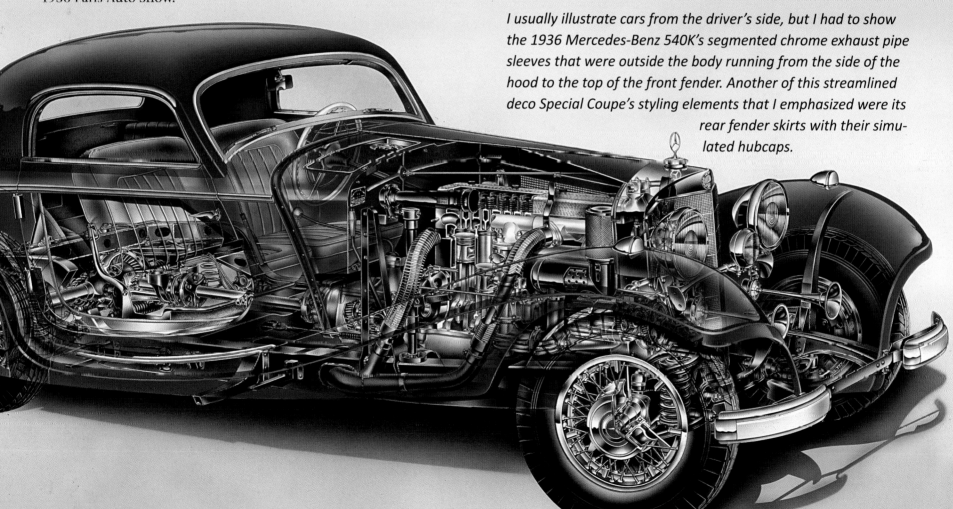

AUBURN CABIN SPEEDSTER

In 1987 I received a surprise package in the mail from Dr. Peter Kesling of La Point, Indiana. It contained a series of photos of his Auburn Cabin Speedster in progressive stages of assembly. These photos were Dr. Pete's way of asking me to do a cutaway illustration of his re-creation of this one-off show car that was destroyed in a tent fire at the 1929 Los Angeles Auto Show. These photos had been taken with amazing insight.

He was obviously confident that I would take the job because he had already arranged for *AQ* to publish my illustration along with an article about the original car and his re-creation. For the additional information I needed, Dr. Pete sent me to his source for the parts and drawings that he used to

build this car. Randy Emma in Orange, California, owned the surviving remnants of Auburn Cord Duesenberg, and was able to answer all my questions.

Featuring an aerodynamic body built by Griswold, the Auburn Cabin Speedster (as in cabin monoplane) was billed as the "sky plane of the highways." Its aviation theme was reflected in the interior with

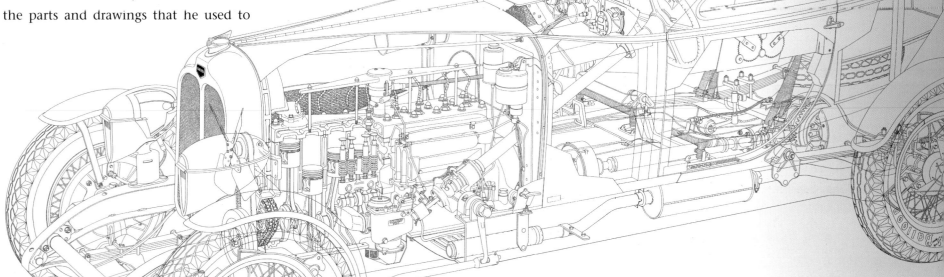

This 1929 Auburn Cabin Speedster is the only illustration project that has ever shown up like a lightning bolt out of the blue in the mail, and it was well worth doing. The photos I received were of a re-creation of the car in progressive stages of assembly and showed a lot of insight into what it took to draw a cutaway illustration.

aircraft-style gauges and wicker seats. It was built on a modified 8-120 chassis and powered by the only flathead I've ever cut away in a car, a Lycoming 247-ci side-valve straight-8 rated at 140 hp and breathing through a single-barrel updraft carburetor.

Coach-built bodies of this period were typically aluminum supported by an ash frame. Dr. Pete sent me a photo of this wooden frame sitting on the chassis, which I included in the illustration. This meant going back to more of a cutaway approach than with the 540K, and although Dr. Pete wanted me to have the sky plane flying over the Auburn factory, I talked him into having it sitting on his stone driveway.

Dr. Peter Kesling had this re-creation of the Cabin Speedster built and sent me the photos of bringing back a car that had been destroyed in a tent fire at the 1929 Los Angeles Auto Show. The Speedster's Pullman green and cream paint scheme was a little understated for Dr. Pete, so he had a second one built as a T-top painted candy apple red.

NATIONAL GEOGRAPHIC PROJECT

Henry Ford was putting America on wheels at his Highland Park, Michigan, Model T factory, and this illustration shows it in June 1913 with the gallows-style body drop in front of the main assembly hall. This was a commission from *National Geographic* in 1987. The magazine provided me with photos from the Ford archive, period magazine articles, and an industrial archaeologist, Dave Hounshell, who guided me in reconstructing this never-before-illustrated scene. I also bought some 1:18-scale plastic Model T kits, which had complete chassis and built them up to different levels of assembly so I could set them up as reference for drawing the cars in the illustration.

About a year later on a trip for General Motors, I made a pilgrimage to this historic site, which had fallen into disuse, and using a transparency of this illustration, I talked my way past the guards. They told me there wasn't much to see, but wandering around the empty assembly hall I discovered that the mint green I had used for the darker lower portions of the walls was spot on, despite having worked only from black-and-white photos.

My work for the car collectors and clients such as *National Geographic* was good fun, but by 1987 I was under so much pressure from the auto manufacturers and advertising agencies that I was forced to wind it down. I enjoy keeping up with the latest technology through my illustration projects but my real passion is technology from the past, and I have managed to squeeze in a few historical cutaways over the years.

My future lies at least partially in the past with me able to choose more of my projects instead of them choosing me, and there is one that I started gathering reference material for in the 1980s that has yet to reach my drawing board. It is a 1911 S76 Tipo 14 Fiat Grand Prix car, a primeval chain-driven monster with a 14.5L 4-cylinder engine. It's still waiting patiently for me.

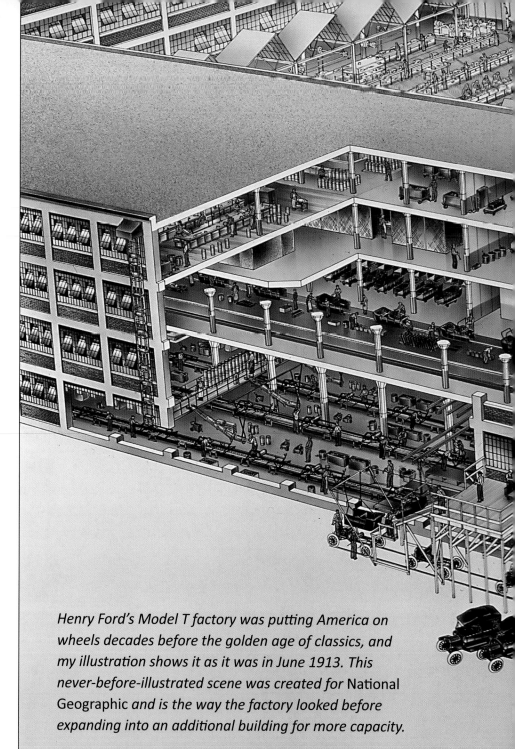

Henry Ford's Model T factory was putting America on wheels decades before the golden age of classics, and my illustration shows it as it was in June 1913. This never-before-illustrated scene was created for National Geographic *and is the way the factory looked before expanding into an additional building for more capacity.*

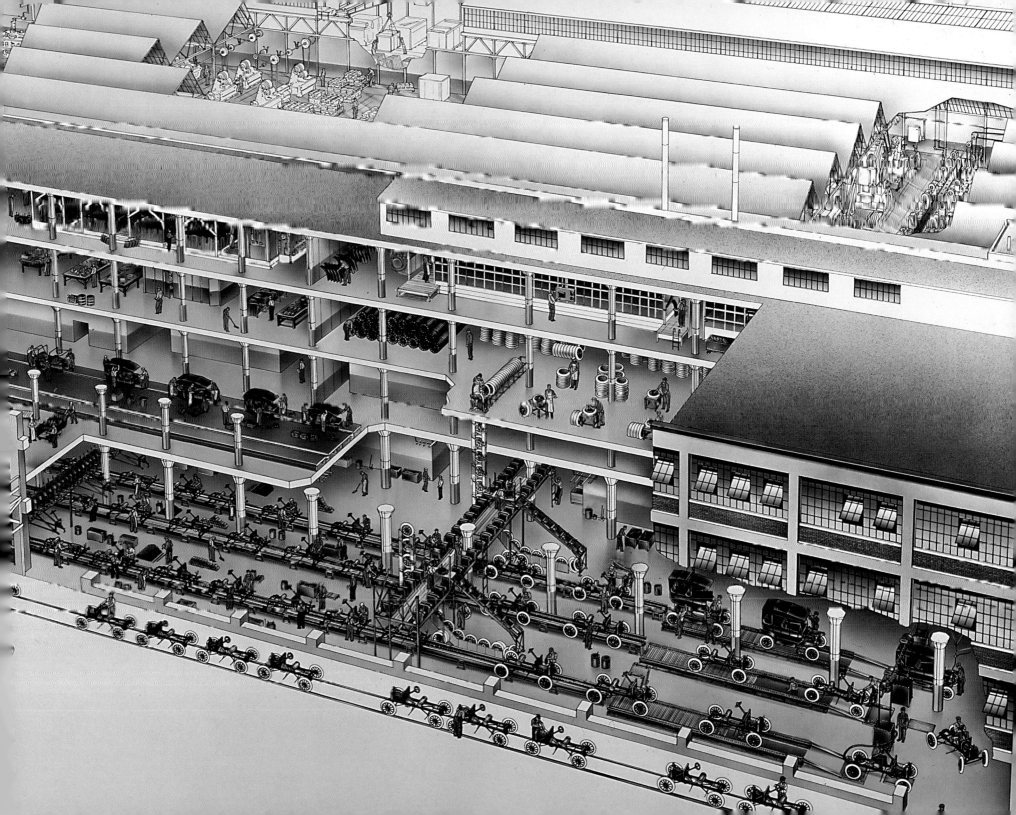

6

TRAVELING THE WORLD TO ILLUSTRATE CUTAWAY CARS

My international travel for illustration projects began in 1982 with a trip to Holland and France, and my last foreign business trip was to Italy in 1995. Air travel got really old, spending 8 to 14 hours at a time confined in an aluminum tube, but it was always exciting once I got there.

THE FRENCH CONNECTIONS

My world travels to take illustration reference photos started in May 1982 with a trip to St. Nazaire in France. My destination was a shipyard and not an auto plant, and my project, the *Nieuw Amsterdam*, floated instead of rolling on wheels. However, my next visit to France was arranged by *Automobile* magazine in March 1987 and took me to Renault's Alpine Plant in Dieppe on the English Channel coast. This trip was coordinated through American Motors, which was owned by Renault at the time.

This was an arrangement that started in 1983 with my cutaways appearing on a series of foldout *Motor Trend* covers. It was *Motor Trend* that put me on the map, and as their staffers moved to other publications they took the idea with them. In only a few years I was working directly for the manufacturers and their ad agencies as well.

I flew to Paris and met with a group of technical writers and technicians who were preparing the American Motors dealers to main-

tain Renault's new sports car, the Alpine, that was coming to the United States. We left for Dieppe in a convoy of Alpines on secondary roads through the French countryside. When it was my turn to drive, the service guy riding with me just wasn't ready for the fun. He started talking about how much he wanted to see his children again as I slid the tail-happy Alpine with a turbocharged V-6 hanging behind its rear axle around the rural roundabouts. As much as I enjoy getting sideways I did eventually slow down, but the service guy was in for an even greater shock the next morning at breakfast.

One of the AMC men who spoke French came into the restaurant with a newspaper that had a lead story about Renault selling AMC to Chrysler. He looked as if he had just been shot. Then everyone began speculating about whether or not they would still have jobs when they returned to the United States.

In a somewhat smaller way I had the same concern, wondering if I still had a project. Although I don't know what happened to the AMC guys, I was there with plenty of film, so I went ahead as though nothing had happened. This was also where the Renault 5 Turbo, a very cool pocket rocket, was built so it was a fun day anyway.

The engineers who showed me around were familiar with my work. I even spotted prints of some of my cutaways on the walls of their cubicles. One of the engineers drove me back to Paris and dropped me off at what I suppose was a very hip hotel, although its sheet metal interior décor made me feel as though I was sleeping in a vending machine.

I flew back to Baltimore and drove to the Harley-Davidson Assembly Plant Museum in York, Pennsylvania, where I photographed the 1949 Hydra-Glide that appears earlier in this book. *Automobile* went ahead with their story and my illustration, even making a poster of it available to their readers. However, I doubt that it sold very well because the Alpine never made it to the United States.

My world travels to take reference photos for illustration projects started with a trip to France in 1982 for the Holland America Lines to do a cutaway of the Nieuw Amsterdam. *This cruise ship was under construction at the shipyard in St. Nazaire where I spent two days documenting her, including going into the dry dock where she was being built.*

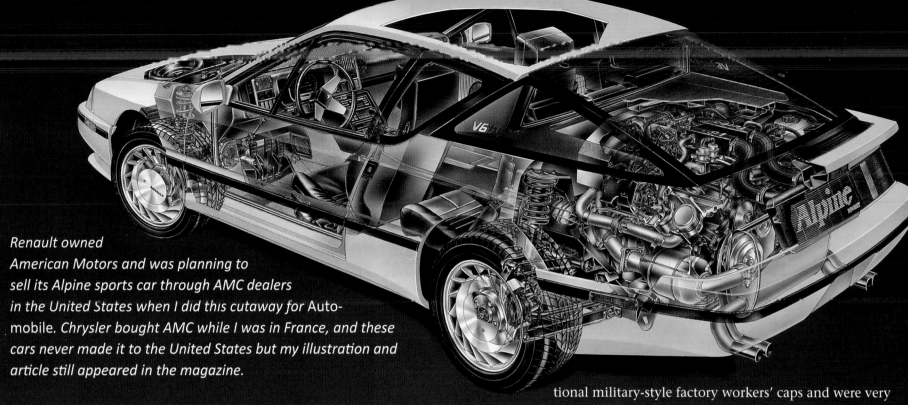

*Renault owned
American Motors and was planning to
sell its Alpine sports car through AMC dealers
in the United States when I did this cutaway for Automobile. Chrysler bought AMC while I was in France, and these
cars never made it to the United States but my illustration and
article still appeared in the magazine.*

MADE IN JAPAN

Motor Trend sent me to Japan for my first visit in July 1983 to photograph the new 300 ZX and its components for a cutaway illustration. Nissan put me up in style at the Imperial Hotel near the emperor's palace. My Japanese adventure got off to a slow start with a public relations man assigned to take me around getting stuck in Tokyo's perpetually near-gridlock traffic. I had given up on waiting in the lobby and was back in my room when Mr. Mitsunaga finally arrived. We headed south with the traffic easing up as we left Tokyo for a Nissan facility in Yokohama.

Here a number of 300 ZXs were on hoists with some of them partially disassembled. A black one was set aside for me in a sort of photo studio. The technicians and their supervisors all wore Japanese tradi-tional military-style factory workers' caps and were very regimented, with Mr. Mitsunaga having to ask each supervisor's permission before I could take photos in his area. After I finished shooting for the day, a black Nissan Cedrick limo took us to their automated Zama assembly plant with the uniformed chauffeur bowing as he opened my door. That was a touch embarrassing, but I liked it.

Zama, according to our tour guide, was the most fully automated assembly plant in the world. When we reached a large group of welding robots with pictures of women taped to them, I asked our guide what was going on. She pointed to some men wearing lab coats who were keeping an eye on the robots as their articulated arms struck like snakes making spot welds. She explained that the technicians "get very lonely and these are pictures of movie stars they have named the robots after."

I was Mr. Mitsunaga's guest at the 1,000-table Mikado Club that evening to see the Marilyn Monroe review with a very convincing

Marilyn dropping her top at the end of the show and getting a rise out of the audience. We went to several other locations over the next two days for me to photograph everything from disassembled engines to driveline and suspension components, and I even managed to get a few hours off for the Tokyo afternoon tour.

For my last evening in Japan a good friend of mine, Dr. Naemura, the U.S. importer of Iwata airbrushes, arranged for me to have dinner with the Iwata brothers. They presented me with an airbrush specially tuned for my work. We had dinner at a restaurant in a 16th-century shogun's fortress that had been moved to downtown Tokyo. Here the owner hand-brushed his business cards in traditional Chinese characters on hand-pressed paper at our table while we drank 100-year-old sake.

After dinner, we descended into a drinking contest and being almost a foot taller than the brothers, I proved the old hot rodders' adage that "you can't beat cubic inches" by being the only one able to stand up without assistance at the end of the evening.

Nissan was very security-conscious, and took each roll of my 35-mm film as soon as I exposed it. A courier met me at Narita Airport with the negatives and proof sheets just before I boarded the plane for the long flight home.

This was my first of so many trips to Japan that I am no longer sure how many there were. But the projects weren't all that exciting, and the other Japanese manufacturers had me illustrate their sporty cars without leaving California. I met Bob Thomas while he was the automotive editor for the *Los Angeles Times*, but when he called me in 1987 he was with Nissan.

He wanted to know if I was available for a trip to Japan to start a cut-away illustration of the all-new 1990 300 ZX.

During those years I always asked if I could drive anything with wheels that I was illustrating. That usually didn't happen, but I did get to drive a gigantic strip mining front-loader in Arizona and the 300 ZX in Japan. Bob Thomas set this up and probably had something to do with my being treated like a minor-league rock star once I arrived in Japan. I was given an impressive hotel suite and a meeting with the 300 ZX engineering team.

Regrettably, I don't remember my public relations minder's name, but I surely do remember the conference room where he took me, with a wall-sized print of my first 300 ZX cutaway at one end. After discussing the engineering team's objectives for my illustration, the

Motor Trend *sent me on my first of many trips to Japan in 1982 for this illustration of the original 300 ZX Turbo through an arrangement with Nissan that also gave them its use. My photos were the first to be taken by anyone outside the company, and my processed film and proof sheets were delivered to me at Narita Airport before I boarded the plane for home.*

meeting ended in a Japanese business card ceremony with each engineer handing me his card with a slight bow in return for one of mine. This was followed by polite questions about my card. One of the engineers discovered that he was out of cards, and the others watched with grave concern as he frantically went through his pockets. Everyone looked relieved when a colleague presented a crumpled one to me. Before leaving the room, I was given a large paint marker and asked to sign the huge print of my 300 ZX illustration on the wall.

Then it was time to go to work, traveling mostly by elevated train to avoid the congested surface streets. We visited several locations around the Tokyo area where I could photograph 1990 300 ZX components before going to a very high-end Chinese restaurant to have dinner with, as I remember, Nissan's director of overseas operations. Mickey, whom I had met at Nissan's U.S. headquarters in Torrance, California, was also there and was the only public relations person I didn't have to call Mister while in Japan. We did some serious bench racing over a lot of sake.

The next day was the high point of the trip with a ride on the 160-mph bullet train to Tochigi. That was a real rush when we passed trains traveling in the opposite direction on a parallel track at a closing speed of 320 mph! Nissan's Tochigi Proving Grounds included several

test tracks, and we were taken to the country road circuit that wound its way through trees, some of which were growing right on the edge of the track.

Nissan had its priorities straight both times I worked with the company in Japan: With my mission in mind, it had me start by photographing a U.S.–market left-hand-drive 300 ZX to use as a base for my illustration before getting involved in anything else. Lunch at Tochigi was a totally unexpected experience, with a

After numerous updates and a re-skin, the 1990 300 ZX was a new platform with styling inside and out that rivaled the Corvette with which it had to compete. The new Z-car's good looks come through in the inking along with its technical content featuring an upgraded 3.0-liter double-overhead cam four-valve-per-cylinder V-6 producing 222 hp.

professional chef preparing our midday meal at our table Benihana-style. I then met the test driver who would be my co-pilot for a few laps around the narrow tree-lined track.

I listened patiently while he nervously explained that I had to be extremely careful and would be limited to 60 kph (about 37 mph) because this car was "much too powerful for an ordinary driver." I was thinking that with 222 hp pushing 3,200 pounds it surely wasn't going to be a stormer. I in turn explained that I owned a 251 Corvette and knew the American racing driver that was doing the ZX's handling development, and had also done some racing myself. Still, no one was impressed, and the 60-kph-limit stood.

On the first lap crawling around the country road circuit I slowed down for the tight corners to calm my nervous passenger, but it was apparent that the only way to find out anything about the car's handling was to maintain 60 kph all the way around. When I didn't back off for the first sharp turn on the second lap I heard a tense, "Dangerous curve; must slow down" from the right seat, so I did. After a few more laps I pulled the Z car in, bringing the only time I drove a car in Japan to an end.

Back in Tokyo I visited Nissan's offices before leaving for Narita Airport to pick up my negatives and proof sheets. I saw Mickey again and he asked me what I thought of the 300 ZX's performance, but all I could tell him was, "I don't have a clue." I found out later that the

Z car I had driven at Tochigi was Nissan's only surviving U.S.–market prototype. The only other one had been wadded up in a crash the day before by the same American development driver I had been so careful to mention I knew. That explained a lot.

In my meeting with the 300 ZX engineering team I had requested orthographic engineering drawings of the car's 3.0-liter 4-cam 24-valve V 6, and before I left Nissan's offices a designer proudly gave them to me. I tried not to show my dismay as I unrolled the drawings and saw that they were three-dimensional wire frames with lines from the back showing through the front surfaces, but I could make out some sections so they weren't a total loss.

I thanked the man and took the drawings back to the United States, realizing that my

The 1990 300 ZX I photographed at Nissan's Tochigi Proving Grounds in 1987 was its only U.S.-market prototype at the time. I drove this Pearl Yellow Z-car on their tree-lined country road circuit with a very nervous test driver as my co-pilot.

request was a long shot anyway. Even though I was a Nissan contractor, foreign manufacturers usually don't release their engineering drawings, and this was a way of saving face. Even without engineering drawings I brought back plenty of information.

While I was finishing the painting Mickey called from Torrance, California, and asked if he could come over. We had a good time and some laughs while he watched me spray on the highlights.

GERMAN ENGINEERING

My first trip to Germany was arranged by *Motor Trend* to illustrate Porsche's new 3.2-liter 911 Carrera Super Sport. My wife, Ellen, and I flew to Stuttgart and took a cab to the Graff Zeppelin Hotel in January 1984. Ellen explored downtown Stuttgart the next day and I took a cab to the Porsche headquarters in Zuffenhausen.

I was met by my public relations contact Tom Nagaba. He told me I would be taking photos on the assembly line and to be careful not to get in the way, jokingly adding that a specified number of 911s were scheduled to be built that day and that if one less rolled off the line by quitting time I would have to pay for it. We both chuckled but I got the point.

After not importing their 911 Turbo to the United States for several years, Porsche offered their U.S. customers the "Turbo Look" in 1984 with the Turbo's tire package and wild bodywork but powered by a 220-hp naturally aspirated engine. Motor Trend sent me to Germany for the first time to illustrate this car that was marketed as the Carrera Super Sport.

We started on the top floor where the 911's flat-6 engines were hand-assembled and worked our way down to the bottom floor where completed cars drove off the end of the line. I must have stayed out of the way because I wasn't asked to pay for one.

The 911 variant was known as the "Turbo Look" because it was equipped with the Turbo's wheel and tire package, suspension and brakes, fender flares, and whale-tail spoiler, but with a naturally aspirated engine for the U.S. market. The next day I photographed one of these 911 Super Sports, as they were officially known, as a starting point for my cutaway.

Because I had previously mentioned to Tom that my first car was a 1955 Porsche Speedster, he showed me the part of the factory where it was built. We then visited the shop where production 911s were converted into GT race cars and custom bodywork was done for customers, along with the 935-style slant-nose conversions.

With my photography wrapped up, Tom offered me a chance to drive a 911 Turbo, a real thrill because they weren't imported to the United States. Tom gave me directions to the closest unrestricted stretch of autobahn and cautioned me to slow down if it started to snow, because the Porsche's Pirelli P7 tires would pack up with the white stuff very quickly and turn into slicks.

I embarrassed myself when I stopped at the security gate on my way out by missing the clutch's engagement point and stalling the car, but once on the autobahn that was quickly forgotten and I headed northeast toward Ludwigsburg. Even on unrestricted sections of the autobahn there were 120-kph limits through the cities. Leaving Ludwigsburg I found myself next to a pair of tricked-up BMWs that appeared to be lining up for a race. When we reached a speed limit sign with a red diagonal line through the 120 kph, we all punched it and the BMWs rapidly turned into specks in my rearview mirror as I reached 260 kph (161 mph) just as it started to snow.

Tom hadn't been kidding, and with the 911 starting to wander and getting tail-happy I relaxed my grip on the steering wheel and slowly backed off. I exited at the first *ausfahrt* I came to and looped around onto the *einsfahrt* heading back to Stuttgart at a reduced pace. I reluctantly turned the car back in and asked Tom to call a cab for me.

Ellen and I had the next day free to be tourists, and because Porsche wouldn't let me keep the 911, we rented an Opel Record. As I watched the Mercedes and BMWs spinning their back tires in the snow, I began to appreciate front-wheel drive for the first time. The Opel would have been a terrible letdown on the autobahn after having driven the Porsche, so we stayed on secondary roads.

After a visit to the Mercedes Museum, we drove through part of the legendary Black Forest to Baden-Baden, exploring every castle we came to along the way. Back at the Graff Zeppelin we watched *Conan the Barbarian* on TV in German, which didn't make much difference because there are only about three lines of dialog in the entire film. Then, finding that we could not sleep, we drove around the area until it was time for our plane the next morning.

Flying back to reality, I found it even more difficult to drive 55 mph on the California freeways after the freedom of the autobahns. However, I enjoyed the Porsche 911 Super Sport cutaway while remembering its speed, because in a way I feel almost as if I own the cars while I'm illustrating them.

Motor Trend worked out a deal with Porsche in 1985 to share the use of a cutaway I was to do of their limited-production 959. This car was never going to be sold in the United States, but it introduced some exciting new technology. I flew back to Deutschland in May and was met at the Stuttgart Airport by a delightful Spanish woman named Begonia who spoke several languages including Japanese, and we had dinner at the Keisersteller, one of the oldest restaurants in the city. The next morning Begonia showed up in a Porsche 928 and after introducing me to Norbert who was driving, we headed for Weissach, the Porsche development center near Ludwigsburg on the same stretch of autobahn where I had driven the 911 Turbo.

Norbert quickly accelerated to about 250 kph (155 mph) and glanced at me for a reaction, but having gone faster in the 911 I was tempted to say, "Is this all this thing can do?" However, I instead commented that I wished we could legally go this fast in the United States.

Weissach was normally closed to the magazines, but I was given access because of Porsche's deal with *Motor Trend*; however, Norbert carried my camera bag until we reached the area where the 959 prototypes were torn down for evaluation after testing. Once I had the camera, Norbert made sure I didn't take pictures of anything but 959 parts, with the chief engineer also watching me most of the time.

When I was photographing a complete engine, he put a shop rag over a bypass in the turbocharger ducting and said, "It's just a heater." The 959's flat-6 had two turbochargers and there was a patent pending on this bypass valve, which took in outside air when manifold pressure dropped below the atmospheric pressure before the Turbo's compressor wheels spooled up. This sensitive assembly was on the right side, so it would have shown in my illustration. Through Norbert's translation the engineer asked me to move it to the left and be sure it didn't show.

Porsche's regular-production 911 turbocharged engine was air-cooled, displaced 3.2 liters, and produced 300 hp with a single turbocharger and single-overhead cams with two valves per cylinder. Only the cylinder barrels of the 959 were air-cooled. Its 2.8-liter engine had liquid-cooled cylinder heads with double-overhead cams and four valves per cylinder with intercoolers mounted outboard of its twin turbochargers, and made 450 hp. I was given an excellent orthographic sectional assembly drawing of this engine, as I had been given for the base 911 the year before. That, along with the internal parts I photographed, ensured my engine cutaway could be both in-depth and accurate.

The 959 had started out to be a rally car for the FIA's ill-fated Group B series and was all-wheel drive, thus taking us to another building where a complete driveline assembly was set up on jack stands. Equipped with Porsche's Steuer Kupplung system, which sent the most power to wheel with the best grip, the transaxle would have made an interesting cutaway, but Porsche asked me to leave it solid, along with the torque tube and front axle.

Lunch at Weissach revealed an interesting aspect of German efficiency: My companions had already begun to clean their plates while I was just getting started, compelling me to shut up and just eat. The décor had a high-tech automotive theme with the dining room chairs upholstered in the same fabrics and leathers used for their car seats, and most of the ceilings had artfully designed exposed ducting painted in varying shades of mauve and gray.

After lunch I was able to photograph a complete pearl white 959 on which to base my illustration. This was a relief because the only fully assembled 959 I had seen up to this point was an engineering car with a large computer in place of a right seat. I did not get to drive a Porsche on this trip, but I did drive a Mercedes-Benz 190 SE with the Cosworth double-overhead cam cylinder head when I went to the Mercedes Museum the next day in Untertürkheim.

After my visit at Porsche I collected information for the cutaway of the 1936 Mercedes-Benz 540K, which appears in Chapter Five. This was a private commission with support from a lot of players, and *AQ* arranged for Mercedes to give me their assistance in Germany.

I picked up the 190 SE, or whatever its designation was, from an airport rental car lot and asked the agent about Heidelberg. She responded, "Why do all Americans want to go to Heidelberg? There's nothing there."

So I asked her, "Why do all Germans want to go to Hollywood? There's nothing there either," and then added, "I hope they all find something we locals don't see."

She told me Heidelberg was about 70 kilometers north and to have a nice drive. Before becoming a tourist, I spent the rest of the day at the Mercedes-Benz Museum. Max von Pine put me in front of a microfilm viewer to pick out 540K engineering drawings that would help with my illustration. Prints were made and shipped to me.

With the 959 photography on 35-mm cassettes in my camera bag and the 540K drawings awaiting me back home, I could be a tourist for a day and so headed for Heidelberg in the little blue Mercedes. The autobahn was only a four-lane, but it was unrestricted and with a top speed of about 220 kph it didn't take long to get there. The trip up was uneventful, but there was a little excitement on the way back.

I decided to take a picture of the gauges with the speedometer and tach almost pegged. As I was driving through my Nikon, a Cadillac Seville pulled out in front of me from between two trucks. I tossed my camera into the passenger seat as the car's first generation anti-lock braking system (ABS) reduced my velocity in a rapid series of jerks. Just as I thought I was going to rear-end the Caddy, our speeds equalized and the Cadillac wandered back into the right lane. When I was alongside, I saw that the driver was an American army bird colonel smoking a huge cigar and steering with the friction of his right wrist. He was completely oblivious to the drama that had just taken place behind him.

In 1989 Volkswagen of America called me from their headquarters in Troy, Michigan, about a cutaway illustration of their new G60 supercharged Corrado sports coupe that was on sale in Europe and coming to the United States in 1990. The woman who called said I would need to go to Osnabruck in Germany where the Corrados were built by Karmann to photograph the internal components, even though it had not yet started producing the U.S. version.

She also told me that there was a U.S.-spec Corrado with the cars that VW was using in their TV commercials. It was at a contractor on the edge of the Burbank Airport. The illustration could be based on it.

She also suggested that I fly Lufthansa to Germany the Friday before the May Day weekend because it offered a discount if I stayed the whole week. That would give me time to drive around and see a lot of the country.

At the Frankfurt Airport I picked up a yellow Corrado with a black interior, just like the one I had been requested to illustrate, except for being a European model. Being interested in naval military history I immediately headed north to see the Kriegsmarine Museum in Kiel. This had been the German navy's headquarters in both world wars and is about 450 kilometers north of Frankfurt on the Baltic Sea.

There was a lot more traffic than I was accustomed to on the autobahn leaving Frankfurt. Reaching the end of the city's 120-kph speed limit, all the other cars accelerated to about 160 kph, but I waited until traffic thinned out to put the pedal to the metal. I was pleased to find that the front-wheel-drive Corrado's 160 horses could pull it to 220 kph. After about 30 minutes of

Motor Trend *worked out a deal with Porsche in 1985 to share my cutaway illustration of their 959, which was not going to be imported to the United States but was the ultimate supercar of its time. This twin-turbocharged 450-hp all-wheel-drive wonder of technology took me back to Germany in 1985 and inside Porsche's Weissach Development Center for my photography.*

missing the scenery while continuously passing cars, I slowed to a 180-kph cruising speed.

After stopping in Hannover for lunch and getting back on the autobahn approach with no one behind me, I stopped on the *einsfahrt* and slipped the clutch enough for a good launch, accelerating through the gears to 220 kph, which was legal because I was buckled up. Traveling through the farmland north of Hannover, I discovered why most German cars have headlights with wipers and washers like their windshields do: Every forward-facing surface of the car was quickly coated with splattered bugs. Fortunately there was enough washer fluid to get through this bug barrage.

In Kiel I visited the Kriegsmarine Museum where I was able to board a U-boat. I then followed the north seacoast down to Wilhelmshaven where I turned inland. Arriving in Osnabruck on Sunday afternoon I checked into the Hohenzollern, a wonderful old hotel where VW had made a reservation for me so I would be ready to go to work at Karmann the next morning.

At that time, Karmann was the largest independent automotive body manufacturer in Germany with close ties to both Porsche and Volkswagen. In the United States it was best known for the VW Karmann Ghia.

My tour started with the first step, a stack of sheet steel being fed into presses, some of which were stamp-

My next visit to Germany was for Volkswagen of America in 1989 to illustrate the supercharged Corrado G60 sports coupe built under contract by Karmann in Osnabruck. The U.S. version wasn't in production yet, but there was a prototype near our studio in Burbank, California, and Neil Nissing photographed it before I went to Germany.

ing our Corrado body panels. The others made body parts for Porsche 911 Cabriolets, which were also built by Karmann. (I later showed this photo to a visitor at my studio, a real Porsche fanatic, who was shocked to find out that Porsches weren't made from some special material.) A Karmann manufacturing engineer took me through the plant and made it possible for me to photograph everything from bodies in white to final assembly along with all the individual components I requested, so I left Osnabruck with a complete package.

Even though it is at the opposite end of the automotive spectrum from the 959 or even the 911, with the impartiality of time I feel the Corrado is a better illustration, my technique having continued to develop.

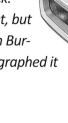

The Italian Jobs

After sending me on my first trip to Germany in January 1984, *Motor Trend* sent me to Italy in December for another first trip to do (what else?) another cutaway illustration, this time of Ferrari's 1984 Testarossa that was coming to the United States in 1985. As with Ferrari's legendary sports racing car of the late 1950s and named for its 3.0-liter V-12's red cam covers, the new Testarossa's 4.9-liter flat-12's cam covers were also painted red.

I flew on Alitalia to Malpensa Airport north of Milano. After wondering slightly about the applause from most of the other passengers following our landing, I rented a Renault 5 for the drive to Modena, about 175 km southeast. My French econobox's performance was similar to the Opel Record I had driven in Germany, which is to say adequate. As I approached my hotel its diminutive size proved to be fortuitous.

Tony Asenza at *Motor Trend* had a lot of contacts in Italy and arranged my trip, which included a reservation at the Canal Grande located on Via Canal Grande, a one-way street,

making the only access to the hotel through a narrow arch at one end. This was a very exclusive hotel owned by the de Tomaso family, whose holdings included Maserati, Pantera, and Innocente, along with Benelli motorcycles. Alessandro de Tomaso's offices occupied the entire second floor.

Tony Asenza had Alessandro's son Santiago contact me, and with a common interest in high-performance cars and American steam locomotives we became great friends. Together we visited every model train store in Modena. In his Innocente, an Italian Mini with a Fiat engine, Santiago also took me through the Maserati factory to see the Quattroportes being assembled, and after a few disparaging remarks about Ferrari's build quality, he cautioned me not to mention having been at Maserati to anyone in Marinello because the old rivalry was still alive.

Marinello is a short drive south from Modena, and Ferrari's main office building looked just as it had in the 1966 film *Grand Prix* when Jim Garner walked through these same gates. After a short wait Doctore Pierro de Franke came to take me around. We started with the assembly building where all of Ferrari's engines and transaxles were put together on the same floor as the Testarossa and 288 GTO assembly line. This was ideal for my photography, but there was one problem. The Testarossas came from Pininfarina partially assembled with only their suspension, fuel system, and

After sending me on my first trip to Germany in January 1984, Motor Trend sent me to Italy in December for (what else?) a cutaway of the new Ferrari Testarossa. This tracing is a composite of photos taken in front of Ferrari's 308 body paint shop with shots of the hood and passenger door both open and closed.

powertrain being installed in Marinello. When I told Pierro I would need to photograph a bare frame he said I would have to go to Torino.

I also asked about engineering drawings of the Testarossa's 4.9-liter 4-cam 48-valve flat-12, at which time Pierro left me for a few minutes. He returned with the chief engineer who told me through a translator, "Of course we cannot give you the secret technical diagrams!"

I knew Ferrari had their own aluminum foundry and asked to see it on the chance that there might be some cylinder block and head castings lying around, and perhaps some of them had been run through a band saw to check for core shifts. Sure enough there was a whole pile of them. Pierro asked me why I was taking pictures of a scrap pile, so I explained that it made an interesting artistic statement, although in reality it gave me the water jacket and port sections that I would have gotten from the forbidden drawings.

A U.S.-spec Testarossa with a stepladder waited for us beside the high-tech 308 body paint shop. Pierro made sure that the shop's over-spray tower showed in my photos, along with the moon that was

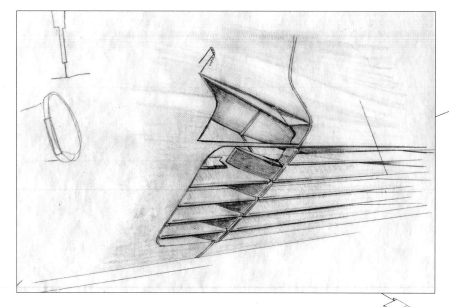

The air ducts behind the Testarossa's signature "cheese grater" side strakes (that feed cooling air to its twin radiators) required a separate layout with a little shading. Small layouts were also done to work out the frame, suspension, brakes, radiator, and engine.

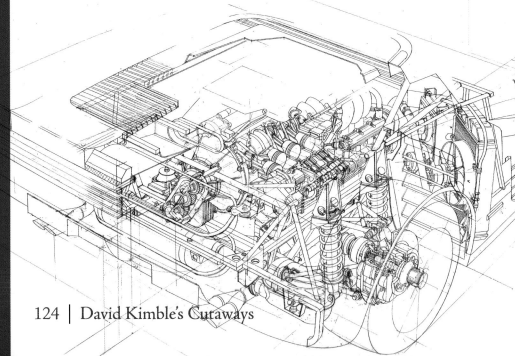

All the small spot layouts were refined and detailed as they were added to this layout of the Testarossa's mechanical and structural components along with the bodywork sections. The 4.9-liter flat-12 was deeply cut into to show its internal architecture, but all I could show of the transaxle, which was under the engine, were the transfer gears that drove it.

the U.S. version having 10 horses fewer than this European Testarossa's 390.

While I was touring Fiorano, Doctore de Franke had Ferrari's office trying to find a hotel room for me in Torino. It took some luck to find a place to stay on such short notice. In the end, the hotel was in Milano about 130 kilometers away, which fit into my plans well. I had intended to spend a day there visiting the Alfa Romeo Museum, an arrangement made possible by *AQ*, even though the museum was closed to the general public. The tradeoff was that I had to get up early to make my nine o'clock appointment at Pininfarina.

I reached the *tangenziale*, which circles the city, in less than an hour and exited on the Via Emanuel, but Italian street signs seem to be hit-and-miss and I could not find the cross street where Pininfarina's headquarters is located. I had passed a rival company, Carrozzeria Bertone, so I went back there and asked for directions. The receptionist summoned one of the most beautiful women I have ever seen who said, "Of course, I should not tell you, but if you turn left at the fire station you will find them."

Pininfarina and Bertone are actually in Gruliasco, south of downtown Torino. They are among the last of the great Italian *carrozzerias*, sustained by production contracts from Fiat, Ferrari, and Alfa Romeo, along with foreign auto makers.

I have owned two Pininfarina-bodied cars, a 1967 Ferrari 275 GTB, and a 1972 Alfa Romeo 2.0-liter Spyder. I was taken to the area where the Testarossa bodies were built and we walked past the Alfa Spyder assembly line. I was surprised to see that the Alfas were mixed in with

about to set. The tower had a large Ferrari prancing horse toward the top and Pierro said, "What a picture! A Testarossa, the Ferrari tower, and the moon. You must use this in your magazine!" So much for art statements; I didn't have the heart to tell him that my photos were only for reference.

Ferrari's restaurant was across the street from the factory, beside the entrance to their famous test track Fiorano where a test driver was waiting with a Testarossa. He had just given a ride to a photojournalist from *People* magazine. The journalist had driven her Ferrari Modena from Rome, and she took some pictures that I still have of me in the Testarossa. Even though the car felt heavy and a little under-shocked it didn't disappoint, with balanced handling and more power than any car sold in the United States at the time, with

Fiat 124 Spyders, which had less in common than my Porsche Speedster and a VW Karmann Ghia, but there they were, nose-to-tail going down the same line.

Although the Alfas and Fiats drove off the end of a moving assembly line as complete cars, the Testarossas didn't get wheels until they reached Marinello, and moved between assembly lines on dollies. The TRs were painted, plumed, wired, and upholstered here, so there was plenty to photograph, but there weren't any bare frames so I was taken to the subcontractor that fabricated them on a side street a few blocks away.

We drove to the small shop and found welding jigs, fixtures, and steel tubing but no frames. The foreman told my PR rep guide that they would be welding up a frame that afternoon so I should come back after lunch.

To pass the time I drove north on the Via Emanuel until it fed into a large piazza de roundabout with streets coming into it from every direction and found some lunch while I watched the street railway cars and other traffic. When I returned to the shop, the elusive Testarossa frame was starting to take shape and these guys were good, with welds that compared to the best race car fabricators in the United States.

The frame was completed in about an hour and I left Torino with everything I needed for the Testarossa project. But my first Italian adventure was not quite over yet, because Malpensa Airport was socked in with fog and the passengers on my flight had to travel by bus to Genova on the Ligurian Sea. I can still see our gleaming white 747 towering over the ancient red tile roofs of the city where Columbus departed as I began my own trip back to the New World.

As improbable as it sounds, my first project for Cadillac took me back to Italy in 1986. Arranged by *Automobile*, it was the beginning of a long relationship that would last through the 1990s with me illustrating most of Cadillac's new models. Neil Nissing was able to accompany me on this trip and the car we were there to document for my cutaway was a real departure for Cadillac. It was a two-seater with Pininfarina bodywork, the Allante.

My approach and technique were evolving quickly when the Testarossa painting was completed early in 1985, and it was my best painting so far. Ferrari made sure I showed the car's fitted luggage and they were surprised at the accuracy of my engine cutaway without the "secret technical diagrams."

The timing of this trip was fortuitous because I was also collecting information to do a Lamborghini Countach illustration for *AQ*, and by arriving in Italy a few days early we could also visit Lamborghini. We flew to Milano Malpensa Airport, and to drive across northern Italy's industrial belt in the Po Valley, we rented an Alfa Sud and headed to Modena where we had reservations at the Canal Grande Hotel.

Lamborghini is located in St. Agata Bolognese, a few kilometers southeast of Modena. We arrived just as the assembly line workers were arriving on motor scooters and liter cars dressed in black coveralls emblazoned with Lambo's gold raging bull logos. We checked in at the security office and Enzo, the production manager, came out to take us into the factory where, as with Ferrari, engines and transaxles were assembled in the same building as the cars.

Enzo had a Countach LP5000S Quattrovalvole brought out for Neil to photograph as a starting point for my illustration before we went to lunch just down the road in St. Giovani. Countachs had a unique powertrain layout with their 5.2-liter 4-cam 48-valve V-12s turned around backward with the transmission facing forward. In the after-

noon we were able to watch one being threaded into the complex tubular space frame.

We were back at Lamborghini the next morning for some additional photography, and then headed southwest on a roundabout route to Maranello where Piero de Franke very obligingly gave us a Ferrari factory tour. From there we drove to downtown Modena and stopped at Maserati to see Santiago de Tomaso, who showed us around. When I asked if we could also see the Pantera factory he said, "Of course, but it's hard to find."

The Panteras were built across town and a driver was going to take a GTI back to the factory, so Santiago had us get in a Maserati Quattroporte that was going to follow him over, and we were off for a wild ride. The Pantera set a torrid pace, splitting lanes and slicing through traffic flat-out. With our driver keeping up with the big Quattroporte, it was like being in an action movie car chase, an unexpected treat.

The de Tomaso Pantera was an affordable mid-engine Italian exotic powered by a Ford 351 Cleveland V-8 when it was

Countach is a Bolognese expletive meaning "wow," and that summed up one of the most outrageous visual statements to ever reach production, making it a car that I had always wanted to illustrate. The 1986 four-valve LP5000S represented the pinnacle of development. Even the two-valve LP5000 that Neil and I managed to borrow in California was a hoot to drive.

sold through Lincoln-Mercury dealers during the 1970s. However, by 1986 it no longer met U.S. safety standards, and was all but out of production. The last of the Panteras were built only to fill individual customer orders in a small building on a side street, and it was interesting but sad to see these exciting cars fading away.

We had time, so we took the scenic route from Modena to Torino, a distance of about 300 kilometers on secondary roads, and unlike my first visit to that city our hotel rooms were booked in advance. We joined Cadillac's director of public relations, Sherry Pirella, and her assistant, Dan Race, for a meeting with Sergio Pininfarina at the *carrozzeria*'s headquarters before their PR guy, Rudy Valentini, drove us to the Allante assembly plant.

We all squeezed into Rudy's Alfa Romeo Berlina sedan and took an autostrada to the new assembly plant with Rudy cruising at about 160 kph and driving with a smooth arms-out style and continuously passing the slower traffic. When nothing was said after we reached the plant the drama continued all the way back.

The Allante program was ambitious with Alitalia 747 cargo planes flying Cadillac parts to Italy and complete cars back to the United States in an operation called the "sky bridge." We had already gone to Detroit and photographed the Cadillac chassis pan, suspension,

The Allante, Cadillac's two-seater wearing an Italian suit by Pininfarina required trips to Detroit and Torino with my cutaway view chosen by Sergio Pininfarina. This is a redo of my original 1987 Allante with the 4.1-liter 170-hp V-8 replaced by a slightly less anemic 4.5-liter engine and new 17-inch wheels for 1989.

automatic front-wheel-drive transaxle, and 4.1-liter V-8 engine along with a prototype Allante for my cutaway. In the meeting with Sergio Pininfarina, he shot down my choice of views, wanting to see the car more from the side, so Neil had to reshoot it in Italy, making this truly an Italian job.

When I was at the Ferrari factory in 1984, the 288 GTOs and Testarossas were being built on the same assembly line and I regretted not having a client for the GTO as well. This would have to wait until after Scott Bailey sold *AQ* to *Road & Track* and they moved *AQ* from Princeton, New Jersey, to Newport Beach, California. Lowell Paddock moved with it and remained editor-in-chief. After the move he was able to have me do some cutaway illustrations directly for *AQ* by sharing them with *Road & Track*. We started with the Countach in 1986 and the next year I suggested to Lowell that we do a double cutaway, something neither of us had seen before. We would have both the 1984 288 and 1962 250 Ferrari GTOs in perspective to each other on a common plane, and Lowell liked the idea.

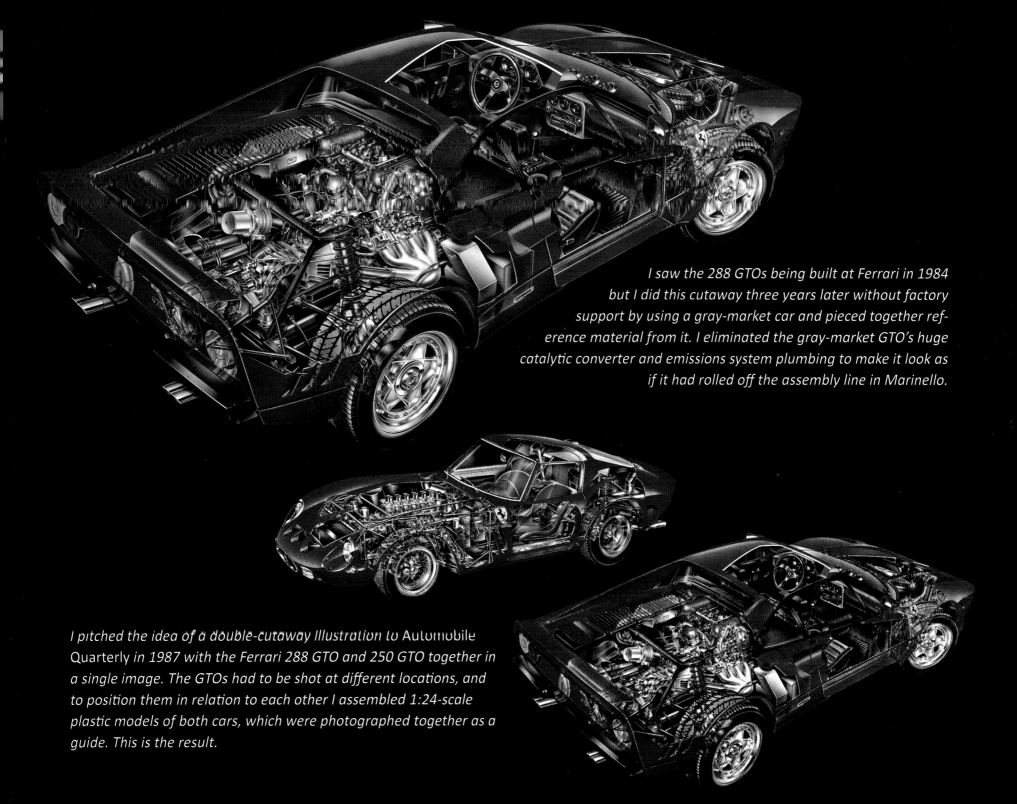

I saw the 288 GTOs being built at Ferrari in 1984 but I did this cutaway three years later without factory support by using a gray-market car and pieced together reference material from it. I eliminated the gray-market GTO's huge catalytic converter and emissions system plumbing to make it look as if it had rolled off the assembly line in Marinello.

I pitched the idea of a double-cutaway illustration to *Automobile Quarterly* in 1987 with the Ferrari 288 GTO and 250 GTO together in a single image. The GTOs had to be shot at different locations, and to position them in relation to each other I assembled 1:24-scale plastic models of both cars, which were photographed together as a guide. This is the result.

With the chances of finding examples of these two rare Ferraris in the same place being slim to none, I started by assembling 1/24 scale plastic model kits of both cars, which Neil photographed together as a guide for taking pictures of the actual cars. Like the Porsche 959, the 288 GTO had started out to be an FIA Group B rally car and wasn't imported to the United States. However, one of Phil Hill's neighbors had a gray-market conversion and agreed to let us photograph it for my illustration. The 1961 Formula One world champion driver had the GTO at his restoration shop Hill and Vaughn, in Santa Monica.

When Neil and I arrived and I asked to have the passenger-side wheels removed while Neil was taking pictures Phil became a little grumpy. It turned out that his neighbor had made him promise that no one else would touch the car, so he had to remove the wheels and then put them back on himself, but he got past it quickly, and I couldn't help thinking sadly about the opportunity I had missed at Ferrari three years earlier.

For the 288 GTO's engine and other internal components I went to see Cris Vandagriff, the owner of Hollywood Sports Cars, a Ferrari dealer since the 1950s, not realizing that he also owned a gray-market GTO. Cris was very enthusiastic about helping, even offering to let me drive his GTO and loaning me the shop manual and the parts catalog, which included exploded views of the engine and transaxle that I copied and

returned. He also arranged for Neil and me to visit Hollywood Sports Car's parts warehouse in Orange County, where he had a GTO 2.8-liter 400-hp turbocharged V-8 and transaxle on a pallet.

Piecing together enough reference material to do a cutaway of a recent car without factory support can be even more difficult than doing a vintage one, and I owe a lot to Phil Hill and Cris Vandagriff for making this one possible.

Synchronicity is a wonderful thing, especially when it works in your favor. While I was gathering reference material for the 250 GTO illustration, Mike McCluskey, who had restored the 1965 427 Cobra that I illustrated, had cut a 250 GTO off its tubular support structure. Mike was restoring the car's body and frame for Ralph Lauren because of his expertise with superleggera-type bodywork, and although he

We caught up with the 1962 250 GTO that Neil photographed for this illustration after it competed in the Monterey Historic Races at Laguna Seca in August 1987. The GTO cutaways were separate full-sized paintings and Neil copied them individually. He also did an amazing job of shooting them together on a single 8 x 10-inch transparency.

Motor Trend *had expected to send Neil and me to Italy for the Ferrari F40 in 1988, but Marinello wanted us to wait, so we ended up at Fiat's emissions lab in Dearborn, Michigan, instead. I tried laying out all the internal detail except the engine and transaxle on the tracing of the photos to save some time, which turned out not to be the way to go.*

didn't have the mechanicals, he knew where we could find an engine.

This lead took us to a small repair garage in Hollywood that specialized in vintage Ferraris, where we were told that the Colombo V-12 they had was almost identical to a GTO engine, but had actually come out of a mid-engine 275 LM. It was on an engine stand, so Neil was able to take some good pictures that could fill in the areas that couldn't be seen under the hood of a complete GTO, and this was the last piece of the puzzle.

The Monterey historic races were coming up in August and at least one 250 GTO was always in the field, so we decided that this would be a fun way to find an example we could photograph for the illustration. Chevrolet was the featured marque in 1987 and I had a new Z51 Corvette, so we decided to go up from Burbank on twisty Highway 1 along the California coast. I drove my 'Vette as if we were competing in the Mille Miglia.

As we had hoped, there was a red 250 GTO in the 1960s sports and GT car race, and after the cars returned to the pits we found the owner. He was happy to cooperate, but suggested we come back on Monday for the Ferrari Owners' Club event when the pits would be less crowded. The photo session couldn't have gone better, and 250 GTOs are well documented, so after a visit to Autobooks in Burbank I had had enough reference material to do justice to this iconic car.

In a meeting at *Motor Trend* early in 1988 I was asked which two high-performance sports or GT cars due to be introduced that year would make the best subjects for cutaway illustrations for their cover. I suggested the Ferrari F40 and the Corvette ZR-1 with everyone agreeing that was a good plan, but access to the F40 would prove to be a problem because Marinello asked me to wait until the car was in production to come to Italy. Naturally *Motor Trend* wanted to be the first magazine with the F40 on the cover, so they found a back door through Ferrari of North America, which gave us access to the Tokyo Motor Show F40 that was in Dearborn, Michigan. The car was at Fiat's emissions lab for federalization studies and fortunately they were willing to remove any parts within reason, because without the factory involved this was all I was going to have to work from for my cutaway.

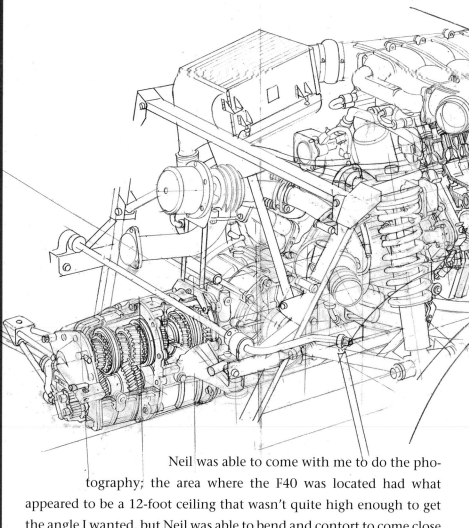

The F40 was hot news and Motor Trend got us access to the Tokyo Motor Show F40 that was in Dearborn to be partially disassembled for federalization studies. It was fortunate that the F40's 2.9-liter twin-turbocharged V-8 was based on the 288 GTO's engine because I had to use GTO DNA for the engine and transaxle internal detail.

neer explained that these were the same titanium wheel nuts used on Ferrari's Formula One cars and they were torqued to an incredible 1,700 ft-lbs, so we needed a longer lever. They found a piece of steel tubing about 8 feet long that would slip over our hand-made wheel nut wrench tube. Four guys, including me, started jumping off the floor to put pressure on the tube until the nut came loose with a screech. A passerby with a clipboard that had been watching this drama commented after the nut was off, "Why did you guys go through all that when all you had to do was leave the car out near Belle Island tonight and just catch up with those wheels after the strippers got 'em?"

The body was split horizontally as is a C4 Corvette, and we were able to get enough of it off to expose the components I wanted to show, but for the engine and transaxle internals I had to use a 288 GTO D.N.A. The F40's double-overhead cam four-valve-per-cylinder 471-hp V-8 was a direct development of the GTO's 2.8-liter 400-hp engine with a new intake manifold and turbocharging system, which accounted for most of the boost in horsepower.

The F40 proved to be my most popular automotive cutaway illustration from this period, and although Petersen Publishing kept all of my original art they eventually returned the publication rights to me and I have received a lot of requests for the use of this painting. Magneti

Neil was able to come with me to do the photography; the area where the F40 was located had what appeared to be a 12-foot ceiling that wasn't quite high enough to get the angle I wanted, but Neil was able to bend and contort to come close enough. When we reached the point of removing the passenger-side wheels, the Fiat crew realized they didn't have a socket large enough for the center-lock wheel nuts. They measured one of them and sent a kid to Snap-on in Farmington to get an 80-mm socket. When he returned it was a jaw-dropper to discover it wouldn't fit because no one had noticed that the nuts were octagons and not hexes.

An Italian engineer in the group laid out an octagon on a steel plate, cut it out, and welded it to a piece of tubing about 3 feet long, but although it fit perfectly the nut wouldn't budge. Another engi-

Marelli featured the F40 cutaway on the cover of an electronic fuel injection brochure with Neil's photo of my Ducati 851 motorcycle appearing inside. This was my favorite secondary use but not the highest visibility. My sales rep, Melanie Kirsch, talked me into letting Adobe scan my F40 line drawing and electronically render it in color to promote their Adobe Illustrator software, and posters of their version kept showing up to haunt me for years. I also used the F40 on my full-color business cards for years because Ferraris are one of the few cars that won't offend other manufacturers, even the Japanese.

The 1980s were the years of foreign acquisitions for the Detroit Three, and Chrysler owned Lamborghini when Neil and I returned to St. Agata Bolognese in December 1989 for another *Motor Trend* project. I also had an assignment from Buick to illustrate their new Park Avenue in the same time frame, so we stopped in St. Louis on our way to Italy and visited the plant where the production pilot cars were being assembled. In stark contrast to this front-wheel-drive midsize GM luxury car, the remainder of our trip was focused on Lamborghini's latest mid-engine raging bull, the Diablo that was going to replace the aging

Countach. We rented a red Fiat Uno at Malpensa Airport and when we reached Modena I felt compelled to follow the Centro Citi signs, convinced that I was doing something wrong because every time they led to a dead end, but at least this dead was very close to the Canal Grande where we again stayed.

Although I knew the Diablo was not in production yet, at Lamborghini the next morning I was dismayed to see how little there was to work with; however, some of the new V-12s were being assembled so Neil could take photos of their internal components.

There was also a fully assembled engine with Lambo's unique driveline bolted to it with the transmission in front and the rear axle driven by a shaft running through the oil pan. Giotto Bizzarini designed Lamborghini's original 3.0-liter 4-cam 2-valve-per-cylinder V-12 in 1963, and with incremental displacement increases over the years it had reached 5.2 liters with four valves per cylinder, and produced 420 hp by 1986. Its replacement, funded by Chrysler, had a similar layout but displaced 5.7 liters and initially made 492 hp with a lot more to come. Sandro Munari gave

Pininfarina designed the F40's high-downforce aerodynamic body, which presented me quite a challenge to keep its features without obscuring the detail underneath. My approach was a complex combination of seethroughs, cutaways, and vignettes. It is a little busy but it works, and this illustration was very popular.

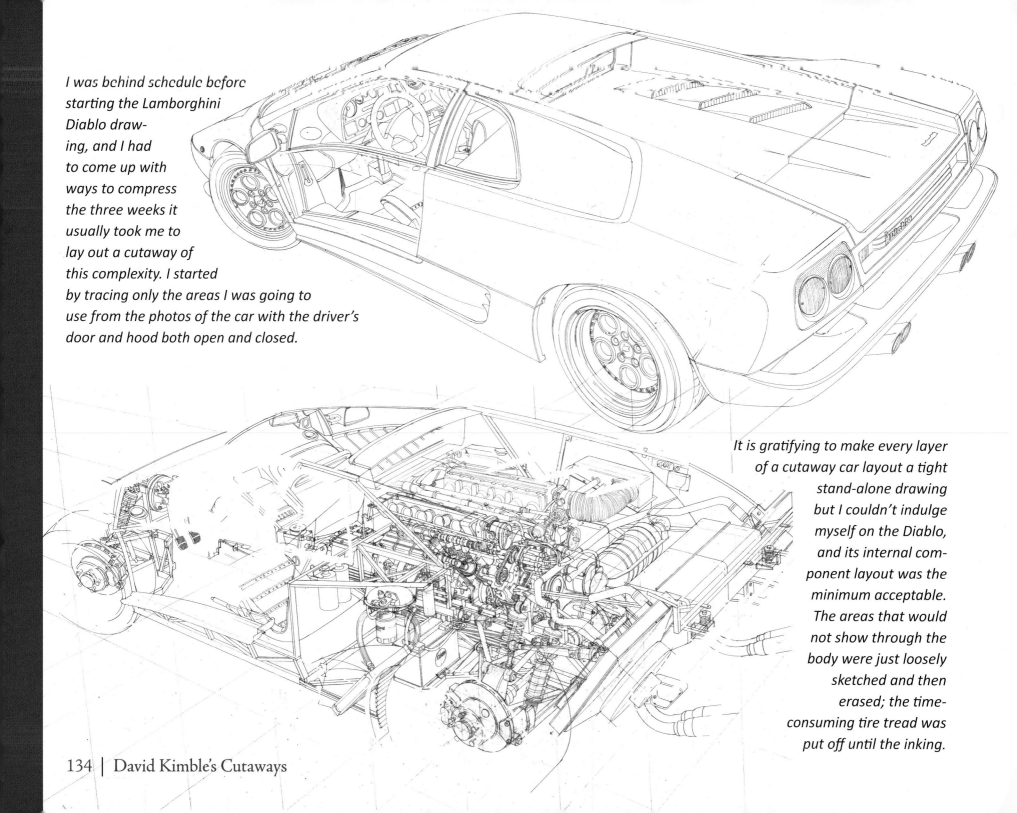

I was behind schedule before
starting the Lamborghini
Diablo draw-
ing, and I had
to come up with
ways to compress
the three weeks it
usually took me to
lay out a cutaway of
this complexity. I started
by tracing only the areas I was going to
use from the photos of the car with the driver's
door and hood both open and closed.

It is gratifying to make every layer
of a cutaway car layout a tight
stand-alone drawing
but I couldn't indulge
myself on the Diablo,
and its internal com-
ponent layout was the
minimum acceptable.
The areas that would
not show through the
body were just loosely
sketched and then
erased; the time-
consuming tire tread was
put off until the inking.

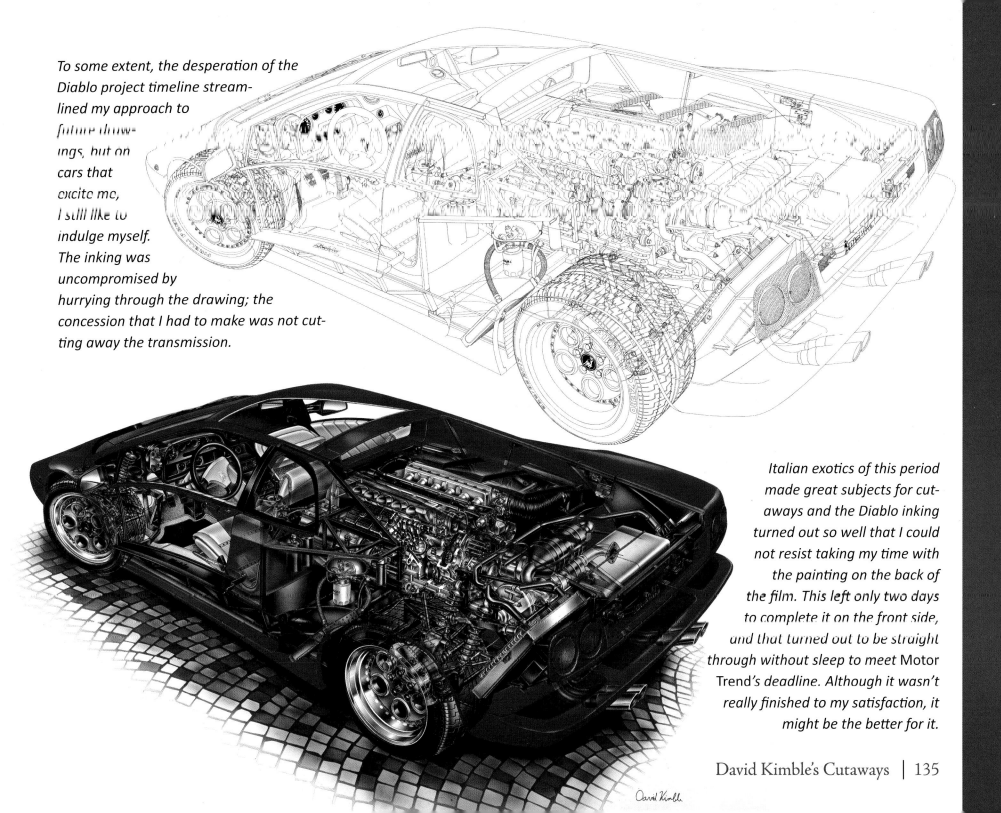

To some extent, the desperation of the Diablo project timeline streamlined my approach to future drawings, but on cars that excite me, I still like to indulge myself. The inking was uncompromised by hurrying through the drawing; the concession that I had to make was not cutting away the transmission.

Italian exotics of this period made great subjects for cutaways and the Diablo inking turned out so well that I could not resist taking my time with the painting on the back of the film. This left only two days to complete it on the front side, and that turned out to be straight through without sleep to meet Motor Trend's deadline. Although it wasn't really finished to my satisfaction, it might be the better for it.

David Kimble's Cutaways | 135

me a Diablo cutaway line drawing done locally that filled in a lot of the blanks.

On this trip, Neil was not only taking my reference photos but also doing the beauty photography for *Motor Trend* of the only Diablo prototype at the factory, which was loaded on a flatbed truck to be hauled to a scenic location. There wasn't much in St. Agata except Automobili Lamborghini with the Lambo tractor factory across the road and a few ruins of ancient frame houses, and our photo safari took us to one of these. A Chrysler PR woman came along with us and I managed to have a stepladder put on the flatbed so Neil could also shoot the photos for my cutaway. That evening I realized that the region's indigenous pattern of street paving bricks under the Diablo would add a lot to the illustration, and Neil climbed a lamp post to get a shot of them at a good angle; however, when I had to add them during the desperate thrash to complete the painting I wished I had never had the idea.

With our assignment from *Motor Trend* wrapped up, Neil and I had a couple of days to see some of the parts of Italy where they did not make cars, and so we headed for Rome but wisely kept our rooms at the Canal Grande. We drove around the ancient city and visited the Vatican, although we arrived too late to see the Sistine Chapel. We decided to stay overnight but discovered we could not check into a hotel because Neil had left his passport in Modena. I told him that the drive north was all his, and with most drivers not paying any attention to the Autostrada's 140-kph speed limit it was similar to sailboat racing, drafting with packs of other liter cars flat-out back to Modena.

With a few hours of sleep we then took off for Venice. After crossing the actual Canal Grande to the city we hired a water taxi for a tour of the canals to top off our look at the historical side of Italy.

In December 1992, a few days after moving into the Palace Theater

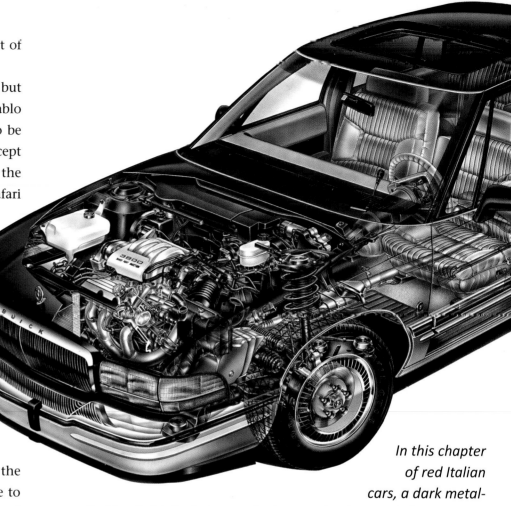

In this chapter of red Italian cars, a dark metallic blue Buick Park Avenue looks completely out of place, but we stopped in St. Louis for this project on the way to Italy. This GM midsize luxury car had to be completed before the Diablo, which really put me in a pinch to meet Motor Trend's *deadline.*

building in Marfa, Texas, I received a call from Fiat's technical director, Alberto Negro, with an offer I regrettably had to refuse. Fiat's proposal was for me to spend some time in Torino illustrating their latest group of new cars, but having just relocated from California and being overbooked with projects from Detroit, the timing could not have been worse. I wouldn't return to Italy until 1995.

Then, like my first French Connection, the next Italian Job floated in the water. It would briefly be the largest cruise ship in the world, the 110,000-ton *Grand Princess*, built by Fincantieri in Monfalcone on the northern tip of the Adriatic Sea. This was one of those places that "you can't get to from here" and I had to fly from London Gatwick to Torino Lanarte and then on to Trieste, where a car picked me up for the final leg to Monfalcone.

I never drove a car on this trip or saw anything exciting on either two wheels or four, but it was interesting with a one-shipyard tonnage war going on between the booming cruise lines at Fincantieri, and I was there for two of these cruise ship illustrations. I had already done a cutaway of the 87,000-ton *Sun Princess*, which was back from sea trials, and my photography of her was to give me more detail for an upcoming illustration of her sister the *Dawn Princess*. I also took photos of a large-scale plaster model of the *Grand Princess*, which, along with a stack of blueprints and interior renderings, would be the basis of the largest cutaway illustration I had done up to that point. The *Grand Princess* painting was 6 feet long and depicted the ship cutting through the water with the hull showing below its wake and over 2,000 happy cruise-goers on board. The only larger painting I have done is the entire Las Vegas Strip at night.

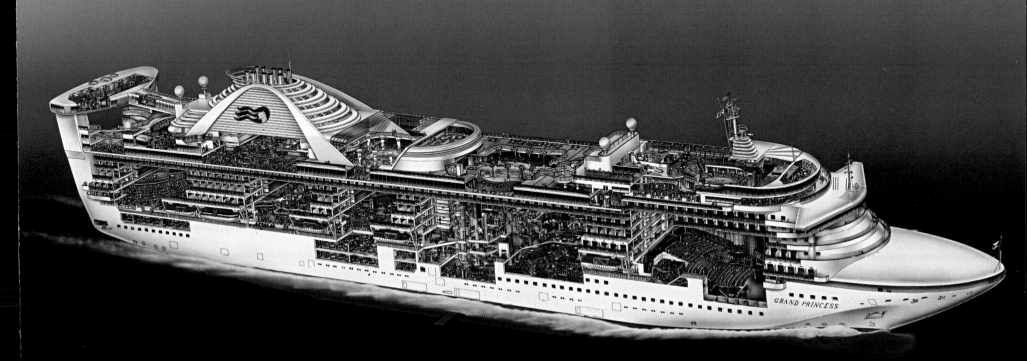

THE CORVETTE YEARS

7

My involvement with Corvettes started when I naively ordered a 1967 Stingray coupe equipped with the radical L-88 package from Mr. Dan, a salesman at Ed Priester Chevrolet in Montrose, California. Mr. Dan was horrified and tried to talk me out of getting one of these monsters, but reluctantly wrote up the order and accepted my deposit. However, his concern was misplaced; the car never came in, and as it turned out only 20 of these street legal but not street compatible race cars were built that year, and only a chosen few dealers had their orders filled.

To discourage casual buyers from ordering the 4-barrel L-88 427-ci engine it was underrated at 430 hp. The street-friendly L71 had three 2-barrels and was rated at 435 hp, so this is what I had to settle for. After waiting several months I found a Rally Red Corvette coupe with black interior that had the same special suspension and brakes as the L-88 I had tried to order, but with an L71, engine at Allen Gwynn Chevrolet in Glendale, and bought that one instead.

FOURTH GENERATION: 1984–1996

Professionally my 25 years of involvement with the Corvette started through *Motor Trend* with a trip to Detroit in November 1982 for a cutaway of the first completely new Corvette in 20 years. Neil Nissing was taking the photos and when we reached Warren, it was a near-religious experience to drive onto the GM Technical Center campus and visit the Chevrolet Central Office for the first time. We met Ralph Kramer, who was handling product information and later would

be public relations director, and he took us to a light metallic blue prototype 1984 Corvette in the Mid-Lux building auditorium. There was also a display powertrain rolling on a set of the new Corvette wheels and tires, with the suspension and exhaust system armatured to the rigid powertrain that had a torque arm mounting the transmission to the rear axle.

Except for the addition of the wheels and tires, this was the way these components were positioned on a fixture at the Bowling Green, Kentucky, Corvette plant ready to be raised into the car, and this offered a unique opportunity. Ralph had a stepladder ready with a technician standing by, and after marking the tire locations with tape on the floor the car was photographed and opened up like nothing else I have ever illustrated.

The clamshell hood pivoted forward and was in the way, so the technician removed it along with the roof panel that was designed to come off, and opened the driver's door along with the rear window hatch. This was all very revealing. The display was then rolled in, taking the car's place, and after it was photographed the technician removed the driver-side wheels and tires and then Neil took a few dozen detail shots, wrapping up the most productive reference photo session we ever had.

I don't remember who gave me the Production Assembly Documents (PADs) that are exploded views showing how every part of a car was assembled, but Chevrolet Pontiac Canada (CPC), later to be GM Powertrain Product Information, gave me the engine info. After Ralph Kramer became director of public relations he also became a client and good friend who has helped me remember some of the information in this book. We did not meet Dave McLellan, the Corvette engineering director at that time, but he also later became a good friend. Dave posed for a photo that appeared in one of the car magazines with my Corvette cutaway drawing that had been submitted for his approval.

This first contact with General Motors was the beginning of several lasting relationships, but with only minor restyling and incremental engineering updates being made it would take the ZR-1 in 1988 to get me more deeply involved with the Corvette.

Two Jim Halls have had an impact on my career. The first was "Texas Jim" Hall of Chaparral fame. I met the other Jim Hall while he was an editor at *Motor Trend* and who later became a client when he worked at Chevrolet.

"Wild Jim" Hall was a brilliant guy with a PhD in astrophysics and a hyperactive sense of humor that extended to the color choice for his company car, a yellow Corvette convertible with a red interior. No one at Bowling Green knew this color combination was even possible because it wasn't on the option list, but Jim managed to get it built.

When his Corvette was seen moving down the assembly line, steps were taken to make sure there would never be another one like it. Jim and I shared a passion for Corvettes, but the first project I did for him was a cutaway of the Chevrolet Express, a futuristic gas turbine powered demonstrator that was actually more of a show car.

Early in 1988 the car magazines were full of rumors and speculation about a super Corvette nicknamed the "King of the Hill" that was going to have 400 hp and be one of the fastest cars in the world. Wild Jim and I were both excited about big horsepower returning to the Corvette and talked about my doing the factory cutaway. Before Chevrolet was ready to show their hand Tony Swan, the automotive editor of *Popular Mechanics* magazine, contacted me. I had done several illustrations for Tony when he was editor-in-chief at *Motor Trend*, and he had figured out a way to give his readers an early look at the King's engine by having me do a cutaway of the Corvette Indy. This was during the years that General Motors owned Lotus, and it built this all-wheel-drive technology demonstrator that took its name from

My professional relationship with the Corvette started with this cutaway of a 1984 prototype photographed at the GM Tech Center in November 1982. This car was actually light metallic blue, but this was a cover illustration for Motor Trend *and they insisted on red because it sold magazines.*

a transversely mounted Chevy Indy car V-8, which had now been replaced by the Lotus-designed LT5.

This meant a trip to Lotus in Hethel near Norwich, England, for Neil and me along with Ellen and our nine-year-old son Jason. We flew into Heathrow Airport and drove to Drayton Woods where we stayed. The Drayton Woods Inn was a delightful place run by a woman from Alsace-Lorraine, and featured a French chef.

The next day Neil and I drove to Lotus, a short distance away on a World War II bomber base. I had been told that we could drive the Corvette Indy on a test track laid out on the runways, but unfortunately the car had been left out overnight and there was snow piled up on the engine's air intake. This meant the complex intake ducting would have to be disassembled to check for water before starting the engine, so we had to be content with just photographing the car for the cutaway. The early LT5 engine development had been done here so there were several of them sitting around, as well as a Corvette Indy chassis sans body that we could photograph.

The next day I went back to Lotus to meet with the LT5 engineering team while Ellen, Neil, and Jason flew over the English countryside in a rented Cessna 172.

I arranged to have an almost complete set of LT5 engineering drawings sent to me in California and then

This partial cutaway of a 1984 Corvette was for a Pennzoil GT Performance Motor Oil print ad and I borrowed a car from Chevrolet Public Relations. I had permission to remove the hood for photography, but I had no idea how difficult it would be to put it back on.

met with Tony Rudd, technical director at Lotus. He had been the BRM Formula I team's technical director, and I wanted to discuss his H-16 3-liter engine, but all he would talk about was his "lightly paid" position with the Imperial War Museum's aviation collection. Then I was given a chance to drive the Lotus test track in a turbo Esprit. I think Neil got a picture of me, because they were flying over the track at about the same time and I was most likely the silver dot following the red dot around the circuit.

We toured Norwich Castle before going down to London that afternoon and I didn't have much trouble driving our little Ford whatever-it-was on the left side of the road, but I did not like shifting with my left hand. It seemed as though I wasn't going to have a problem navigating on London's one-way streets until I couldn't find the cross street where the Hilton was located and finally gave up and hired a cab to lead us to the hotel.

It turned out that the portion of the street that ran in front of the Hilton had a different name at the

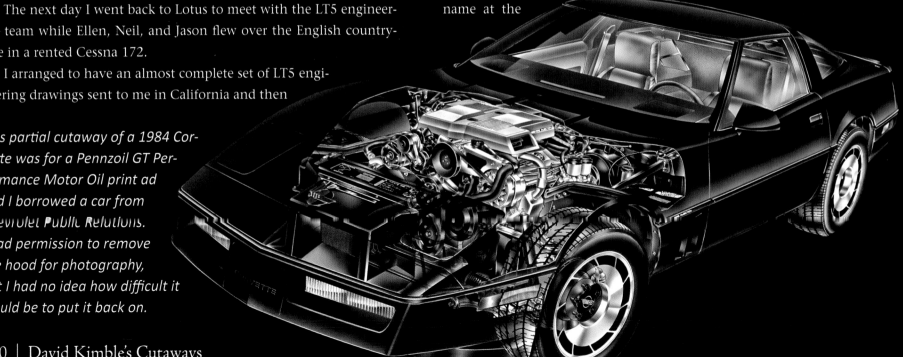

140 | David Kimble's Cutaways

place we were crossing it. Surprisingly, there wasn't a parking garage on the hotel property, and we became helplessly lost trying to find the closest one, having to hire another cab to find where to park the car. That night we rode the underground to the wild West End with some amazing guys who had safety pins hanging from their ears, shiny black plastic motorcycle jackets, and spiked hair in primary colors. We then spent the next day touring museums before flying home.

There had not been an ultimate high-performance Corvette since the L-88 and ZL-1 in 1969, which were combined engine and chassis packages intended for racing. The ZR-1 and its LT5 engine were

After I illustrated the Chevrolet Express technology demonstrator for Jim Hall in Don Runkel's group at Chevrolet in 1987, Jim made it possible for me to do a cutaway of the ZR-1 Corvette. The Express was really more of a show car and looks very simplistic as a line inking; it filled in nicely to become a painting.

Ducking under the Chevrolet Express raised canopy was awkward, but once seated, the driver had a digital instrument display and a navigation screen as well as a rearview video screen at the top of the center stack. The throttle pedal controlled a gas turbine engine and, similar to a Corvette, this car rolled on Goodyear Gatorback tires.

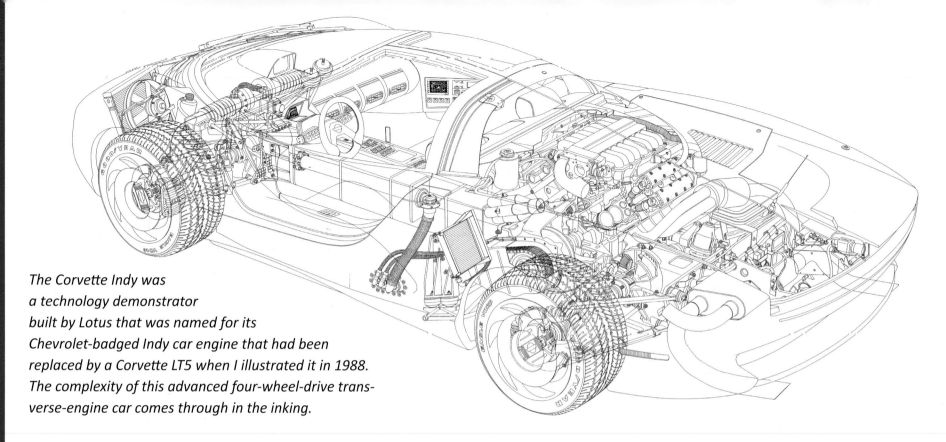

The Corvette Indy was a technology demonstrator built by Lotus that was named for its Chevrolet-badged Indy car engine that had been replaced by a Corvette LT5 when I illustrated it in 1988. The complexity of this advanced four-wheel-drive transverse-engine car comes through in the inking.

for the street. I had commissions from both Chevrolet and *Motor Trend* for complete cutaways of the "King of the Hill" super Corvette, and one from *Automobile* for its LT5 engine. I had also written the technical press release on the engine for Chevy Public Relations.

Even though there were development challenges in meeting emissions and noise standards, the Z-1 was scheduled for a 1989 introduction with the base Corvette's L98 pushrod 16-valve 5.7-liter V-8 rated at 245 hp. That year its 4-cam 32-valve 5.7-liter LT-5's goal was 400 hp. Corvettes in 1989 rolled on P275/40R17 tires, and to get the additional power to the road the ZR-1's rear tires were P315/35 R17s. To avoid fender flares the rear fenders were 6 inches wider across the back with tapered doors that were also wider at the back.

Jim Hall at General Motors was my facilitator in making this ambitious program possible. He met Neil and me at the Nashville airport

and drove us to Bowling Green, Kentucky, where a batch of 1989 pilot ZR-1s were being built under tight security. This was our first look at ZR-1s, which were moving down the assembly line mixed in with mere mortal L98-powered Corvettes and we all expected to have a chance to drive one on the small road course behind the plant.

Unfortunately, this didn't happen. LT5s had a complex induction system that had eight primary fuel injectors and eight secondaries, which could be turned off with a valet key when one of these cars was left with a parking attendant. Port throttle plates under these secondary injectors closed when they were deactivated, but the problem was that these plates were not opening at all. With fuel puddling on them and then catching fire, several ZR-1s had burned spots on their hoods. The singed cars didn't take long to repair, but none of the other ones could be started until this problem with the new engine control

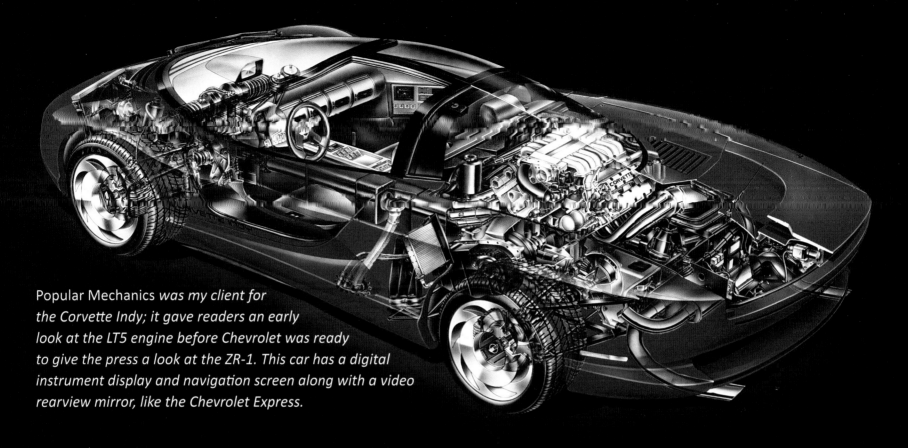

Popular Mechanics *was my client for the Corvette Indy; it gave readers an early look at the LT5 engine before Chevrolet was ready to give the press a look at the ZR-1. This car has a digital instrument display and navigation screen along with a video rearview mirror, like the Chevrolet Express.*

module was corrected, and so the first ZR-1 I was able to drive was two years later, after I bought one.

Except for having to push the car into position, the photography for my cutaways went well with a front view for *Motor Trend* and one from the back for Chevrolet to show off the product-specific wide convex rear fascia with its LT5 badge.

From Bowling Green it was back to Nashville and after flying to Oklahoma City, Jim rented another car and we drove to Stillwater, where Mercury Marine's MerCruiser plant was building the LT5 engine for CPC Powertrain. MerCruiser converted GM engines for marine applications and this program was contracted to them because with the LT5's low volume and all-aluminum construction it wasn't a good fit for any of the GM engine plants.

At Lotus the only up-to-date LT5 I had seen was in the Corvette Indy, and the internal components in that cutaway were done from the engineering drawing, but after our visit to Mercury Marine I had photos of every part. I'd never had this much information on an engine before. With two LT5-powered Corvettes to illustrate from opposite ends and a cutaway of the engine without a car around it, it gave me the flexibility to treat them all differently.

It also turned out that through my travels I had more LT5 information than Tom Quinlan, who was doing the factory cutaway, was able to get in-house, so I loaned him some of the Lotus engineering drawings. I was glad to help Tom with his engine illustration because I was doing the complete ZR-1 for Chevrolet and my own engine cutaway for *Automobile* to support what had now become a holy cause.

After suffering through the dark decade of the 1970s with Corvettes hitting bottom in 1975 (the year catalytic converters were introduced) with only a 165-hp 350, horsepower junkies eagerly watched as the numbers started climbing again in the 1980s. No one who didn't live through this horsepower-starved era can appreciate how much the ZR-1's promise meant to high-performance enthusiasts around the world.

This was evidenced by my fold-out ZR-1 Corvette *Motor Trend* cover overshadowing the Ferrari F40 I did for them that same year. Both Chevrolet and *Motor Trend* wanted their ZR-1s to be red, but after having illustrated nine red cars in a row I talked Chevy into steel-blue metallic and *Motor Trend* into letting me make their cover Corvette yellow, even though that color was going to be canceled in 1989.

My factory ZR-1 illustration appeared in more than 80 magazines around the world. Then it was announced late in 1988 that the special performance package was not going to be released until the 1990 model year.

The ZR-1's 1990 introduction coincided with a redesigned instrument panel that replaced all the fourth-generation Corvette's "video arcade" digital displays except the speedometer with analog gauges in a restyled dash. This made my Chevrolet ZR-1 cutaway out of date, and although Neil and I were in Detroit for some other projects Jim Hall gave us an early look at a 1990 Corvette interior mock-up. This was in the highest-security building at the Tech Center Design Staff headquarters.

Jim also took us in to meet Chuck Jordan "The Chrome Cobra," GM's vice president of design who had a print of my *Motor Trend* Ferrari F40 behind his desk. Both public relations and Campbell Ewald, the agency that did the Corvette brochures, wanted an updated ZR-1 cutaway, and I did it with a film positive of just the changes, which were painted white on the back and overlaid on the original art.

When a dream becomes real, reality sometimes falls a little short, and when the 1990 Corvettes with the ZR-1 special performance package reached production, their LT5 engines were rated at only 375 hp. Despite this small shortfall these ultimate Corvettes did not disappoint

I was able to do more with the LT5 engine cutaway in Motor Trend's *ZR-1 illustration that came out a few months later than the* Popular Mechanics Corvette Indy, *but* Motor Trend *had the whole car. This was a fold-out cover of a 1989 ZR-1 in yellow, a color that was being canceled for that year, but they liked it because yellow was next best to red for selling magazines.*

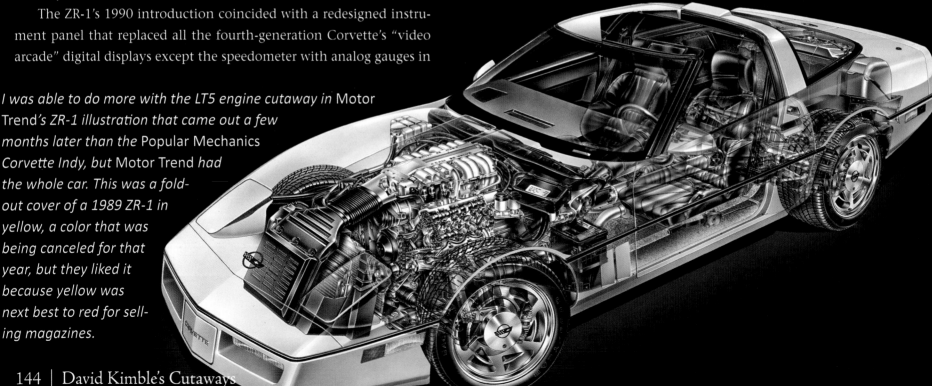

the car magazines' road test editors. This started a feeding frenzy at Chevrolet dealers eligible to sell the ZR-1s, with enthusiasts and investors alike clamoring to get one.

ZR-1s could only be ordered as coupes with a base price of $31,979, and the ZR-1 package added another $27,016, making the minimum price for a stripper ZR-1 $58,995. Most dealers put value-added premiums on these scarce cars and $100,000 was not unheard of. I had a black 1987 Corvette equipped with the Z51 performance handling package and stopped at a red light next to a ZR-1. After eye contact with the gold-chain guy driving it, he blew my doors off and confirmed that I had to have one when they cooled off.

In October I heard that the public relations press ZR-1s were ready to be sold and I was told that Chevrolet wanted me to have one and that there were two to choose from in the press fleet

The ZR-1's introduction was pushed back to 1990, which coincided with the replacement of the Corvette's "video arcade" digital instrument display, making my illustration out of date. This is the inking of my 1990 conversion layer, which included the new dash, wheel centers, and a ZR-1 badge, which replaces the LT5 on the rear fascia.

In street racing terms, the ZR-1 was a "sleeper" with the same-style wheels as a base Corvette and subtly tapered body sides to cover the wider rear tires. I did Chevrolet's cutaway from the rear to show its only distinctive styling clue, a wide convex rear fascia with squared-off taillights, and an LT5 badge for 1989.

David Kimble's Cutaways | 145

Vista Group in Van Nuys. Both ZR-1s were red, and one had a saddle interior with a low VIN and 17,000 miles on it. The other was low in mileage with a high VIN and a red interior, but it hadn't been as fast in road tests. Naturally I chose the faster one and bought it through Valley Motors on Van Nuys Boulevard where it had been maintained.

A few days later I drove my ZR-1 to John "Brute" Force Racing in Yorba Linda for an illustration project. Winston had commissioned me to do a cutaway of John Force's Oldsmobile Funny Car and he was wound up as tight as he is on TV while he took parts off his Funny Car for me to photograph. Then he noticed my ZR-1 and asked me, "Hey, Kimble, is that your ZR-1?"

When I proudly answered yes he said, "How would you like to tell your friends that John Force drove your ZR-1?"

Looking around the shop at all the blown-up parts I thought, "Oh my God!" but fortunately he became distracted and never got back to his request.

On Halloween night, I threw my leathers and other riding gear into the back of my still-new-to-me ZR-1 and drove up the coast on twisty Highway 1 to Monterey, turning into the switchbacks so hard the Little Richard CD I was listening to changed tracks. I was preparing to go motorcycle road racing and went up there for a two-day Keith Code racing school at Laguna Seca. I had been hop-

ing for some four-wheel track time as well, but Keith said his insurance wouldn't allow it. I went back down Highway 1 in the daylight and was stopped by the highway patrol, but the officer was a sport and did not write me up. Instead he just kept repeating, "A real ZR-1! I can't believe it!"

At that time I was an unrepentant sociopathic compulsive street racer and found I could usually beat the Porsche 911 turbos, which were being imported again, as well as Ferrari Testarossas, but mostly I raced pesky kids in

A few days after buying a ZR-1 of my own, I drove it to John "Brute" Force Racing to do a cutaway of his Funny Car for Winston. John noticed my Corvette and asked me, "Hey, Kimble, how would you like to tell your friends that John Force drove your ZR-1?" I thought, "Oh my God!" but he then became distracted and never did drive it.

5.0-liter Mustangs. The kids were used to beating up on base Corvettes with drivers that impulsively raced them without knowing how to get the most out of their cars, but they were in for a rude surprise when they took on the ZR-1.

In 1991 I realized the ZR-1 was about to have a domestic rival when Chrysler contacted me about doing a cutaway of their upcoming Viper, a latter day big block Cobra that was going into production in 1992. The second-generation Shelby Cobra was a minimalistic sports car powered by a Ford 427-ci engine. It appealed to extreme performance enthusiasts, and with only 260 of them sold between 1965 and 1967, they had a lasting impact far beyond their numbers.

The Dodge Viper RT/10 was designed around Dodge's V-10 8.0-liter truck engine, but with an aluminum block and heads topped by a wild-looking twin throttle body cross-ram intake manifold, and it made the 400 hp missed by the 5.7-liter LT5. CPC Powertrain contin-

ued developing the LT5 and bested the Viper's V-10 in 1993 with 405 hp, but the additional 30 hp didn't increase performance because the ZR-1 also gained weight. I had to miss the Viper press event at Willow Springs where I raced motorcycles because of indecision over the placement of the nose badge, so when I expected to be flogging an RT/10 around Willow I was sitting at my drawing board moving the badge instead.

My last chance to drive a Viper came late in 1992 when I was able to borrow a press car. It was sitting quietly next to my ZR-1 in our studio parking lot on a quiet Sunday when a motorcycle racing buddy of mine came by and suggested we do a comparison test. Flower was a two-lane industrial street without any traffic on weekends. We went off from a slow roll and the Viper was ahead at about 100 mph when the Corvette passed and was pulling away just as we ran out of room, but it was still close.

Big-block second-generation 427 Cobras were the inspiration for Dodge's Viper and had a coil-spring chassis designed by Ford, but were still built by AC Cars in England. This is a 1965 SC, which is one of the 51 competition Cobras built, with mufflers in its side pipes so it could be sold through Ford dealers and driven on the street.

After moving to Marfa, Texas, in December 1992 I received several requests and offers that would have taken me away before getting completely moved into the Palace and I turned them all down, but a request from Chevrolet just would not go away.

I had recently done a cutaway of the fourth-generation Camaro for Tom Hoxie, deputy director of public relations. The car's press introduction was going to be at the Jonathan Beach Club in Santa Monica, California. Tom asked me to attend the event and sign posters of my illustration, and although I felt bad about it, I turned him down. Within minutes his boss, Ralph Kramer, called me and asked what it would take to get me out there. At that point I realized I had better go, and because I had never driven a Corvette equipped with either the LT1 engine or traction control, both introduced in 1992, I said I would

like to have a 1993 Z51 to drive while I was there.

When I arrived at LAX the evening before the event, a 40th Anniversary Edition Z51 Corvette was waiting for me at a rental car garage. I drove it to the hotel where everyone was staying, on a cliff overlooking the Pacific Ocean. The next morning after giving the valet my parking stub, I noticed Chevrolet's general managers Jim Perkins, Ralph Kramer, Tom Hoxie, and some other guys all squeezing into an Astro van and felt very relieved when my Corvette didn't show up until after they left.

The event was a lot of fun with a fourth-generation Camaro and Firebird parked on the sand near the Jonathan Beach Club, and I met a lot of old friends while signing posters. Chevrolet had good luck with the weather because it didn't start to rain until after the event. It was still raining when I left Los Angeles, giving me plenty of opportunities to test the 1993 Corvette's traction control but not the LT1's power.

The 1992 Viper RT/10 was designed around Dodge's V-10 8-liter truck engine, except with an aluminum block and heads topped by a wild-looking cross-ram intake manifold. It had 400 hp and was almost as minimalistic as the Cobra with no air conditioning or cruise control and with side curtains instead of roll-up windows.

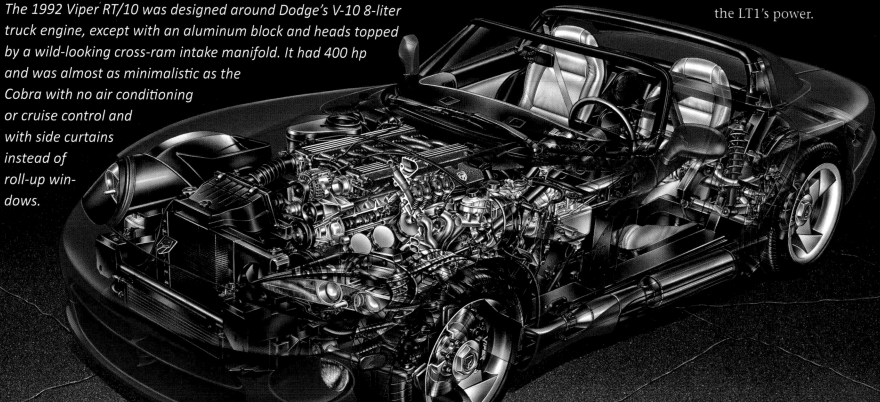

ZR-1 production ended with the 1995 model year, and with enough cars built to satisfy anticipated demand the last one rolled off the assembly line in May. There was a big event at the National Corvette Museum to commemorate the passing. Bill Hagee, the service manager at Jack Sherman Chevrolet in Midland, Texas, and I decided we couldn't miss this get-together, and another ZR-1 owner who was also one of Bill's customers wanted to come along. Bill had managed the Corvette Challenge Racing Series mechanical support from Chevrolet, and was a friend of Jim Minneker, the Corvette Group's powertrain engineer. Jim was organizing the display cars for this event at the museum and wanted my early ZR-1 for display in the museum to represent the first year of production.

We headed for Bowling Green with Bill as my co-pilot and Tim Tangen's wife, Diane, riding with him in his red 1994 ZR-1. We were joined on the interstate by two more ZR-1s before leaving Texas. I guess there must really be safety in numbers, because our formation of four Texas Corvettes cruised most of the time between 80 and 100 mph

and no one was stopped. I was proud when my car took its place in the row of ZR-1s representing all six years of production, but I soon found out the downside, as this made me only a spectator at the ZR-1 Nationals held at a local drag strip as well as all the street racing.

Ralph Kramer had moved up to GM Corporate Public Relations Director in 1994, and Bill O'Neil (with whom I had worked at Cadillac) had taken his place. We had a meeting in a conference room during the event, and Bill gave me the assignment to illustrate the C5 Corvette. I also had a private audience with Zora Arkus-Duntov, whose wife, Elfi, had to translate because after a second stroke his speech was slurred. I wished I had talked more about Corvette history with him in the past.

As with most other cars, every successive generation of Corvette has been characterized as "all new," including the third generation, which was a new body on the second-generation chassis. But the fifth generation actually was completely

Motor Trend hired me to do several solid versions of my cutaway cars to be used as holographic cover illustrations that changed from solid to transparent. The Viper's upper body surfaces are darker than I would have liked to cover the detail underneath when it was viewed as a solid surface.

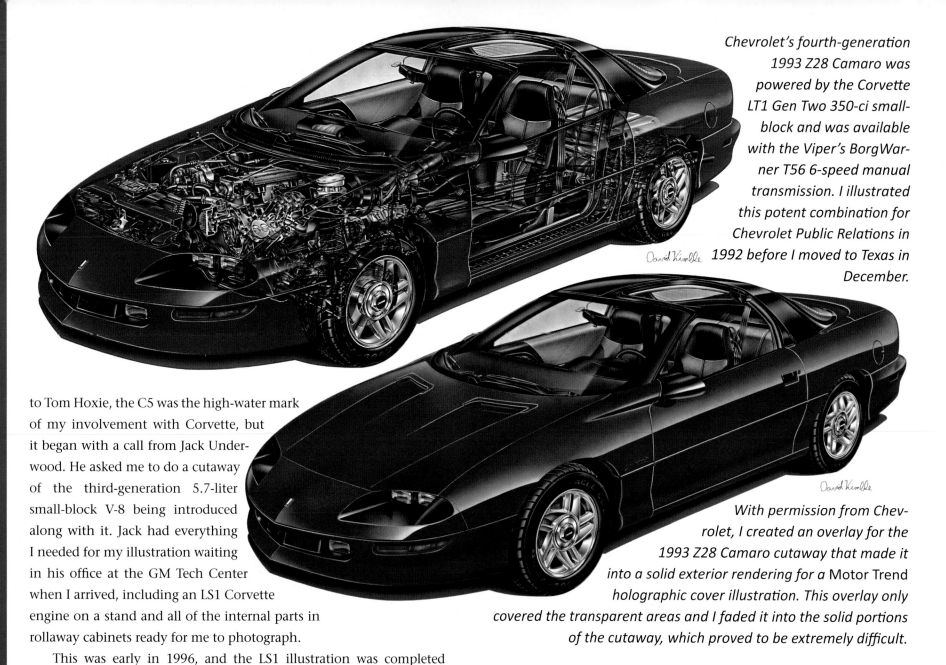

Chevrolet's fourth-generation 1993 Z28 Camaro was powered by the Corvette LT1 Gen Two 350-ci small-block and was available with the Viper's BorgWarner T56 6-speed manual transmission. I illustrated this potent combination for Chevrolet Public Relations in 1992 before I moved to Texas in December.

With permission from Chevrolet, I created an overlay for the 1993 Z28 Camaro cutaway that made it into a solid exterior rendering for a Motor Trend holographic cover illustration. This overlay only covered the transparent areas and I faded it into the solid portions of the cutaway, which proved to be extremely difficult.

to Tom Hoxie, the C5 was the high-water mark of my involvement with Corvette, but it began with a call from Jack Underwood. He asked me to do a cutaway of the third-generation 5.7-liter small-block V-8 being introduced along with it. Jack had everything I needed for my illustration waiting in his office at the GM Tech Center when I arrived, including an LS1 Corvette engine on a stand and all of the internal parts in rollaway cabinets ready for me to photograph.

This was early in 1996, and the LS1 illustration was completed before I returned in late April for the C5's Immersion Day Presentation. The goal of the event was to familiarize GM employees who were outside the Corvette group (but would be involved in its launch) with its details.

This event was held in the same Mid-Lux building auditorium where Neil had photographed the C4 for me 14 years before, and was organized by Janine Fruehan under tight security. It seemed that I was the only outsider. The presentation went on all day with engineers in charge of every aspect of the car including structure, suspension, and powertrain doing a show-and-tell with a complete car, a rolling chassis, and a uniframe on stage.

I came back the next morning and the stepladder I had requested was there but I was on my own, so even though the uniframe was on a dolly I decided to trust my well-calibrated eyeballs to maintain the same angle on each part I photographed. Although only the C5 coupe was going on sale in 1997, I was doing two illustrations, one from each end, for a potential double cutaway, and I moved the ladder between shots instead of trying to shove this stuff into position by myself.

A single cutaway illustration could not do justice to the Gen Five Corvette's innovative mechanical and structural layout, so I did it in three layers. The powertrain, with the rigid torque tube on its mounting cradles along with the exhaust system, suspension, wheels, and tires were the base layer.

FIFTH GENERATION: 1997–2004

Janine arranged to have a full set of PADs shipped to me, which filled a dozen loose-leaf notebooks. With the addition of the uniframe to photograph, this gave me more to work from than I had had on the C4 but it still wasn't enough. With Bowling Green still producing C4 Corvettes, the pre-production C5s were being assembled under high security in the Mid-Lux building basement, but they weren't far enough along to be of much help and Janine said she would let me know when to come back.

I returned to the Tech Center a couple of weeks later and she gave me a letter of permission to take my cameras where no outsider's camera had

The second layer added the uniframe with hydroformed frame rails and included this car's automatic transmission's gear sector and the pair of wedge-shaped fuel tanks. This structure had a center backbone channel that necessitated moving the transmission to the back.

gone before. Janine took me into the C5 inner sanctum where I had to show my photo pass so often I finally pinned it to my shirt. There were not only C5s at every stage of assembly, but sub-assemblies being put together as well, giving me not only what I needed but also a look at two future projects, the 1998 convertible and 1999 hardtop.

There was no way to do justice to the new Corvette's innovative structural and mechanical layout with a conventional cutaway illustration, so Tom Hoxie supported me in doing a double cutaway in three layers. I did both views on black backgrounds so they could more easily be combined, similar to the double Ferrari GTOs, with the wheels, tires, suspension, exhaust system, and powertrain on the base layer.

The front view was equipped with an automatic transmission and the middle layer added the uniframe with RPO F-45 selective real-time damping, which gave the driver adjustable ride control with its wheel position sensors mounted to the hydroformed frame rails. This layer also included the automatic transmission gear selector and linkage on the uniframe's center backbone and the wedge-shaped pair of plastic fuel tanks with their crossover behind the passenger compartment bulkhead.

The solid portions of both the uniframe and body layers were painted over with opaque white after they were airbrushed on the back of the film, including places where nothing showed through to give them a uniform appearance. It was about 3:00 am on the morning I had to ship the front view, which was

With the addition of the top layer, the stack of film positives becomes a 1997 Torch Red fifth-generation Corvette coupe, which appears to be a conventional cutaway illustration. I lost track of how many car magazines this cutaway appeared in, but there was one that arranged something different.

done first, when I put the body layer over the other two and saw how gray and murky it looked.

With FedEx typically picking up around 2:00 pm, I put a wash rag over my studio clock so I wouldn't panic over the time, and only the first light of dawn reminded me as I desperately added highlights, shadows, and density until around noon when it looked good enough to ship. Neil Nissing did a remarkable job of copying this stack of film positives. With polarizers on the lens of his 8 x 10–inch–view camera and studio strobes he made it look like a conventional single-layer cutaway.

David E. Davis, founder and publisher of *Automobile*, knew my C5 Corvette cutaways were modular illustrations and assured Tom Hoxie that if I would do another body layer in Nassau Blue metallic he would put it on a double-page spread. Tom asked me to do this second body layer for David E., and Neil shipped the painting back to me instead of to Chevrolet Communications. After I painted the new body I could put it over the bottom layers and add the shadows and highlights in context.

Neil was a successful commercial photographer and sometimes had other commitments when I needed him to copy a painting, so I found a big photo studio in Detroit that was more than happy to do a test for me, and I sent them the blue Corvette overlay. The results were disappointing, but it is fortunate I didn't pitch this transparency because it shows how the overlays worked and also Neil's ability to get the most out of my paintings.

Even though none of the parts were the same, RPO Z51, the performance handling package, was available with the new platform. I equipped the rear view with it along with the BorgWarner T56 6-speed manual transmission. This was the first American-made 6-speed transmission, with the C4's 6-speed made by ZF in Germany and debuted in the RT/10 Viper, but for the C5 it was assembled into a rear-mounted transaxle. This assembly was mounted to an 11-inch-diameter aluminum torque tube by an empty bellhousing with the clutch remaining in its usual location bolted to the engine's flywheel and driving the transmission through a semi-flexible shaft. The manual transmission's gear shift lever and its linkage are added to the illustration along with the uniframe on the second layer, and this rear view gives a clearer look at the innovative architecture of the C5.

Most of the car magazines preferred the front view, but Chevrolet's advertising agency, Campbell Ewald, used my rear view of a 1997 Sebring Silver metallic coupe with a red interior as a double-page spread in that year's Corvette brochure.

Top: Automobile *wasn't satisfied with having the same 1997 Corvette cutaway as their rival publications and made a deal with Chevrolet Communications. They guaranteed a double-page spread if I painted a second body layer in Nassau Blue metallic.*

David E. Davis, the founder of Automobile, *thought of blue as the traditional Corvette color, and the 1997 coupe proved to be extremely popular in magazine articles. In books, the art directors have consistently chosen my blue 1997 Corvette over the red one.*

Side-impact door barriers had been a government mandate for years and my clients were no longer insisting I show them by 1997, but these were just simple tubes so I decided to put them in to define the doors' presence on both C5 cutaways. The rear-window defogger grid, instrument panel, and other lettering are Chromatechs, which are custom rub-down transfers made from inkings in PMS colors, including the Pantone I used to use, and now I regret not spraying a little more tone on the white center stack button graphics.

I was really impressed with "the best 'Vette yet" and arranged to buy a red Z51 press car with a manual transmission as soon as it became available. Unfortunately, the Chevrolet Dealers Association stepped in and these cars were auctioned off to the dealers, so I had to wait.

With the C5's transmission assembled into a rear-mounted transaxle, the back view of the Gen Five Corvette offered the best look at its innovative layout. This car is equipped with the same BorgWarner T56 6-speed manual transmission as the current Z28 Camaro and Viper, and is bolted to a Getrag rear axle.

The addition of the uniframe to the rear view makes it clear why the C5 was the most rigid removable-top car of any class at the time. When the convertible was introduced in 1997 removal of the "halo bar" hoop did not require any additional reinforcement.

The Sebring Silver 1997 Corvette coupe cutaway with red interior didn't appear in many magazines, but Chevrolet's ad agency, Campbell Ewald, used it for a double-page spread in the brochure. As in my rear view of the ZR-1, its Michigan license plate was taken from a friend's Corvette.

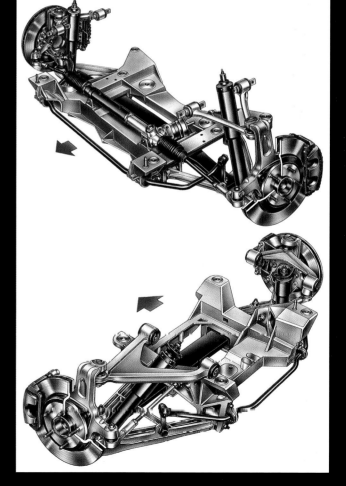

The Gen Five suspension warranted stand-alone illustrations and took a similar approach at both ends, but with the rack-and-pinion steering mounted to the engine cradle. The fiberglass leaf spring and anti-roll bar were mounted to the bottom of this cast-aluminum sub-frame and the lower control arms were mounted to the sides.

Out back was a similar transaxle cradle, and I cut segments out of the brake rotors at both ends to show the aluminum uprights (knuckles in Detroit-speak). These were used at all four corners with the lefts and rights trading places front to back and their stub axles replacing the C4's front spindles.

Tom Hoxie had only mentioned a C5 convertible in passing when I was taking photos of the C5 coupe pilot build in the Mid-Lux building basement, but I did take some pictures of the already assembled convertibles. In 1997 Tom asked me to do a convertible conversion of the rear-view C5 coupe illustration.

I started by drawing the drop-top's rear deck and hard tonneau cover along with portions of the interior under the roof of the coupe. This was then inked and composited with the coupe body inking to make a film positive of a complete convertible body that was given a black background to cover the upper portion of the coupe's rear window and roof. With the film positive airbrushed and sprayed white on the back, I had a red Z51 Corvette convertible. I ordered one just like it from Jack Sherman Chevrolet, taking delivery of it in January 1999.

When Tom Hoxie called me in January 2000, he had retired from General Motors and was working for Chevrolet Communications as a contractor to help introduce the ultimate high-performance version of the fifth-generation Corvette. I had done more illustrations for Tom than for any other client, and when he asked me to do one more (even though I already had a full schedule), between the subject and my appreciation I could not turn him down.

This car was an unprecedented separate model based on an unprecedented third body style, the hardtop that was lighter and more rigid than the coupe or convertible, making it an ideal starting point. This model was named for a famous regular production option, RPOZ06, the Stingray racing package, and in 2002 it would outperform the ZR-1 except in top speed

for only a $2,175 premium over a base convertible. Tom told me I would be working with Bob Tripolsky from Chevrolet Communications, and when I called him, Trip asked me to also do a cutaway of the C5R endurance racing Corvette.

I met Trip at GM's Milford, Michigan, Proving Grounds for the Z06 project on a cold morning in early February and we were taken to the F and Y car garage where the Camaro and Corvette were developed. They had one Millennium Yellow Z06 prototype along with most of the special parts made up the package. After I took pictures of them the sky brightened and I asked to photograph the car outside even though it was still very cold.

I was planning to use my three-layer front view 1997 Corvette coupe illustration as a starting point for a single-layer Z06 cutaway, and having not previously drawn the hardtop, I made an effort to match the angle of my original drawing. After lunch we visited Pratt & Miller where the pair of C5Rs were being torn down after Daytona for my first look, but I would have to come back before they left for Sebring to photograph them reassembled for my illustration.

A. J. Foyt returned to NASCAR as a team owner in

With everything under the fiberglass skin of this 1998 Corvette convertible unchanged from the coupe, except for having to lose the "halo bar," this illustration was done with a film positive overlay. It appeared in a Chevrolet print ad as well as the Corvette brochure, and I bought one just like it in 1999.

Named for the 1963 Stingray's racing package RPO, the Z06 was the ultimate fifth-generation Corvette and this drawing was based on my three-layer 1997 coupe. The 2001 Z06 was a single-layer cutaway with the hardtop roof and all of this model's high-performance modifications. I still have a Millennium Yellow 2002.

2000 with backing from Conseco, and their advertising agency contacted me about a cutaway of the Conseco Pontiac, which took me to Mooresville, North Carolina. I managed to time this trip so I could fly from Charlotte to Detroit a couple of days before the Corvette team was scheduled to leave for Sebring. Visiting these race shops was really exciting for a lifelong racer such as me.

As it turned out, I brought back what I needed to do both projects but it was ugly with both racing teams under intense pressure and my visits forced on them by their backers and sponsors. I was about as welcome as a swarm of ants at a picnic. My timing at Pratt & Miller was good in a way, though, because a pair of second-generation C5Rs were under construction and revealed details that couldn't be seen in the completed cars.

Actually Gary Pratt did everything he could to help me, but a crisis had developed, with the C5Rs needing new hub carriers machined from billet aluminum before their rear suspension could be put back together, and his machining center had broken down. I went to Katech in Clinton Township where the 427-ci racing engines were built and tried to stay out of the way until the No. 3 car was ready for my wheels and body on-and-off photography about 9:00 in the evening the day before the team had to leave for Sebring.

I could not have been more in the way at this point, with the car ready to go on their set-up pad while I was tying both it and the crew up with my photo session. Although things became really tense the guys did what I asked and I left in a hurry.

The C5R paint scheme in my illustration had transitioned into overall Millennium Yellow by the end of the 2000 American LeMans (ALMS) season. This was the lead color for the Z06 when it came out in 2001. Although the Z06 lacked the ZR-1's charisma, it was a remarkable car that took a minimalistic approach to increasing performance through weight reduction and hot-rodding the base 350-hp LS1, transforming it into the 405-hp LS6 in 2002. My reaction when I saw the Z06 was, "I gotta get me one of them!" but I was aware that it

Chevrolet wanted to link the Z06 to the C5R endurance racing Corvettes even though they were based on the coupe's low-drag body. I revived the idea of a double cutaway and did this comp for a suggested poster, which was eventually published.

My C5R cutaway was of the lead No. 3/63 car that ran at LeMans as the No. 63, which was denoted by a red band at the top of the windshield. The No. 4/64 team car had a black band. The graphics, including the numbers, were on an overlay so they could easily be changed for different events.

was a work in progress and waited until the 2002 model year to order one through my friend Craig Horton at Jack Sherman Chevrolet.

Bob Tripolsky arranged for this to become a Corvette brand manager's order, which sped up delivery of this hot-selling car. A yellow Z06 with a black interior showed up in Midland, Texas, in late September 2001. I'd had my 1999 Torch Red Corvette convertible for 32 months when the Z06 came in, and it was in pristine condition with less than 10,000 miles on it so I offered the car to Neil. He still has it and I still have the Z06.

After missing out on the second-generation Viper, I was contacted by Mark Malmstead at Dodge about doing a cutaway of the third generation. Of course I jumped at the chance to get involved again with America's other sports car, and although the latest version was not

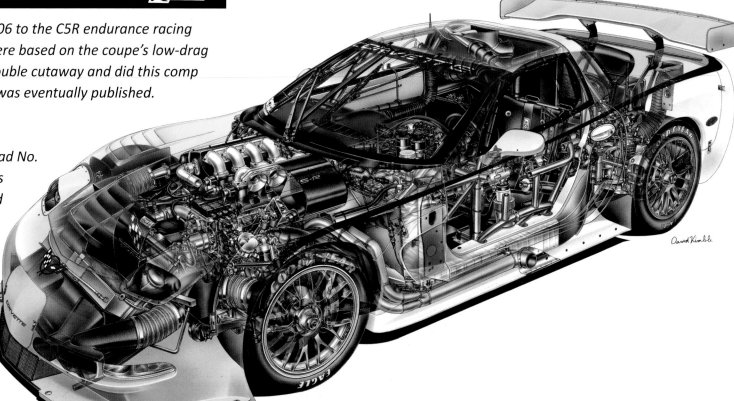

a clean break with the past, it was a huge advancement over the car I had illustrated 11 years earlier. The new 2003 Dodge Viper SRT/10 pilot cars were being built on the same assembly line as the outgoing second-generation Vipers when I visited DaimlerChrysler's Conner Avenue toy factory in early 2002, tactlessly wearing a Z06 Corvette polo shirt.

The new Viper's 505-ci 500-hp V-10 was impressive, with a single two-bore throttle body feeding a twin plenum cross ram intake manifold. I chose a very high-angle front view to make that the focal point of the illustration.

The Corvette stagnated on the same chassis for 20 years with the same body on it for 15, the fourth generation lasting 13 years and the C5 Corvette only 8 before the 2005 introduction of the sixth generation. This platform and the fourth-generation 6.0-liter 400-hp small-block came out together based on the previous Corvette's architecture, but with a lot of refinement and very few parts carrying over.

Bob Tripolsky asked me to do a pair of three-layer illustrations of the new Corvette in 2003. This time the rear view started out as a convertible with the drop-top introduced along with the coupe. Trip remained my primary contact with Chevrolet Communications, but with the new Corvette sharing its chassis with the Cadillac XLR the introduction was being managed by a project coordinator.

After I moved to Texas Neil Nissing continued to copy my paintings and make large prints for me to draw from, but we had not had many opportunities to work together for years when he met me in Detroit to photograph the C6 Corvette. There was a Gen VI coupe as well as a convertible ready for us in the Black Lake garage next to Milford's flat expanse of black asphalt, and the ceiling was high enough that Neil could shoot the views I wanted from the indoor roof of the office.

By this time General Motors had set up a dedicated plot model assembly operation across Twelve Mile Road from the Tech Center campus, and unlike in the C5 basement pilot build, it wasn't possible to take many useful photos. Although there were plenty of the new Corvettes at various stages of assembly, they were on a waist-high conveyor, putting their upper surfaces above eye level and there wasn't much to stand on. After I asked the supervisor

When the C5R team arrived at LeMans in 2000, they were the first Corvettes to compete in the 24-hour race since 1995, and this is the No. 3/63 car's package at that event, except with the addition of an American flag on the nose. This car finished a respectable fourth in class and eleventh overall.

escorting us to start bringing out parts from inventory for Neil to photograph, it wasn't long before he said, "I have something I want to show you," and it was the door!

At least the photo session at Black Lake had gone well, but the tone of this visit was very different from my C5 experience, because the Corvette and XLR product coordinator had given the XLR cutaway to my digital rival near the Tech Center. He would have had them do the Corvette illustrations as well, but the Corvette brand manager had insisted on me, so I made sure my artwork received maximum exposure by writing a 10-page article to go with it for *Road & Track*.

The computer generated cutaway of the Cadillac XLR lacked technical content even though it was done from the math data files that the car's tooling was made from, and the photos Neil was able to take would have been adequate for this approach. For the in-depth illustrations I was going to do, far more information was needed and fortunately I had already done a cutaway of the LS2 engine and was able to have a complete set of production assembly documents sent to me.

As with the sixth-generation Corvette, my illustrations took the same approach with similar views as the fifth generation. Although this wasn't very imaginative it was effective. But this time around there was no thought of using both views together. The cars were on white backgrounds and both views had 6-speed manual transmission now made by Tremec.

The front view was equipped with the Z51 package that included cross-drilled brake rotors and asymmetrical-tread tires. The powertrain, suspension, brakes, wheels, and tires were again on the base

After missing out on the second-generation Viper I was asked to illustrate the third, and chose this high angle to make its 505-ci 500-hp V-10 the focal point of the illustration. My photos were taken at the Conner Avenue Viper plant where the engines were assembled on the same floor as the cars, as is also done at Ferrari and Lamborghini.

film positive. With the gear shift now mounted to the torque tube it was included and both the transmission and the Getrag rear axle were cut away. I felt the C5 uniframes looked incomplete, so I added the steering wheels and columns mounted to their cast-magnesium supports, along with the seats and windshield frames.

SIXTH GENERATION: 2005–2013

After 42 years with concealed headlights, the 2005 Corvette's were exposed and fared into its rounded fenders with Ferrari-influenced

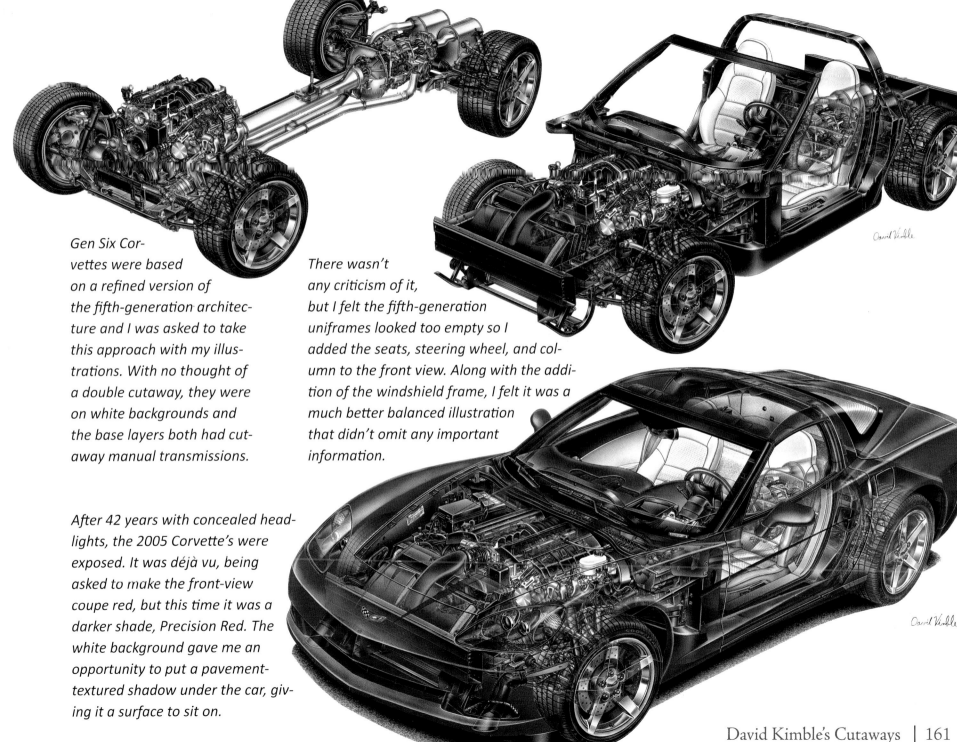

Gen Six Corvettes were based on a refined version of the fifth-generation architecture and I was asked to take this approach with my illustrations. With no thought of a double cutaway, they were on white backgrounds and the base layers both had cutaway manual transmissions.

There wasn't any criticism of it, but I felt the fifth-generation uniframes looked too empty so I added the seats, steering wheel, and column to the front view. Along with the addition of the windshield frame, I felt it was a much better balanced illustration that didn't omit any important information.

After 42 years with concealed headlights, the 2005 Corvette's were exposed. It was déjà vu, being asked to make the front-view coupe red, but this time it was a darker shade, Precision Red. The white background gave me an opportunity to put a pavement-textured shadow under the car, giving it a surface to sit on.

Tremec had bought BorgWarner's transmission business by the time the C6 reached production, but the old drawings that I worked from were still close enough to do a credible transmission cutaway. Along with the cutaway Getrag rear axle, this approach added a lot of interest to the C6's rear-view powertrain.

This was my first convertible uniframe illustration, with the C5 drop-top done only as a complete car. It includes the composite floor panels along with the seats. This view gives a better look at the magnesium steering column mount with the clutch and brake pedals hanging from it.

body-color surrounds. This presented quite a challenging see-through vignette on the left side. Being asked to make the C6 front view red (as was the fifth generation) was a déjà vu experience, but although Torch Red was on the option list it was never actually available and my painting was Precision Red, a much darker shade that was called Cobalt Red on the color sample.

I was not able to do as much as I would have liked with the highly sculpted body contours without obscuring too much internal detail, but I made up for it on the rear view, which I had more time to finish. I missed FedEx on the Friday I had to ship and it doesn't pick up in Marfa on Saturday, so I had to take it to the closest FedEx station, which was in Midland, 200 miles away. Because I had not finished the painting until 3:30 pm, my Kamikaze Courier Service had to go into action, where I either ship or end up in jail; I shipped.

My photos of the new Corvette's rolling powertrain and uniframe from seven years before were close enough to matching the angle of the complete C5 that I could use them as a starting point for my draw-

ings, but there wasn't anything similar to this for the C6. It was necessary to plot everything inside these cars' bodies geometrically, which seemingly took forever, especially the rear view, which remained the most revealing.

The transmission and rear axle cutaways are from BorgWarner. The Getrag sectional orthographic assembly drawings that Jack Underwood had given me for the C5 project were not quite up to date,

The C6 made a great-looking convertible, and from the rear I was able to show the C2 Stingray-inspired fender strakes without obscuring too much internal detail. Unlike with the C5, I had good photos of the new folded-down drop-top so I could include it along with the first power-top mechanism available in 42 years.

but they look impressive from this vantage point. The C5 uniframe had looked empty from the back, but with the addition of the seats, steering, and magnesium steering support with brake and clutch pedals hanging down from it, it was more pleasing.

I felt the LeMans blue convertible was the more impressive of my two 2005 Corvette cutaways, and *Road & Track*'s design director Richard Baron agreed with me and spread it across the first four pages of my September 2004 article. It was possible to show the original Stingray-inspired fender strakes above the wheelwells as vignettes. Before being ejected from the pilot model build, Neil had managed to get a photo of a folded-down convertible top, so unlike the C5 I could put it in this time. As with the exposed headlights, this was the first Corvette in 42 years to offer an optional power convertible top; I was also able to include its mechanism below the folded drop-top.

My rear-view 1989/1990 ZR-1 cutaway had GM Jim Hall's Corvette's license plate on it, but I didn't get to have any fun with the

2005 convertible's license plate. However, a street map showing the Corvette plant can be seen on its navigation screen.

When I first spoke with Bob Tripolsky about the Z06 cutaway in 2000 he had also asked me to illustrate the C5R. Trip was very much aware that I wanted to illustrate its successors the C6R and the Gen VI Z06 when he called in December 2004. This was the good news phone call: I had the C6R endurance racing Corvette project. But my client was GM Racing, and when I called my contact Kevin Luchansky he gave me the bad news. They wanted my cutaway in time to print posters for Sebring in March. Kevin said the pair of C6Rs were still under construction but there was a show car that I could use for my illustration.

We met at Pratt & Miller in New Hudson, Michigan, early in January 2005. Their new facility was a huge step up from the two units in a Wixom industrial park that I had visited five years earlier. After the success of my C5R cutaway Gary Pratt was glad to see me again.

GM Racing had consolidated all of their production-based road racing programs here, and Pratt & Miller also built cars for individual customers who raced GM products, so the main building where the C6Rs were being put together was quite large. The C6R race cars weren't as far along as I expected. Kevin and I took a good look before walking to the back to see the show car, which was being measured and photographed by Revel-Monogram for a plastic model kit.

I had less than two months to complete this illustration and that was a squeeze so I was counting on the show car as a starting point, but it was a caricature with a modified C5R chassis that still had its original engine. The Revel guys were listening when I explained the situation to Kevin and none of them seemed to think it was a big deal, but for me if the illustration did not represent an accurate C6R race car, there wasn't any point in doing it.

The way around this dilemma was to start with a photo of the show car, salvaging what little was correct and shooting a matching photo of one of the race cars, and then combining them on a single tracing. This involved process was a lot more than I had bargained for and took longer than I had anticipated, even with the help of an assistant. The cars were not completed in time to have anything in print by Sebring anyway, and photos of them gave us a chance to get the final details correct.

The 2005 C6Rs were an unpublicized preview of the 2006 Z06's wide body styling and velocity yellow, which became the Corvette team's racing color for the remainder of the decade. These Gen VI endurance Corvettes continued the Gen V's near-domination of the GT1 class, with their only real opposition coming from Prodrive's Aston Martin DBR9s. The Corvettes won their last race, the 2009 24 Hours of LeMans.

The new Z06 project came my way a few months later, with Bob Tripolsky again giving me the word and letting me know I would be working with Wendy Clark, the Product Communications Performance Team's manager. She took my call from Bob Bondurant's driving

When I started drawing this C6R, it was still being built, and this cutaway was based on photos of a show car that was on a modified C5R chassis. This illustration is of the No. 3 C6R, the way it looked at the 2005 12 Hours of Sebring.

school and we met a few days later in the pilot build complex parking lot, where Wendy climbed out of a machine silver C6 Corvette.

I was concerned after my last visit, and was relieved to see that the 2006 Z06s were not on a conveyor. They were being assembled individually in the same manner as the C5 pilot models. I came away with everything I needed.

A humorous situation came from my photo session. Someone leaked a picture on the Internet that was supposed to be a new Z06. I had been the only outsider to take pictures of them. I was told GM Corporate Communications went absolutely nuts looking for the leak, and although no one pointed a finger at me I felt defensive until I finally saw the photo. It was an earlier design study and not the real deal. Whew!

This was my last Corvette cutaway and I had intended to illustrate the 2009 ZR-1 at a new angle but that wasn't possible, so I based it on my 2006 Z06. This loose blue pencil body contour drawing was done on tracing vellum over my Z06 layout with the slight opacity of the vellum making it easier to see how I was doing.

ZR-1s had more aggressively styled wheels and a Michelin Pilot Sport tire package that was roughed out on vellum and traced onto this layout along with the body contour drawing. The parts shared with the Z06, such as the headlights and outside rearview mirrors, were also traced in, making this a complete exterior layout.

When I interviewed Corvette Chief Engineer Dave Hill for my *Road & Track* article and asked about the next Z06 he said, "It will move up market." He wasn't kidding. The C6 Z06 was powered by a 505-hp 7.0-liter V-8 and built on an aluminum uniframe wrapped in wild bodywork. This was such an extensive makeover of the base Corvette that I wrote a follow-up article for *Road & Track* in 2005. It featured my cutaway, which, similar to the last Z06, was based on my three-layer front view, but which stayed a coupe this time. With weight reduction coming from the aluminum uniframe, some carbon fiber body panels, and a magnesium engine cradle, the hardtop did not return, and despite its added content this Z06 only weighed a few pounds more than its predecessor and had another 100 hp.

RPO ZR-1 originated as a racing package for 1970 350-ci 370-hp LT-1–powered Corvettes. The 1990 through 1995 ZR-1 remained a regular production option but it came to signify the ultimate Corvette and returned in 2009 in that context as a separate model. This was the first supercharged production Corvette and the most powerful up to that point in time, with its 6.2-liter LS9 engine rated at 638 hp. It wasn't the lightest with the supercharger, and its built-in separate cooling system adding about 200 pounds.

The ZR-1's chassis and bodywork were based on the Z06 but took it to another level with even wider tires and a recontoured all carbon fiber body to accommodate them that included a clear polycarbonate window in the hood. This was for maximum gawker appeal, to show off the supercharger plenum cover in the spirit of the F40

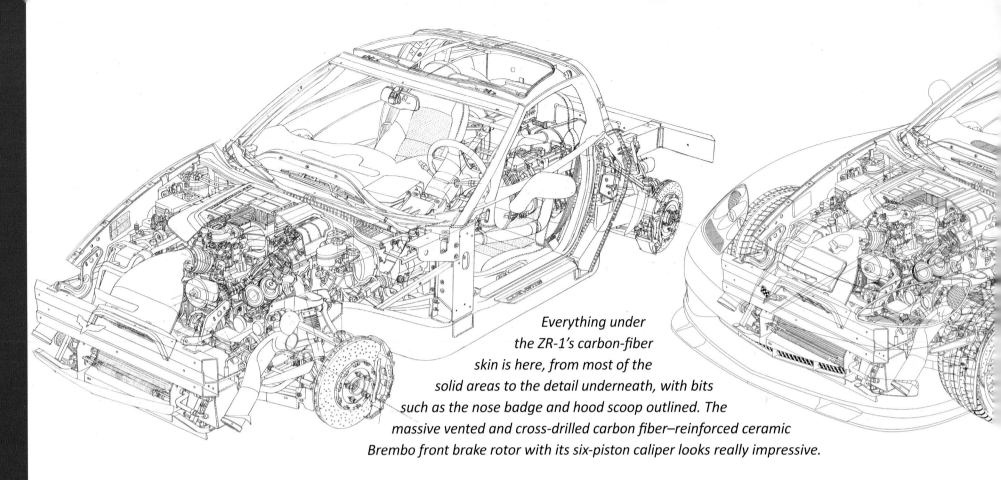

Everything under the ZR-1's carbon-fiber skin is here, from most of the solid areas to the detail underneath, with bits such as the nose badge and hood scoop outlined. The massive vented and cross-drilled carbon fiber–reinforced ceramic Brembo front brake rotor with its six-piston caliper looks really impressive.

Ferrari with its intercoolers and intake manifold on display through its rear window.

This time I worked directly with Bob Tripolsky at GM's Milford Proving Grounds, and within its high-security confines Trip drove me to a parking lot full of the latest Corvettes including a ZR-1. There was no stepladder handy so I couldn't take photos at a high enough angle to base an illustration on, but I was able to shoot plenty of exterior close-ups in the bright sunlight.

Then we visited the F and Y car development garage where there were several ZR-1s in various stages of disassembly, but although they had a stepladder there wasn't enough room around the cars to shoot a useable view here either. I made the decision to base the ZR-1 cutaway

on my Z06, and as a visual reference only I was able to get a high-angle photograph of a Velocity Yellow ZR-1 sitting on a hoist, making it easy for the technician to take the wheels off and on.

Early supercharger development for the ZR-1 began with a blue fifth-generation Z06 that was caught on film by famous spy photographer Jim Dunn, as it was tear-assing around Milford faster than anything he had ever seen. This car was soon nicknamed the "Blue Devil," which was reflected in the ZR-1's logotype with the engine covers and brake calipers being blue instead of red as were the C5 and C6 Z06s. I suggested to Trip that in this spirit with my base C6 coupe in red and Z06 in yellow, I should paint the ZR-1 cutaway that was based on the same view in Jetstream Blue, a new color introduced in 2008, and it was approved.

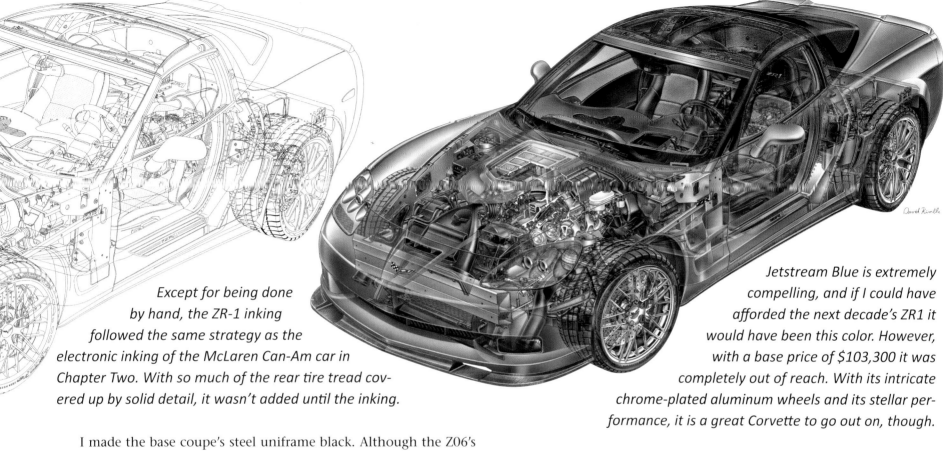

Except for being done by hand, the ZR-1 inking followed the same strategy as the electronic inking of the McLaren Can-Am car in Chapter Two. With so much of the rear tire tread covered up by solid detail, it wasn't added until the inking.

Jetstream Blue is extremely compelling, and if I could have afforded the next decade's ZR1 it would have been this color. However, with a base price of $103,300 it was completely out of reach. With its intricate chrome-plated aluminum wheels and its stellar performance, it is a great Corvette to go out on, though.

I made the base coupe's steel uniframe black. Although the Z06's and ZR-1's uniframes were also painted, I had left them in natural aluminum to highlight their lightweight construction. All of the ZR-1 wheels I had seen were powder coated silver until my latest *Autoweek* came with a photo of a ZR-1 with chrome wheels that looked so good I called Trip and he gave me an extra day to change them. It was worth the hassle.

The 2009 ZR-1 was the sixth-generation Corvette's last major technical development and would be Trip's and my last Corvette project, with Trip being transferred from Chevrolet Communications and retiring not long after that. Computer generated cutaways, such as the one of the Corvette-based Cadillac XLR that lacked technical insight, artistic judgment, and content soon trivialized the art form. After a

flood of them appeared in the car magazines, they all but disappeared. Computer-generated imagery (CGI) had taken the magic and the wow factor away and people not familiar with how I work started asking, "What software do you use?" instead of, "How can you possibly do something such as this?"

SEVENTH GENERATION: 2014–

I still do cutaway illustrations of most of The General's new engines and transmissions including those for the seventh-generation Corvette. But they chose not to have anyone do a cutaway of the complete C7 car.

8

But Wait, There's More

This chapter is a catchall that allows me to include a couple of categories of automotive cutaways that weren't large enough for a complete chapter. It's also an opportunity to wrap up with my latest factory car cutaway without it seeming out of context and give credit to the people who have worked with me.

NASCAR from the Inside Out

I grew up on open-wheel oval-track racing and didn't have much interest in NASCAR stock cars, but when I inherited a couple of press passes from *Road and Track* for the January 20, 1963, NASCAR event at Riverside I decided to go and see this race. Riverside International Raceway was a nine-turn 3.4-mile road course that was shortened to 2.7 miles for this event by running the cars straight across from turn six to turn eight, eliminating turn seven completely.

Even with this simplified course there were plenty of off-track excursions with at least one of the big-block road boats churning up clouds of dirt at all times, making my companion and me laugh our heads off. Actually this nearly six-hour 500-mile race was a good show, with eventual winner Dan Gurney driving a Holman and Moody Ford and battling with A. J. Foyt's Ray Nichols 1963 Pontiac and Fireball Roberts' Banjo Matthews Pontiac. Foyt finished second, 36 seconds behind Gurney. Among the many wrecks, two were spec-tacular with point leader Jim Paschal flipping his Plymouth seemingly a dozen times and Danny Weinberg crashing his 1962 Pontiac heavily in turn six.

In 1961 ABC TV started including highlights of selected Grand National races on their *Wide World of Sports*, but I still didn't get really interested in NASCAR until CBS Sports televised the 1979 Daytona 500 live. I have been following it ever since.

When I started working with *Motor Trend* and *Hot Rod* on a regular basis in 1982, I also started doing a lot of traveling. Neil Nissing accompanied me to take the pictures when he was available, and *Hot Rod* sent us to Atlanta, Georgia, in November. With support from Richard Petty's primary sponsor STP we were there to cover the November 7 *Atlanta Journal* 500 NASCAR Grand National Winston Cup race in Hampton. It was also an opportunity for me to gather reference material for a cutaway illustration of "the King's" No. 43 Pontiac and write an article about it.

It had been almost 20 years since I had seen NASCAR stock cars live, and this time they were in their element on a high-banked oval track and it was really exciting watching them entering the turns. Richard's Pontiac was next to Darrell Waltrip's No. 11 Buick in the garage, and I was able to talk to Darrell long enough to realize that when he became a TV commentator his "good ol' boy" persona was just a ruse and he was actually quite articulate.

Another future TV personality I came across in the pits was Dr. Dick Bergerand, the editor of *Speed Sport News* and *Open Wheel* magazines, which had published my Edmunds midget cutaway as a center spread the previous year. He gave me a good-natured hard time about my Edmunds sprint car appearing in *Hot Rod* that year, and I pointed out that if I were still working with him instead of *Hot Rod* I wouldn't be standing there with him.

The fans did not have access to the pits and there weren't any areas where they could watch the crews' activities or get the drivers to sign autographs as there are today with NASCAR's greater awareness of marketing. I was surprised to see what rock stars they were, with fans running to line up 10 deep on both sides of the pit gate whenever a driver, no matter how obscure, walked through it.

Richard Petty had won his last of seven Grand National championships in 1979 and his career was winding down at this point. He only won five more races in the last 10 years of his 35-year career, but he was and would remain "the King." Richard qualified 13th in the 40-car Atlanta 500 starting field and led 54 laps looking as if he was going to break a 38-race losing streak when he spun on lap 313, but he recovered to finish 15th in the 328-lap event.

There were 45 lead changes among 14 drivers with Bobby Allison in the No. 88 DiGard Buick taking the lead from Darrell Waltrip driving Junior Johnson's No. 11 Buick with 24 laps to go. Bobby finished 0.5 seconds ahead of Harry Gant's Mach 1 Racing Buick, with Waltrip finishing in third place. I wanted to include the results of this race in my technical article about the Petty Pontiac, so we stopped by the pits to ask some questions before heading to Petty Enterprises in Level Cross, North Carolina.

It was a straight shot northeast on Interstate 85 from Atlanta to Greensboro, and then due south on 220 to Level Cross, which looked too small to be on the map, but maybe Richard Petty put it there. Petty Enterprises' group of one-story buildings were

Richard Petty finished fifteenth in the 1982 Atlanta Journal 500 driving this Petty blue and STP red No. 43 Pontiac, which was photographed for this illustration at Petty Enterprises. Similar to all Winston Cup cars of the time its stock body panels were hung on a surface-plate-built tubular steel frame.

set back from the street in a vast expanse of grass. After talking to Richard, Neil and I went to work, starting with the photos of the Atlanta race car to base my illustration on. With the last race of the 1982 season on the road course at Riverside, this speedway car was going to be torn down. The team offered to start right away by removing the hood, windshield, window net, and left-side wheels for Neil's second shot. This was unexpected good fortune but the photo session became even better when the guys rolled out a complete frame on a dolly and replaced the car with it right in front of Neil's camera.

Petty Enterprises was a family operation, and Richard's first cousin and longtime crew chief Dale Inman showed us some partially disassembled cars along with suspension and driveline components. Richard's younger brother Maurice ran the team's engine shop where Neil was able to photograph everything from complete to partially assembled engines and all of their internal components. We also met Richard's 22-year-old son, Kyle, who had driven the team's No. 42 car in Winston Cup racing since 1979 and was speculating about putting license plates from a wrecked Pontiac Grand Prix on an old race car.

The Petty family home was next to the shops, and the patriarch of the family, Lee Petty, was sitting on the porch when we followed a fresh No. 43 Pontiac Winston Cup car onto the grass in front of his house. Before Neil went to work photographing the car for *Hot Rod*, we talked with Lee for a while and he told us about his early years of racing in NASCAR, which started with their first race in 1949. NASCAR's first official strictly stock race was on June 19 at a 3/4-mile dirt oval in Charlotte, North Carolina, and Lee remembered how he "put a roll bar made of plumbin' pipe and a seat belt in my Buick and drove it to Charlotte for the race."

The car was a 1946 Buick Roadmaster and Lee crashed on lap 105 of 200, which was good enough for 17th place in the 33-car field. After collecting $25 in prize money he was able to drive the Roadmaster back home. Lee Petty went on to compete in NASCAR's top-tier series for 16 years, winning his last three Grand National championships in 1959, the same year he won the inaugural Daytona 500 in the Petty Engineering No. 42 Oldsmobile.

While Neil was taking his pictures of the famous No. 43, cars started parking along the edge of the road. One awe-struck fan motioned me over and asked if I would tell Mr. Petty that he "admired his drivin'." When I relayed the message Lee just waved to him.

Winston Cup Grand National stock cars still had production body sheet metal in 1982, but otherwise were purpose-built racing cars with tubular frames fabricated on a surface plate, as can be seen in my illustration. After giving up on Chrysler products during 1978, Petty Enterprises switched to General Motors and settled on Pontiacs in 1982. They continued to be painted Petty Blue and day-glow red, the team's colors since STP became a major sponsor in 1972.

I was told that Lee's Oldsmobiles were white with blue numbers and when Richard wanted to paint the old race car he was going to start driving in 1958, there wasn't enough of either color in the shop to do the job so he mixed them together to create his signature racing color.

Cup cars then weren't the rolling billboards they are today, but with the partial cutaway approach I took for this illustration I could not keep all the sponsors' decals. Richard made sure that I knew which ones were most important.

In 1990, R. J. Reynolds Tobacco (RJR) contacted my sales agent Melanie Kirsch. RJR wanted me to do cutaway illustrations of three vehicles from racing series it either sponsored or was involved with in some way. My cutaway of John Force's NHRA Funny Car appearing in Chapter Seven was part of this deal, along with a cutaway of the Winston Eagle Unlimited Hydroplane, and of course it wanted a NASCAR Winston Cup car. RJR was the title sponsor of the Cup series through its Winston Cigarette brand, and even though Richard Petty hadn't won a race in 10 years he was still NASCAR's best-known driver and RJR chose his No. 43 Pontiac Grand Prix Cup car.

So it was back to Level Cross again after eight years. Neil and I flew into Winston-Salem, North Carolina, to meet Arnold Gambel, an art director from RJR's advertising agency, and he went with us to Petty Enterprises.

When we reached Level Cross Richard Petty was expecting us, and I was pleased to see that he had a framed print of my last cutaway of his Cup car hanging in his office and that both Dale Inman and Maurice were glad to see us again. A No. 43 1990 Pontiac Grand Prix Winston Cup car was waiting for us in about the same location that Neil had photographed the last one, and with a similar red and blue paint scheme, but with the colors reversed this time.

Arnold Gambel was calling the shots and I wasn't terribly pleased with the view he picked, but it turned out all right. However, this go-round there was a catch. Richard Petty wanted the illustration to be of his 1991 Daytona car. The next year's Grand Prix styling had been freshened up and all he had at this point was one of the new bodies hung on a frame, but it wasn't much of a problem to draw, unlike his new sponsors' decal package, which was a real pain.

It had been almost 10 years since my last NASCAR project when Melanie called with another one in February 2000. This was an

R. J. Reynolds commissioned me to illustrate Richard Petty's famous No. 43 for a second time eight years later in 1991. This car had a similar paint scheme but with the colors reversed. The only production body panels remaining were the hood, roof, and deck lid; the remainder of the now doorless body was fabricated by the team.

opportunity to do both cutaway and exterior illustrations of the Conseco Pontiac for the financial and insurance company's ad agency. These illustrations were for a brochure, with the exterior of the Conseco Pontiac on a cover that was going to open in the middle revealing the cutaway. This was a great concept and I had to do it, even though the Z06 and C5R Corvette projects were due in the same time frame.

This was a start-up team for A. J. Foyt Racing who had not competed in NASCAR since 1994 and was in a new building in Mooresville, North Carolina, where the majority of NASCAR's traveling series teams were located. Foyt's old NASCAR crew chief Waddell Wilson ran Team Conseco with his son building the engines. He bought a Joe Gibbs Pontiac Cup car for ideas in building their own cars and to use as a baseline comparison.

Having overbooked myself, I needed all the drawing board time I

could get and took the latest flight possible to reach Charlotte before midnight so I could visit A. J. Foyt Racing in Mooresville early the next morning. This trip was timed to give me a couple of days at Pratt & Miller in Wixom, Michigan, before the C5R Corvettes left for Sebring. That meant I had to leave North Carolina that evening for Detroit, and that was not good timing for Foyt Racing, with the team testing at Rockingham that day.

At least the shop crew and foreman were there along with several green-as-money Conseco Pontiacs emblazoned with A. J. Foyt's famous No. 14 racing number, and I was able to have one rolled outside to get it out from under the shop lights for my photos. While I was outside, the shop foreman very matter-of-factly told me that the car being used for the test was the only one with up-to-date decals. This put me back in the same spot as I had been with Richard Petty's 1991 Daytona car.

My skills had progressed along with NASCAR's stock cars when I drew this cutaway of A. J. Foyt's No. 14 Conseco Pontiac in 2000 for the sponsor's advertising agency. A. J. returned to Winston Cup after a four-year hiatus to field this single-car team run by Waddell Wilson, his old NASCAR crew chief.

While I was taking pictures of suspension and driveline components the shop foreman got a call from Waddell in Rockingham and he told the crew, "We got some work to do, boys. Mike's done it again; the car's comin' back with the right side flat and the left side puffy."

In 1999 A. J. Foyt, the only driver to win the Indy 500, Daytona 500, and the 24 Hours of LeMans, had announced his return as a Winston Cup team owner. His driver was Mike Bliss, a USAC Silver Crown champion and standout in the Craftsman Truck Series. Mike got off to a shaky start, qualifying 35th for the Daytona 500 and finishing 33rd. He then failed to qualify for the next three races and was briefly replaced by Cup veteran Dick Trickle who made two starts and moved on. Rick Mast, another Winston Cup regular, then took over the ride for the remainder of the season, making 24 starts and scoring two top-10 finishes.

I was told not to put any driver's name on my illustrations, and I don't believe the brochure was ever even published.

After my Viper cutaway in 1991, Chrysler became my biggest client for several years until the "merger of equals" with Daimler-Benz; and Larry Crane, who had become a friend when he was art director for *Automobile*, put me back in touch with DaimlerChrysler in 2000. Larry was designing and producing a magazine advertising insert and a hardbound book to promote Dodge's return to Winston Cup racing after competing for several years in the Craftsman Truck Series. Larry was working for Mark Malmstead at Dodge Communications and asked me to contact Mark.

This led to the largest single illustration project I have ever done: 10 Dodge Intrepid R/T Winston Cup car cutaways and a rolling chassis. Dodge had four established Winston Cup teams under contract to race their cars. The company had also lured Ray Evernham, Jeff Gor-

don's crew chief, away from Hendrick Motorsports to start a fifth team that also supplied Dodge parts to the other four.

This massive project ended the first work draught I had suffered since 1978. It started with a visit to DaimlerChrysler's Tech Center in Auburn Hills, Michigan, and then to Evernham Motorsports in Liberty and Mooresville, North Carolina. I had agreed to do the Dodge Winston Cup car cutaways in August 2000, with the two Evernham Dodges due in November for the magazine insert, and the other eight due in January 2001. This was a challenge made even more difficult by the fact that none of the cars had been completed.

The only way I could pull this off was to take advantage of NASCAR's "aero equal" bodies, which were all alike except for the window outlines and fascias. I also had the good fortune to learn that both Foyt and Evernham used Ronnie Hopkins frames. I used the Conseco Pontiac drawing as a starting point for

Conseco is a financial and insurance company and the Cup car it sponsored was as green as money. I did this solid exterior view for a brochure cover that opened in the middle to reveal the cutaway inside flanked by advertising on the back side of the cover.

laying out a complete Evernham rolling chassis, a stand-alone illustration that also appeared under the body overlay of each of the 10 cars. This was a compromise, but no one complained.

My Dodge NASCAR project almost ended before it started when I called Evernham Motorsports to arrange a visit. After explaining that I needed to take reference photos for cutaway illustrations of their cars I was told they would call me back when the cars were finished. I had to get started right away to have any chance of meeting the deadlines, so I filled in Mark Malmstead on my dilemma and Dodge quickly got the project back on track.

Then I received a heated call from Ray Evernham. Ray said, "How can we be holding you up when there aren't any finished cars to photograph yet?" I explained as I had before that I didn't need a completed car to piece together a cutaway illustration. Once he understood, Ray had no problem with my taking pictures of the cars being built or in his engine shop and I was able to combine this trip with the visit to DaimlerChrysler's NASCAR Engineering Group.

Dodge returned to the NASCAR Winston Cup series in 2001 with 10 cars and I illustrated all of them as body overlays on this rolling chassis. None of the Dodge Cup cars were completed when I drew this rolling chassis, and, like the Conseco Pontiac, they had Ronnie Hopkins Industries frames, so I used that as the starting point.

Manufacturers of cars competing in the Winston Cup Series only provided the racing teams with cylinder blocks, heads, intake manifolds, and some body parts. The rest of these "stock cars" came from speed equipment manufacturers or were made by the team. Dodge's main focus was the engine, and I spent several hours looking over senior designer David James' shoulder as he showed me math data files of individual parts along with complete assemblies, sectioning them at my request and printing out the ones I asked for. There were also digital models of the Intrepid R/T NASCAR body and chassis, which he also printed out for me. These would be a big help in making the unfinished cars I was going to work from look the way Dodge intended.

My day in Auburn Hills ended in the dyno lab where I was given a thorough tour of the engine's development including an explanation

of their spin dyno that measured parasitic losses. This made me feel almost a part of this racing program.

I met Larry Crane for dinner at Detroit Metro Airport and showed him the math data print-outs before I left for Charlotte and drove up Interstate 85 to Liberty, which is near the track that was then Lowe's and is now Charlotte Motor Speedway. At Evernham Motorsports headquarters the next morning I was met by Sarah Nemecheck (Front-row Joe's cousin), who was Ray's PR person. She took me to the engine shop where they were machining raw castings from Dodge for all the teams.

When I finished taking pictures Sarah gave me directions to the team's fabrication shop on appropriately named Performance Road in Mooresville, about 15 miles northwest on two-lane roads through idyllic countryside that rivaled anything I had seen even in France. There was a stack of Ronnie Hopkins Industries frames, a race car in the early stages of assembly, and the team's test mule to work from, which was enough, but I needed help moving stuff around. Just then Chad Knaus, who was going to be one of Ray's crew chiefs, walked in and had some of the busy fabricators give me a hand. Although Chad soon returned to Hendrick, he was with Evernham at the right moment for me.

Jeff Gordon's crew chief Ray Evernham left Hendrick to start Dodge's lead team that provided technical support and parts to the other four Dodge teams. The No. 19 Dodge Intrepid was driven by "Awesome Bill from Dawsonville" Elliot, and it qualified on two poles while winning one race and leading 171 laps during the 2001 season.

I made Larry Crane's deadline for the magazine advertising insert featuring my cutaways of Bill Elliot's No. 9 and Casey Atwood's No. 19, Evernham Motorsports' Dodge Intrepids, but the real battle was just beginning. This was the factory team and Mark Malmstead put me in touch with the contractor doing the graphics who was also working for Dodge, but the other four teams were all a problem.

Petty Enterprises was no longer a laid-back family business and referred me to a disinterested contractor for their No. 43, 44, and 45 cars' graphics. Bill Davis Racing's No. 22 and No. 93 paint schemes were being done in-house. The Coors Light graphics on Chip Ganassi Racing's No. 40 driven by Sterling Marlin were complicated, but at least they didn't change; Jason Leffler's No. 01 switched to Singular Wireless at the last moment. Melling Racing's No. 92 driven by Stacy Compton had the most challenging graphics of all, but the only Dodge single-car team was the least difficult to deal with.

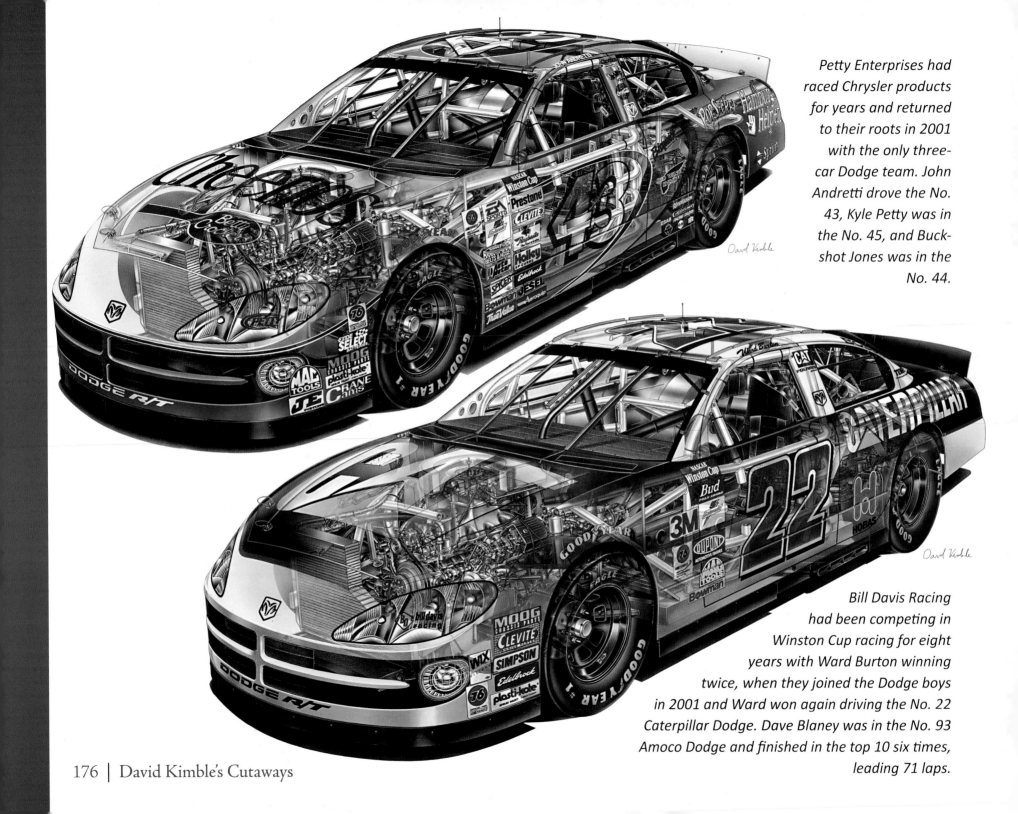

Petty Enterprises had raced Chrysler products for years and returned to their roots in 2001 with the only three-car Dodge team. John Andretti drove the No. 43, Kyle Petty was in the No. 45, and Buck-shot Jones was in the No. 44.

Bill Davis Racing had been competing in Winston Cup racing for eight years with Ward Burton winning twice, when they joined the Dodge boys in 2001 and Ward won again driving the No. 22 Caterpillar Dodge. Dave Blaney was in the No. 93 Amoco Dodge and finished in the top 10 six times, leading 71 laps.

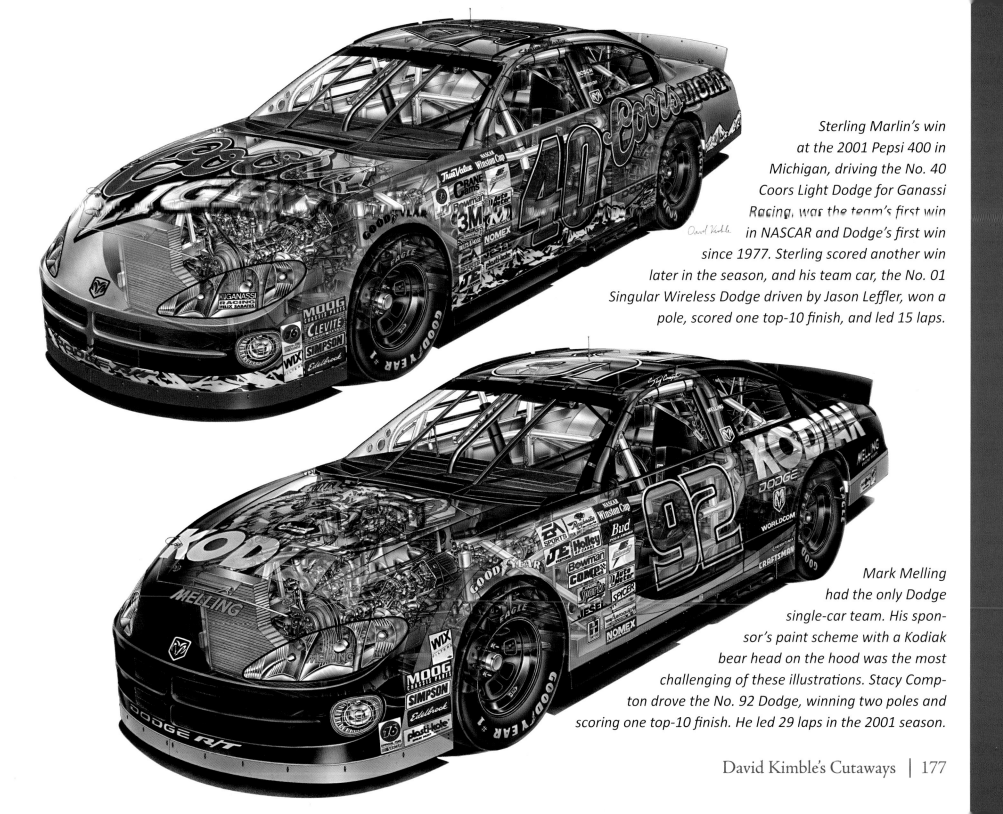

Sterling Marlin's win at the 2001 Pepsi 400 in Michigan, driving the No. 40 Coors Light Dodge for Ganassi Racing, was the team's first win in NASCAR and Dodge's first win since 1977. Sterling scored another win later in the season, and his team car, the No. 01 Singular Wireless Dodge driven by Jason Leffler, won a pole, scored one top-10 finish, and led 15 laps.

Mark Melling had the only Dodge single-car team. His sponsor's paint scheme with a Kodiak bear head on the hood was the most challenging of these illustrations. Stacy Compton drove the No. 92 Dodge, winning two poles and scoring one top-10 finish. He led 29 laps in the 2001 season.

David Kimble's Cutaways | 177

GM's Electrifying Interlude

Although the Dodge Winston Cup cars remain my largest single automotive project, and the 1997 Corvette illustrations weren't far behind, another automotive project that didn't involve racing or high-performance cars came close and was almost as exciting. This was a series of cutaways for a program that GM Corporate Management didn't believe could ever be profitable but felt compelled to try because of a California Air Resources Board mandate that 2 percent of cars sold in the state by 1998 be emissions free. This mandate increased to 10 percent by 2002. With GM's Impact electric concept car receiving a favorable reaction in 1990, it was decided to put it into production.

My involvement started with a call from Dick Thompson in 1993. I had done some cutaways for Dick when he was at Buick. He felt my illustrations were a good way to introduce a new era in GM technology and show that the Impact was a real car, not just a full-bodied golf cart.

With the California Air Resources Board (CARB) mandating that 2 percent of new cars sold in the state be emissions-free by 1998, increasing to 10 percent by 2002, General Motors built 50 Impact plug-in electric cars. This one is parked next to a charging station. These cars were loaned to private individuals for testing and feedback.

This was my first full year in Texas, and it seemed as though I was spending more time traveling than at the Palace when I left for Detroit in February with Neil Nissing coming from California to do the photography for the Impact project. After a meeting at the GM Tech Center in Warren, Greg Major, an electric vehicle development engineer, took us to GM Advanced Technology Vehicles in Troy. Here 50 Impacts were going to be hand-built for real-world testing by selected private individuals.

After Neil finished his photography we were given a chance to drive a white Geo Storm powered by an Impact electric motor. It had a surprising amount of power, easily spinning its front wheels in the light snow and sounding like a slot car as it accelerated.

Dick Thompson wanted in-depth cutaways of all the Impact's electrical components, so the next stop was Delco Remy in Anderson, Indiana, and Greg Major flew with us to Indianapolis and took us out to the plant where the motors were made. We were surprised to see the extent of GM's electric propulsion system research with everything from battery-powered pickup trucks to city buses under development, along with gasoline and diesel hybrids.

Neil was able to photograph every stage of Impact motor assembly. With the Impact's chassis, batteries, and engine covered, that left only its power control system. After going our separate ways from Indianapolis, we all met a few days later at Hughes Electronics, which was owned by General Motors in Torrance, California. I had yet to drive one of the new Camaros, so I borrowed one from Chevrolet, a 6-speed Z28. After I picked up Neil we met Greg at Hughes where project manager Mike Milani took us through the control and charging systems, completing our cross-country odyssey.

In 1995, with feedback from drivers of the loaned-out Impacts and engineering evaluation of their performance, this car evolved into the EV1 for production. The Reatta Craft Center in Lansing, Michigan, was chosen because it was intended for low volume. Introduced in 1988, the Reatta was Buick's answer to

Cadillac's Allante, a sporty two-seater body on a high-volume front-wheel-drive chassis that in this case was powered by their 165-hp 3800 V-6 with more than 3,500 pounds to haul around.

With a power-to-weight ratio of 22 pounds per horsepower, performance was not one of the Reatta's strong points, but when I visited the Craft Center in 1987 for my cutaway illustration I was impressed with the sports coupe's build quality. I think at least part of the problem was that Buick was trying to position the Reatta as an "adult sports car." When I borrowed one in California it was explained to me that adults do not care about acceleration. But I was 43 years old and it really pissed me off when a BMW blew the Reatta's doors off!

After selling only 22,000 examples including convertibles, the Reatta was canceled in 1992, clearing the way for EV1 production. This was not only The General's first electric vehicle, but also the first-ever passenger car to wear a GM badge. Even though the body, interior, and

Introduced in 1988, the Buick Reatta was a sporty two-seater built at the Reatta Craft Center in Lansing, Michigan, a low-volume assembly plant. The Reatta was canceled in 1992 and its low-volume Craft Center was ideal for assembling the EV1, a production version of the Impact electric car.

chassis carried over essentially unchanged, everything electrical (that is to say everything else in the car) was redesigned, and Dick Thompson had me do a complete set of new illustrations.

On a snowy morning another development engineer, Bill Shepard, drove me from GM AVT headquarters in Troy to Lansing to photograph some of the first red, dark green, and silver EV1s on the assembly line, and by the time I finished the weather had cleared. We walked to the large parking lot behind the building where a silver EV1 was waiting. I was given a chance to drive it, and found that, except for the absence of sound when stopped, an EV1 drove like a refined subcompact gasoline car.

As with the Impact before it, the EV1 was a two-layer illustration with its propulsion system, suspension, heat pump, air conditioning unit, and charge port rolling on Michelin Momentum low-rolling resistance tires on the base layer. The 137-hp AC induction electric motor with its reduction drive gearing is flanked by the front suspension's aluminum control arms and visually joined to the tubular rear axle by 20 lead-acid batteries on a T-shaped tray.

Everything possible was done to minimize weight, with cast-magnesium wheels and across-the-car support for the air bags, seat frames, and motor cradle mounted in an aluminum unitary chassis with a plastic body. The car weighed just 1,776 pounds without batteries. That was impressive, but the Delphi lead-acid battery pack weighed 1,310 pounds and stored the energy equivalent of one and one half gallons of gasoline, giving the first EV1s a range

of just 60 miles, which was a stretch for many suburban commuters.

In addition to the vehicle, I did stand-alone illustrations of all the propulsion system's major components, with the Delco Remy electric motor appearing in Chapter Four and the Hughes power control module. This module was mounted above the motor and they both needed cooling, which was handled by a conventional aluminum automotive radiator. As with the other ordinary car parts the radiator did not receive any special attention.

I was asked to do a close-up cutaway of the Delphi battery pack, and later would do another one with GM Ovonic nickel metal hydride batteries, which were 178 pounds lighter and extended the range of the 1999 Gen II EV1 to 160 miles. Hughes was responsible for the charging system, and I cut away a vehicle charge port with a paddle suspended above it, along with three different chargers, including one that was kept in

Similar to the Impact, the EV1 was a two-layer illustration. This car's propulsion system, heat pump, A/C unit, and charge port rolled on special low-resistance Michelin Momentum tires. The 137-hp electric motor and its reduction gearing were joined to the rear axle by 20 lead-acid batteries on a T-shaped tray.

the EV1's trunk and could be plugged in anywhere.

Between 1996 and 1999, 1,117 EV1s were built; 457 of those were extended-range Gen IIs. They could only be leased through Saturn dealers and had a retail price of $34,000, although they could not be purchased. On February 7, 2002, GM Advanced Technology Vehicles notified lessees that General Motors would be removing the vehicles from the road, and late in 2003 General Motors CEO Rick Wagoner officially canceled the EV1 program.

There are a lot of conspiracy theories about why General Motors pulled the plug, but the economics of this experimental program are enough to justify it. Lease payments were based on the car's perceived value of $34,000, and it is estimated that they cost The General between $80,000 and $100,000 each. Another key factor was that from the beginning of the program General Motors was counting on scaling up polymer lithium hearing aid battery technology, which would have dramatically reduced both the batteries' cost and weight while extending the range, but it never happened.

After the EV1 was in production, GM AVT continued some development including the NiMH battery pack. Dick Thompson had me illustrate this and several

unrelated projects, but no complete cars until 1999 when he invited me to Troy, Michigan, for the Precept. It was a technology demonstrator and show car being built in response to the Partnership for a New Generation of Vehicles, a U.S. Department of Energy initiative. I had to base my illustration on a full-scale mock-up without a body.

Metalcrafters in Fountain Valley, California, was putting the Precept body on the actual aluminum ladder frame and Hughes, now a part of GM ATV, was developing its parallel hybrid power control system in Torrance, California. This was a worst-case scenario, having to piece together a car that wasn't going to be finished in time to work from, but I was able to photograph the mock-up and the hybrid propulsion system components before leaving Troy.

The EV1's body and interior were essentially carried over from the Impact but everything electrical (that is to say everything else in the car) was redesigned and I chose red from the three colors in which it was available. The other two colors were dark green and silver, which I felt lacked impact, and my client agreed.

David Kimble's Cutaways | 181

My red 1999 Corvette convertible was only a few months old and I hadn't had much time to drive it, so with the Precept body almost finished, going to Metalcrafters was a good excuse for a road trip. I thoroughly enjoyed the 1,100-mile drive to Southern California. I stopped at Neil Nissing's studio in Burbank, arriving about noon. I hung out until mid-evening and drove to Fountain Valley where I found a motel close to Metalcrafters, avoiding getting stuck in early morning traffic. This California *carrozzeria* was well-known for building concept car bodies including the Viper and I had a bit of luck getting there early because the Precept was almost ready for paint and would then have been inaccessible for hours.

Then it was up the 405 Freeway to Torrance, where I met Mark Selogie, the product manager at the GM AVT power electronics operation. Seeing my Corvette, Mark said that if he could drive it I could drive his EV1 and assured me we didn't have to worry about the cops. He explained that most of them knew him and that GM's facility was the last large industrial employer in the city, so as long as we didn't get too crazy they would leave us alone.

I got to find out how a Gen II EV1 handled at its speed-limited 80-mph terminal velocity. The Precept's main hybrid power unit is covered in Chapter Four, but I did not include any of the electronic power control illustrations because they're just boxes full of circuit boards and after 16 years I can't remember what any of them do. This trip wrapped up my photography for this project and the blanks were filled in with math data, except for the interior, which was done from CGI renderings with the scene on the rearview video screen based on a sketch of Highway 90 done while returning to Marfa.

The Precept's propulsion system was developed from the experimental EV1 parallel hybrid, and had an Isuzu three-cylinder turbocharged diesel that could drive the rear wheels unassisted through a solenoid-shifted manual transmission. It also ran a motor-generator that could drive the rear wheels while providing power to the front wheels' drive motor and at the same time charge a nickel metal hydride battery pack under the front seats. This offered a bewildering array of combinations that

The Precept was a GM technology demonstrator and show car built in response to the Partnership for a New Generation of Vehicles, a U.S. Department of Energy initiative. It was a parallel hybrid built by GM Advanced Technology Vehicles Division (ATV) with a body by Metalcrafters in Fountain Valley, California. It reminded me of a Citroën DS19.

David Kimble

were automatically selected and continuously adjusted by the power control system computer to achieve 80 miles per gallon with the help of the body's incredibly low 0.16 coefficient of drag.

The car is shown on a stylized set of wheels and tires that were just for show with the wheel spoke outline extending onto the tires' sidewalls and across the tread. The Precept's mileage numbers were set on Michelin Momentums. I have always liked this illustration, not for its technology but because I'm a sucker for the styling of weird French cars and this one reminds me of a Citroën DS19.

THE REBORN VIPER AND BEYOND

As the global economic meltdown accelerated into 2009 with both General Motors and Chrysler filing for bankruptcy and the other markets for my work such as Las Vegas and the cruise lines also in the tank, I was completely out of work in May. America's sports cars that I had regularly illustrated were also suffering from the Great Recession. Corvette sales dropped from 35,310 in 2008 to 12,194 in 2010, and the Viper was canceled with the last snake rolling off the assembly line on July 1, 2010.

After reorganization both companies downsized, and with many of my clients at or near minimum retirement age most of them were given their retirement packages or laid off. Unfortunately only one of my relationships with these companies survived. This was with GM Powertrain where my contact, Ron Bluhm, was handed his package but I was able to keep the account; however, it took until 2012 for things to come back to life. Working with Lea George, it has been solid ever since.

Early in 2012 photos of a fifth-generation Viper that was going into production for the 2013 model year appeared in the magazines, and it wasn't long before I heard from my old friend Vince Muniga who had moved from General Motors to Chrysler. I had last worked with Vinnie in 2008 on a cutaway of the 2010 Camaro. He asked me to do the same with the new Viper late in 2011, and after it broke cover he called with an update, but this was the last I heard from him or anyone else about the project for months.

By late July I was sure the Viper illustration wasn't happening and was loaded up with GM projects, when I received a call from Dan Reid, manager of SRT communications. He asked me if I could illustrate an SRT Viper GT3 coupe by October, and I had to tell him that it was impossible. With the workload I was already committed to I couldn't possibly go to Detroit, but with everyone at SRT wanting a Kimble cutaway of the new Viper we came up with a plan.

Chrysler had an excellent computer graphics group, and with Joe Kelly, the Viper Group's lead designer making math data assemblies, it would start with the powertrain and add parts in stages, making a series of illustration-sized prints for me to use as a starting point. This was a gamble because no one involved, including me, had ever attempted anything such as this before. It worked perfectly with Joe Kelly emailing me several views of a complete car.

Joe then eliminated layer after layer of parts from the master digital model down to the powertrain, and I picked six stages of assembly to be enlarged by the graphics group to working size with the Viper body 36 inches in length. The prints arrived at the Palace on August 6. After confirming that all the layers matched in size and perspective so they would fit together, I called Dan Reid to let him know that if nothing unexpected happened the Viper cutaway could now be completed by the end of October.

I guess it really shouldn't have been unexpected that once I got into the project a few months before the start of production I found that the new Viper was a moving target. It had a myriad of parts that were not finalized, such as the inside rearview mirror. This sounds trivial but it shows very prominently in the illustration along with the radio antenna above it on the interior side of the windshield.

This was another problem that sucked up a lot of time, but the SRT guys were incredibly helpful. They kept me up to date with photos and math data of the latest changes and developments. They also did extensive photography on finished pilot-build Vipers, allowing me to do something I had never done before, which was to illustrate a car that I had never actually seen the way it would look rolling off the assembly line. That was something no one had seen at that point in time.

With the Viper project squeezed into an already full schedule, I completed a GM LT1 Gen V small-block V-8 drawing for the C7 Corvette and started the preliminary Viper layout on the same day, completing it 16 days later on August 22. With the layout submitted to SRT Engineering for review, I painted a film positive of Rick Terrell's electronic inking of the LT1, which took 14 days, and then shipped my final layout of the Viper to Rick on September 22, giving him just two weeks to ink it.

Rick had to bring in another digital artist to help, but they finished and I began painting the new snake on October 12. Working 18 to 20 hours a day with an October 28–29 all-nighter, I shipped the painting in 18 days. If this had been a few years earlier the drama would have ended when FedEx picked up on Monday, with Neil Nissing shooting 8 x 10-inch color transparencies on Tuesday and Chrysler receiving the art and trannies on Wednesday, but now it's not that simple.

Reproducing artwork done by hand in this digital world is a challenge that requires a flatbed laser scanner large enough to accommodate the painting. This is hard enough to find, but the difficulty does not stop there. These scanners don't see the art the way our eyes do, so the digital scan has to be corrected. That is another art form in itself. I asked Steve Constable, who digitizes and prepares my GM illustrations, to do the Viper. Rick Terrell volunteered to work with Steve on the correction of the Viper scan and this turned into a three-day around-the-clock marathon. Steve's wife, Patty, delivered the art to Chrysler on Friday.

Time constraints had forced me to ship the Viper before I was ready. Along with the usual color and value corrections this team very obligingly pumped up the metallic red body and some of the blacks the same way I would have if I had had more time. For that I am grateful.

By the time I was asked to illustrate the 2013 Gen V Viper, I realized that a cutaway of the 2014 Gen VII Corvette would not be done by me or anyone else. Because my history with these cars went back 30 years, I was relieved to be involved in the powertrain work and not entirely left out. In a way it was a push illustrating the new Corvette's powertrain without the entire car and the complete Viper but not its powertrain.

Chrysler's snakes have always made great subjects for cutaways with their massive V-10 engines. The aluminum V-10's displacement increased from 8.0 to 8.3 liters in 2002 and to 8.4 liters for the Gen V version, which was the first to have a plastic intake manifold. This, along with additional cylinder head and camshaft development, gave the Viper 640 hp, topping the ZR1 Corvette's 638. Intake air for the 2-barrel throttle body continued to come through the hood scoop that had inspired

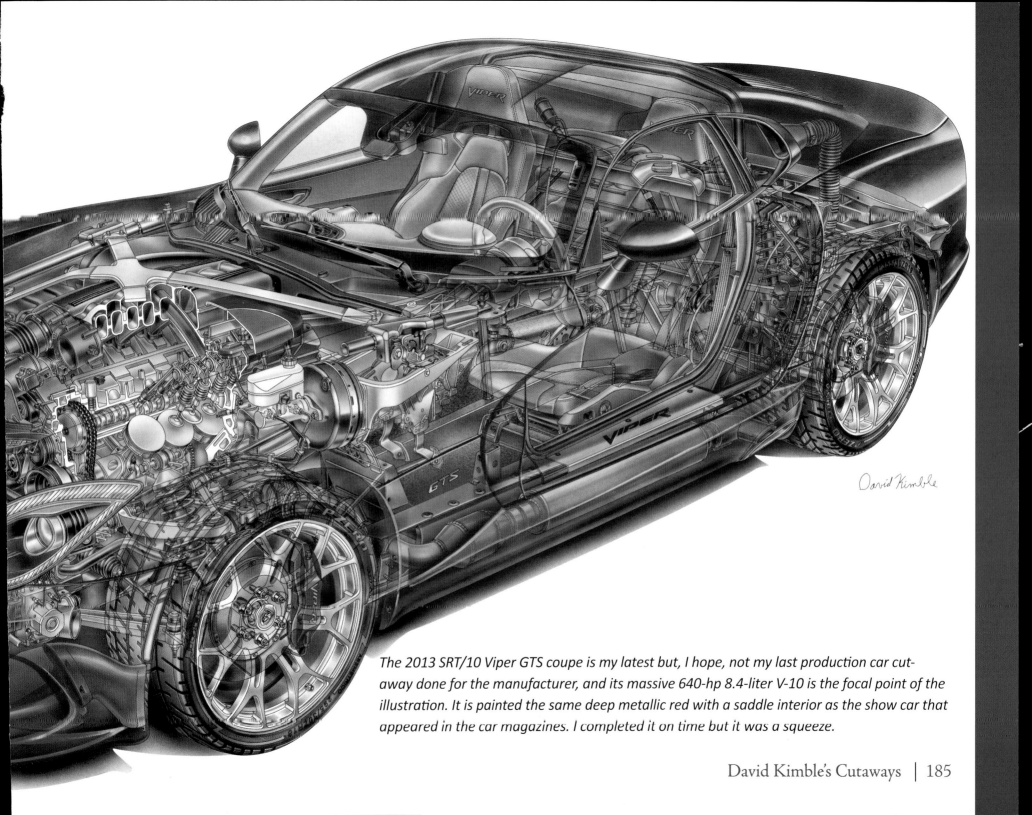

The 2013 SRT/10 Viper GTS coupe is my latest but, I hope, not my last production car cutaway done for the manufacturer, and its massive 640-hp 8.4-liter V-10 is the focal point of the illustration. It is painted the same deep metallic red with a saddle interior as the show car that appeared in the car magazines. I completed it on time but it was a squeeze.

David Kimble's Cutaways | 185

the 2006 Z06 'Vette's scoop, which just blew cool air into the engine compartment.

We made the deadline for the poster and press kit that were going to be handed out at the production Viper's introduction to the automotive media, but I was concerned about seeing it in the magazines because the new Viper had received so much publicity. I didn't mention it to Dan Reid, but I felt my cutaway should have been available for the first wave of publicity early in the year the way Vince Muniga had intended, but Vince was no longer with Chrysler. I suspected Dan felt the same way and perhaps he was hoping my cutaway would lead to another round of magazine articles, but it never had a chance.

Instead of being featured it was buried, appearing on the poster down in one corner. This meant that the enthusiasm for the project that I shared with everyone I worked with at SRT did not extend to Chrysler's marketing and advertising people. My chosen art form all but disappeared from their mainstream media.

I have been told that my artwork contributed to the popularity of cutaways in the 1980s and 1990s, with it making a difference in the perception of the cars I illustrated, which is very gratifying and I would like to think it is true. The most important thing, though, is that this is what I am motivated to do, and I rode a wave of popularity that lasted more than 20 years with enough interest in my work to keep me busy today.

Still, it is a shame that the Viper is the only car I have done for a manufacturer since the industry recovered from the recession, but at least there is not some other cutaway artist illustrating all of the hot cars I used to do, and I remain ready to take on some more. As I am beginning to choose more subjects for my Jurassic art than are choosing me, I think back to the only self-commission I have done that wasn't a car. It is an 1868 Schenectady American-type locomotive, and my future just may lie in America's steam-powered past.

With a Little Help from My Friends

To retain an account, any business has to be able to fulfill its customers' needs. In the almost 40 years since I left engineering to start David Kimble Illustration in January 1976, I have relied on help from many friends. I freelanced for a while before leaving my day job, and my largest client, the Willis Oil Tool Company, wanted me to take over their series of airbrushed black and white sectional oil field valve illustrations, even though I had never used an airbrush.

I remembered an industrial designer I had worked with at Monogram Industries and stayed in touch with because we were both street racers; he was teaching airbrush classes at Los Angeles City College. I agreed to take the offer from Willis, and fortunately Dick Bruton was up for it, with me doing the drawings he would airbrush. This worked out well until he wasn't available in time to meet one critical deadline. Having looked over his shoulder and seeing how it was done, I was able to do the painting myself.

This had been the only time I had hired someone to do something I couldn't do myself, and I was again working alone when John Steinberg started representing me in May 1976. He soon brought in so many projects that I couldn't keep up and he strongly suggested I find some help.

I had already been contacted by Ken Elliott, a talented and versatile technical illustrator with whom I had worked in the late 1960s. Ken was also a raging alcoholic prone to disappearing on benders and even though he had been a friend I regretfully turned him down.

Instead, Dave Destler, another technical illustrator who shared my interest in sports cars, came on board to help with the drawing and inking, but after a few months he started a British sports car magazine, and so I called Kenny. He had already told me that he had quit drinking and was a member of AA, and now there wasn't any choice. Working with Ken turned out to be one of the best decisions I ever made.

Ken Elliott was a product of the technical illustration sweat shops that took in contract work from aerospace companies around Southern California, but unlike most job-shoppers he was a real artist and doubled my productivity for more than 20 years. He had his limitations in not understanding descriptive geometry or the physics of how things work, but with me getting his drawings started and guiding him, Kenny became a second pair of hands and our skills grew together. He eventually reached the point of being able to both draw and ink the simpler cars including the countless front-wheel-drive sedans we illustrated in the 1980s, with me doing only the painting.

Ken worked at home, bringing his drawings in every few days for a review, and I had been going to his house when he was in a tight spot, so moving to Texas worried me a little, but it worked out fine for a while. However, he was 12 years older than I and he began losing altitude in the late 1990s. Even though I felt terrible about it, I had to stop working with him altogether in 2000.

Stan Goldstein ran a small ad agency specializing in speed equipment manufacturers and was both Neil's client and mine. When I needed additional help in 1982 Stan suggested Steve Swaja, whose cutaways I had seen in *Hot Rod*, and Steve was happy to work with me.

I stopped working on the drawing of this 1868 Schenectady American-type steam locomotive when I was asked to do the plans for the models for Star Trek: The Motion Picture. *It took me 17 years between paying projects to finish the painting, but I enjoyed every minute and there may be more steam power in my future.*

He didn't have his own studio and I had two drawing boards in mine, so for the first and only time I had an in-house assistant. This was fun because we both liked to talk, but after a few months it became obvious that Steve and I together were getting less done than I had by myself.

During this time the *Valley News* had run an article about me, and Hanna-Barbera Studios called to find out if I would be interested in designing spacecraft and military vehicles for their animated action cartoons. I had discussed with Steve how counterproductive our incessant talking was, but neither of us had managed to shut up, so I recommended him to Hanna-Barbera and he found a home working there for years.

My staff was back to just Kenny and me in 1986 when John Steinberg oversold our capabilities by bringing in all the illustrations for Acura's first brochure. This left me understaffed and over committed so I ran a help-wanted ad in the *Los Angeles Times* and received more than 80 responses by mail. I picked the 20 or so most promising-sounding ones and held a marathon interview session, finding that the higher their degree from an academic institution, the less capable they were. I finally picked eight undereducated technical illustrators that I hoped would be good enough.

I then found myself managing a full-blown production studio, coordinating all of these guys' efforts while instructing the better ones and reassigning the work given to no-hopers. I had become an administrator! I only had time for a little painting at night, and when the project was completed with the deadline met and the client satisfied, I told John Steinberg, to his disappointment, that I was never going through anything like that again.

I didn't completely walk away from car brochures, but the ones we did involved fewer illustrations with more time. I continued to work with the two best illustrators from the Acura brochure crew for a while, but they weren't in Kenny's league. Another illustrator, Michael Kester, who did have talent found me about this time and while I had doubts about working with him because he was in Ashland, Oregon, it worked out fine. Michael would not be my only assistant from that state, however, with Tom Johnson in Portland working with me for 16 years.

In 1988 I taught a class at *Airbrush Action*'s magazine's first Airbrush Getaway in Tampa, Florida, and Tom was one of my students, attending my class a second time at the next Getaway in Key West six months later. I taught at these Getaways for about three years, and at the next one Tom was my teaching assistant. Starting in 1992, he became the only illustrator I ever worked with who could handle the whole package: drawing, inking, and painting as well.

In 1992, David Kimble Illustration fanned out across the country from the West Coast. Melanie Kirsch moved to Rhinelander, Wisconsin, in June and I moved to Marfa, Texas, in December, making both Tom Johnson in Oregon and Ken Elliott in California long-distance assistants. By 1997 Kenny was fading fast and Melanie found an Art Center graduate named Eric Fulghum from South Pasadena, California, who looked promising. I worked with both Tom and Eric until the meltdown in 2009, and by the time I needed help again in 2012, they had moved on.

Rick Terrell started doing electronic inkings for me in 2005 and continues today as my only assistant. We have become an effective team, but in a way I am back where I started with Dick Bruton doing my airbrushing. Not being computer-oriented in any way, I again have to hire something done that I cannot do myself.

50 YEARS OF KIMBLE CAR CUTAWAYS 1964-2014

Not counting numerous pickups, SUVs, and vans, I have done 139 car cutaway illustrations over the past 50 years and look forward to doing a lot more.

Line and Tone

1964	Halibrand Shrike Indy car
1964	Magic Car NHRA Slingshot Dragster
1965	Halibrand Shrike Indy Car
1965	Harrison Special Indy Car
1966	Edmunds 4-Bar Midget
1966	Edmunds 4-Bar Sprint Car
1966	Edmunds 4-Bar Super Modified
1968	McLaren M8A Can-Am Car
1969	Edmunds 4-Bar Sprint Car
1969	Penske Camaro Trans-Am Car
1969	Reynolds McLaren M8B Can-Am Car
1971	Motown Missile Dodge NHRA Pro Stock Car
1972	1932 Ford Model B Roadster Street Rod
1973	Hot Rod Magazine Street Rod of the Future

Full Color

1976	Stapp 4-Bar Sprint Car
1976	Honda Civic
1976	Honda Civic Wagon
1976	Honda Accord
1976	Ferrari 308 (black & white rendering)
1978	Stapp 4-Bar Sprint Car
1979	Toyota Corolla
1980	1939 Duesenberg-Powered Indy Car
1981	Edmunds 4-Bar Midget
1982	Edmunds Coil-Over Sprint Car
1982	Alston Camaro NHRA Pro Stock Car
1982	1983 Nissan 300 ZX
1982	1984 Corvette
1982	Pontiac No. 43 NASCAR Cup Car
1983	Camaro Show Car
1983	1984 Pontiac Fierro (front view)
1983	1984 Pontiac Fierro (rear view)
1983	1927 Miller 91 Front-Drive Indy Car
1984	March 84C Indy Car
1984	Porsche 911 Carrera
1984	1965 427 SC Cobra
1984	1985 Ferrari Testarossa
1984	1931 V-16 Cadillac Dual-Cowl Phaeton
1985	Porsche 959
1985	Ford Mustang NHRA Funny Car
1985	1930 Model J Duesenberg Speedster
1986	Mercedes-Benz 540K Special Coupe
1986	1987 Cadillac Allante
1986	Fat Jack Street Rod
1986	Chrysler LeBaron Convertible
1986	Chrysler LeBaron Coupe
1986	Lamborghini Countach LP500S
1986	Mazda RX-7 Turbo II
1987	Mitsubishi Starion ESI-R
1987	Toyota Supra
1987	1988 Buick Reatta Coupe
1987	1929 Auburn Cabin Speedster
1987	1984 Ferrari 288 GTO
1987	1962 Ferrari 250 GTO
1987	Chevrolet Express Gas Turbine
1987	1988 Cadillac Deville
1987	1988 Cadillac Eldorado
1987	Renault Alpine
1988	1989 Ferrari F40
1988	1989 4.5-Liter Cadillac Allante
1988	Corvette Indy Technology Demonstrator
1988	1989 Corvette ZR-1 (rear view)
1988	1989 Corvette ZR-1 (front view)
1988	1990 Buick Reatta Convertible
1988	Ford Turbo Thunderbird Coupe
1989	1991 Northstar Cadillac Allante
1989	1990 Lexus LS 400
1989	1990 Buick Park Avenue
1989	1990 Toyota MR2
1989	1990 Isuzu Impulse SE (ed)
1989	1990 Isuzu Impulse SE (white)
1989	1992 Isuzu Impulse SE (black)
1989	1992 Isuzu Impulse SE (blue)
1990	Lamborghini Diablo
1990	Nissan 300 ZX
1990	1991 Dodge Intrepid
1990	1991 Jeep Eagle
1990	1991 Chrysler Concord
1990	1991 Chrysler LeBaron
1990	1991 Chevrolet Caprice
1990	1991 Pontiac No. 43 NASCAR Cup Car
1990	Oldsmobile NHRA Funny Car
1990	1992 Dodge Viper RT/10
1991	Dodge Stealth R/T Twin Turbo
1991	1992 Acura NSX
1991	1992 Acura Legend
1992	1993 Camaro Z28
1992	1993 Lincoln MK8
1992	1993 Lincoln Town Car
1993	1993 Camaro Indy Pace Car
1993	1994 Oldsmobile Aurora
1993	Cadillac Concord
1993	Camaro Convertible
1993	GM Impact Electric Car
1994	Mustang GT
1994	Mustang V-6
1994	Dodge Cirrus
1994	Plymouth Stratus
1994	Dodge Neon
1994	Chevrolet Caprice Police Car
1995	Mustang GT
1996	Chevrolet Monte Carlo
1996	GM EV1 Electric Car
1996	1997 Corvette (rear view)
1996	1997 Corvette (front view)
1996	1997 Chevrolet Monte Carlo
1996	1997 Chevrolet Impala
1997	1998 Oldsmobile Intrigue
1997	NHTSA Ford SVO Taurus
1998	Ford SVO Contour
1998	Cadillac Deville
1998	Corvette Convertible
1999	Lincoln LS V-8
1999	Lincoln LS V-6
1999	Mustang Cobra
1999	GM Precept Parallel Hybrid
2000	2001 Corvette Z06
2000	Corvette C5R Endurance Racer
2000	Pontiac No. 14 NASCAR Cup Car
2000	2001 Dodge No. 9 NASCAR Cup Car
2000	2001 Dodge No. 19 NASCAR Cup Car
2000	2001 Dodge No. 43 NASCAR Cup Car
2000	2001 Dodge No. 44 NASCAR Cup Car
2000	2001 Dodge No. 45 NASCAR Cup Car
2000	2001 Dodge No. 22 NASCAR Cup Car
2000	2001 Dodge No. 93 NASCAR Cup Car
2000	2001 Dodge No. 40 NASCAR Cup Car
2000	2001 Dodge No. 01 NASCAR Cup Car
2000	2001 Dodge No. 92 NASCAR Cup Car
2001	1966 Chaparral 2E Can-Am Car
2002	2003 Viper SRT/10
2003	Cadillac CTS V
2003	2005 Corvette Convertible
2003	2005 Corvette Coupe
2005	2006 Corvette Z06
2005	2006 Corvette C6R Endurance Racer
2007	2009 Corvette ZR1
2008	2010 Camaro SS
2012	2013 Viper SRT/10
2014	1968 McLaren M8A Can-Am Car

INDEX

Additional books that may interest you...

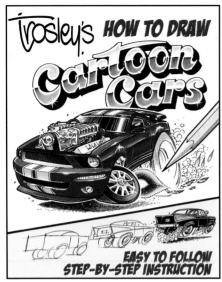

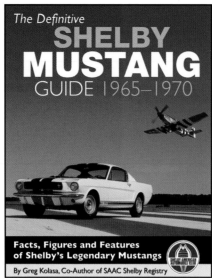

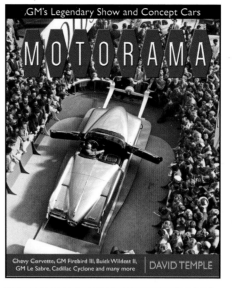

TROSLEY'S HOW TO DRAW CARTOON CARS *by George Trosley* The author takes you through the process step-by-step of drawing your favorite cars, starting with the basics such as profiles, point of view, speed, attitudes, custom graphics, and coloring. You learn to draw components including wheels, engines, and accessories. Then you are treated to step-by-step lessons on many different body styles: Corvettes, Mustangs, pickup trucks, off-road trucks, muscle cars, hot rods, and a few race cars as well. If you are a budding artist, closet cartoonist, or just want to learn how to draw your own hot rod or muscle machine, this book shows you how it's done. Trosley is one of the best in the business today. Softbound, 8-1/2 x 11 inches, 144 pages, 462 color and b/w illustrations. *Item # CT557*

THE DEFINITIVE SHELBY MUSTANG GUIDE: 1965-1970 *by Greg Kolasa* Shelby American Auto Club (SAAC) historian and registrar Greg Kolasa details the specifics on the performance and appearance alterations. This book gives a detailed look at both the performance and styling characteristics of each year of the 1965–1970 Shelby Mustangs in text, photographs, and charts/graphs. It clears up many myths and misconceptions surrounding these legendary pony cars. In addition to his firsthand knowledge, Kolasa relies heavily on factory documentation and interviews with Shelby American designers, engineers, stylists, fabricators, and race drivers. Hardbound, 8.5 x 11 inches, 192 pages, 500 color photos. *Item # CT507*

MOTORAMA: GM's Legendary Show & Concept Cars *by David Temple* Motorama expert and experienced author David Temple has comprehensively researched the show, the cars, and the personalities to create a fascinating story with new photos of these magnificent cars. Temple goes into detail on the body, frame, engine, drivetrain, and special features of each showcase model. He has also retraced the ownership histories of some of these cars. This book features fascinating period photography of Motorama cars at the show, in development, and at different locales. No other automotive show rivaled the extravagant and elaborate Motorama for stunning productions and awe-inspiring cars. Hardbound, 8.5 x 11 inches, 192 pages, 400 color and b/w photos. *Item # CT533*

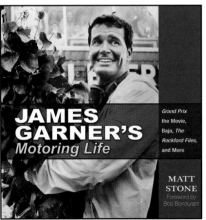

JAMES GARNER'S MOTORING LIFE: *Grand Prix* the Movie, Baja, *The Rockford Files,* and More *by Matt Stone* From starring in the movie *Grand Prix,* tackling the rigors of Baja off-road racing, forming his own road racing team called American International Racing, driving the Pace Car at the Indy 500, all the way to his stunt driving in *The Rockford Files,* James Garner was a true enthusiast. *James Garner's Motoring Life* covers the cars he owned and drove, the cars he raced, his tour of duty as a racing team owner, his great racing film, the drivers on his team, as well as the drivers he competed against. Hardbound, 9 x 9 inches, 160 pages, 200 color and b/w photos. *Item # CT529*

www.cartechbooks.com or 1-800-551-4754